A Faith of Their Own

A FAITH
OF THEIR OWN

*Stability and Change in the Religiosity of
America's Adolescents*

LISA D. PEARCE

MELINDA LUNDQUIST DENTON

OXFORD

UNIVERSITY PRESS

2011

OXFORD
UNIVERSITY PRESS

Oxford University Press, Inc., publishes works that further
Oxford University's objective of excellence
in research, scholarship, and education.

Oxford   New York
Auckland   Cape Town   Dar es Salaam   Hong Kong   Karachi
Kuala Lumpur   Madrid   Melbourne   Mexico City   Nairobi
New Delhi   Shanghai   Taipei   Toronto
With offices in
Argentina   Austria   Brazil   Chile   Czech Republic   France   Greece
Guatemala   Hungary   Italy   Japan   Poland   Portugal   Singapore
South Korea   Switzerland   Thailand   Turkey   Ukraine   Vietnam

Published by Oxford University Press, Inc.
198 Madison Avenue, New York, NY 10016

www.oup.com

Oxford is a registered trademark of Oxford University Press

Library of Congress Cataloging-in-Publication Data
Pearce, Lisa D. (Lisa Deanne), 1971–
A faith of their own : stability and change
in the religiosity of America's adolescents /
Lisa D. Pearce, Melinda Lundquist Denton.
p.   cm.
Includes bibliographical references and index.
ISBN 978-0-19-975389-5
1. Teenagers—Religious life—United States.
I. Denton, Melinda Lundquist. II. Title.
BL625.47.P42   2011
200.835'0973—dc22
2010013243

1 3 5 7 9 8 6 4 2

Printed in the United States of America
on acid-free paper

With endless gratitude for my parents,
Eldon and Mary Ann Pearce, and my sister, Megan
L. D. P.

With all my love to Jason, Lukas, and Everett
M. L. D.

Contents

Acknowledgments

This book comes out of the National Study of Youth and Religion (NSYR). The larger project of the NSYR and the specific work of this book reflect the efforts of a great number of people to whom we owe our gratitude and thanks. We thank Chris Coble and the Lilly Endowment Inc. for their very generous support of NSYR. We are extraordinarily appreciative of Christian Smith for inviting us to be a part of this groundbreaking project, mentoring us professionally, and providing feedback during the process of writing this book. Terri Clark, the project manager for NSYR from Wave 2 on, has been absolutely invaluable, constantly going above and beyond in her management of the data collection, research team activities, funding proposals, reports, Institutional Review Board applications, and management of communication and media requests. We cannot imagine a more skilled, wise, or trustworthy assistant than Terri. Debby Pyatt served as the point person for keeping track of our youth respondents across time—not an easy task! Her diligent tracking efforts led to an admirably high retention rate for the second wave of data collection. Thank you to Emily McKendry-Smith, Beth Latshaw, and Kyle Longest for assisting with these efforts.

We also owe a great debt of gratitude to all of those involved in the collection of the NSYR Wave 2 survey and semistructured interviews. Thank you to those at the Odum Institute for Research in Social Science, especially Teresa Edwards, Michelle Temple, Jessica Hardie, and Gerald Lackey, as well as the interviewers, for their tireless efforts in support of our telephone survey. Kim Manturuk lent her excellent leadership to the fielding of our 122 in-person, semistructured interviews, assisted by an outstanding team of interviewers: John Bartkowski, Tyson Brown, Dan DeHanas, Korie Edwards, Richard Flory, Youn Ok Lee, Alexis Pankey, Norman Peart, Mark Regnerus, David Sikkink, Christian Smith, Steve Vaisey, Ria Van Ryn, and Todd Wilkins. We are grateful to Laura Boutwell, Laura Hoseley, Diane Johnson, Sandi Osterkatz, Robyn Richie, and Pam Roberts for transcribing the interviews. And we thank Emily McKendry-Smith and Youn Ok Lee for formatting the transcripts for analysis in ATLAS.ti.

We would also like to thank all those who contributed time and effort in data analysis and research tasks, including Christopher Ball, Ian Conlon, Dan DeHanas, Tracie Gesel, Gretchen Gooding, Jessica Hardie, Taylor Hargrove, Leigh Howell, Hannah Jefferies, Stef Knauer, Beth Latshaw, Youn Ok Lee, Jamie Lewis, Emily McKendry-Smith, Jessica Pearlman, Niobra Peterson, Monica Pyles, Shradha Shrestha, Ria Van Ryn, and Heather Wendt.

Karolyn Tyson and Michele Berger provided invaluable feedback, advice and moral support during the writing of this book. Mark Chaves and Margarita Mooney, along with the students in their Sociology of Religion classes, similarly offered helpful reactions to and suggestions for drafts of the book. E. Michael Foster provided excellent guidance in the use of latent class methods. Thanks also to Heather Tirado Gilligan for providing exceptional editorial assistance in the final stages. We are grateful for the feedback of the anonymous reviewers whose comments helped shape the direction of the final manuscript. Thank you to Cynthia Read, our editor at Oxford University Press, for guiding us through the publication process.

Another key constituency in the development of this book is the William T. Grant Foundation, which generously supported Lisa through a Scholars Award as the book was being written. This award comes with a network of incredibly supportive and encouraging junior scholars, foundation staff, and selection committee members. The mentorship, advice, and camaraderie developed in the past five years have been invaluable to this project. Thanks especially to my senior program advisor, Tom Weisner as well as Bob Granger, Ed Seidman, Vivian Tseng, Irene Williams, Renee Spencer, Rachel Dunifon, Rob Crosnoe, Stefanie DeLuca, Dina Okamoto, and Brian Mustanski. Your support has meant the world.

Pearce's year as a Fellow at the Stanford Center for Advanced Study in the Behavioral Sciences (2007–8) was where the writing of this book launched. Thank you to all the CASBS personnel and fellows (especially my H Block friends) for the rich year.

We extend thanks to our home departments and colleagues, the University of North Carolina at Chapel Hill's Department of Sociology and the Carolina Population Center, as well as the Clemson University Department of Sociology and Anthropology, for their support as we undertook this process, from proposal writing, to data collection, through the completion of this manuscript. Thank you to prior mentors and colleagues as well, including our undergraduate advisors at Whitworth University, Robert Clark, Don Liebert, and Raja Tanas, and Seattle Pacific University, Cynthia Price, David Diekema, and David Caddell. Many of the ideas that formed this project and book are rooted in important conversations and social support from close friends and colleagues William G. Axinn, Jennifer Barber, Dirgha Ghimire, Kathie Harris, Arland Thornton, and Scott Yabiku.

We wish to extend an especially heartfelt thanks to our families for scaffolding us with their never-ending love and support as we worked on this book: Eldon and Mary Ann Pearce, Megan, Brian, Kathryn, and Emily Smith, Jason Denton, Melvin and Gracie Denton, Gregg and Virginia Lundquist, Marla Conser, Melody Barrera, and Kelley Tegen.

Finally, this book would not have been possible without the generous cooperation of the many parents and youth who continue to participate in the National Study of Youth and Religion. We are forever indebted to your willingness to share your lives with us. You have taught us much.

A Faith of Their Own

Introduction

It is the summer of 2005 and we are each on our way to the first of many in-person interviews with adolescents all across the United States, in coffee shops and public library meeting rooms. Digital recorders in hand and thoughts of a book on religious change in adolescence looming, we begin to wonder: How will Rachel, now 17 years old, and Chelsea, now 16, have changed since we interviewed them two years earlier?[1] I (Lisa) had taken an immediate liking to Rachel's bubbly enthusiasm as she described her good friends, how they swap clothes and help each other choose boyfriends. I wonder, will her already waning attendance at the family's Methodist church have fallen off further? Maybe her mother's boyfriend will have moved in and succeeded in convincing her mother that church attendance is pointless. Will Rachel still be proud of how well she communicates with God through prayer, or will the increasing busyness of adolescence have crowded that out of her life? When I (Melinda) first met Chelsea, she was a young 13-year-old with an outgoing personality, a quick wit, and an innocent view of the world. At the time she was confident that she could embrace both her mother's Jewish heritage and her father's Presbyterian roots and be "Christian with a hint of Jewish." I wonder if she has been able to maintain the delicate balance through age 16, or if she has given up on religion altogether. Will her mother still be her best friend, the person in whom she confides about everything? Did the transition to high school dull her youthful optimism?

The journey through adolescence is typically equated with an assertion of independence and individuality. In the United States the teen years and early twenties are a time to search for freedom. Youth push the boundaries of conventional style and language. They seek leisure time away from their parents and find jobs that give them a taste of financial independence. Rachel confessed in the second interview to spending a lot of time at parties with youth her age, drinking the occasional wine cooler and smoking pot. She works at an amusement park in hopes of saving enough money to buy her own car and pay for insurance. Chelsea's weekend activities include going with friends to movies and having sleepovers, where they have water fights and play truth-or-dare. At 16 she classifies herself as "a pretty boring child" but is beginning to assert her independence and desire for autonomy. Aware of her parents' financial struggles, Chelsea has taken it upon herself to maintain a superb academic record in order to win scholarships and pay her own way through college. She has recently had a falling-out with her mother, who insists on "babying" her though Chelsea is ready to be treated as an adult. Religious beliefs and practices can appear contradictory to this adolescent quest for autonomy: getting up early for church when their bodies are begging for more late-morning sleep, submitting to the watchful eye of coreligionists and clergy, spending precious time reading scriptures or praying instead of studying, working, or socializing. Adults and teenagers alike often say that an active religious life seems relatively incompatible with adolescence.

Yet when asked, teenagers offer a view of their own religiosity that reveals a significant inclination toward the spiritual. Indeed, as we show in this book, youth are overwhelmingly likely to say they have remained as or gotten *more* religious during adolescence. Only a small minority of adolescents say they became *less* religious in their teenage years.

Rachel is one of those youth who describes herself as overall having stayed the same religiously in adolescence. She says that she prays about the same amount these days, but when we talk about public religious practice, she says that she attends religious services less often than she did two years ago. Rachel explains that this is primarily because her mother's boyfriend, who has still not proposed marriage or moved in with them, sleeps over every Saturday night. As he has no interest in attending church, none of them goes when he is around. When we talked specifically about the cognitive aspect of her religiosity, here is how she describes why she feels stronger in her religious beliefs:

> It's because I'm more knowledgeable of what it really means to me, like um, and a couple years ago I'd just be like okay, well I could just

do this, ask for forgiveness, and he'll forgive me. I've kind of grown up you know. That's really not the point—why he forgives you and everything—and so that doesn't give you an extent to where you can do it, and just say, "Oh, I'll ask for forgiveness later, so it's okay."

Many of the youth we interviewed feel that they have matured to the point that their faith is their own, and that makes it deeper and stronger. In some cases, much like Rachel, they feel this balances out decreases in their religious practice, so that their overall religiosity has stayed the same. In other cases they feel that this personal ownership outweighs and overpowers any decreases or stasis in religious practice, so that ultimately they perceive themselves to have become more religious.

What do we as a society really know about religious change during adolescence? When anyone asks us what our book is about and we say "How religiosity changes in adolescence," nine times out of ten the response is some variant of "Oh, how much does it decrease?" No one asks whether or not religiosity decreases in adolescence, they just ask how much it decreases. That we will tell a story of religious decline among adolescents seems to be a foregone conclusion. But we wonder if common wisdom has exaggerated the extent to which religious beliefs and practices decrease during adolescence. Worse yet, are we sending young people false messages about what a normative adolescent experience might be? Yes and no. Like most social processes, paths to adulthood and religious life trajectories are intertwined and complex.[2] Part of the complexity arises in the attempt to define and understand what it is that makes someone religious. The term *religious* is applied regularly to describe individual identity, but regularity does not imply uniformity of meaning. Sometimes being religious means that a person believes strongly in God or some sacred, supernatural being. Yet some youth who believe in God do not call themselves religious, whereas others do. This ambiguity in the definition of religion reflects the many dimensions of religion and religiosity. Understanding the trajectories of religious change among adolescents requires that we start by recognizing this multidimensional nature of religiosity. Religiosity has many aspects; three of the main dimensions are the *content* of religious belief, the *conduct* of religious practices, and the *centrality* of religion, or what we develop as the three *C*s in chapter 1.

Although they do not use this language, youth are also aware of the multidimensional quality of religion. As Chelsea talks about her religion she is quick to distinguish her religious *conduct*, whether or not she gets up for church in the morning, from her religious *content* and *centrality*, her belief in Jesus and the importance of her relationship with God:

> I go to church once a week, but if I haven't been getting a lot of sleep, I might sleep in, um, and I guess the whole reason for that is I don't think I need to go to church to prove that I'm a Christian and I believe in Jesus Christ as my Lord. I think people that say that you have to go to church, it's a ridiculous statement. I mean I know that I love God, and God knows that I love God.

In this book we examine what happens to the multiple dimensions of religiosity and spirituality in adolescence by conceptualizing religiosity and spirituality as tile mosaics that individuals create and continually modify based on their own definitions of the important dimensions of religiosity, the intensity or importance of each of those dimensions, and the religious patterns that have been modeled for them to this point in their life. We identify and illustrate five common but unique profiles of religiosity, or types of religious mosaics, in the population of America's adolescents that we call the five *A*s: the *Abiders*, the *Adapters*, the *Assenters*, the *Avoiders*, and the *Atheists*. We examine how the lives of youth with different religious mosaics vary in other ways. We also consider how religious mosaics change over time and how youths' parents, peers, and religious institutions factor in the refinement taking place in adolescents' religious lives.

This book is intended to speak to a variety of audiences about the nature of religiosity and spirituality in adolescence. Scholars of religion in everyday life will be interested in our alternative conceptualization of American religiosity as falling into five main profiles and the social characteristics that tend to define each group. Parents and others who work with adolescents (in religious settings or elsewhere) will be able to use this typology of five religious profiles to better understand, communicate with, support, and challenge adolescents.

Adolescence is a Latin word derived from the verb *adolescere*, meaning "to grow into adulthood."[3] Adolescence is typically used to refer to that period in life when individuals are moving from the immaturity of childhood into the maturity of adulthood, and this involves many dramatic biological and social changes. Adolescence involves puberty, interest in sex, autonomy from parents, increasing abilities to make independent and wise decisions, growing self-awareness and a concern for the future.[4] Adolescence is also marked by key life transitions, including driving, working, and voting. In the two years between our in-person interviews Rachel moved from middle school to high school, got her driver's license, started working, and became sexually active. Chelsea also transitioned to high school, embraced a liberal political identity, and experienced an increasingly strained relationship with her mother. These changes all have implications for how Rachel and Chelsea are religious (or not) and the changes and refinement that occur to their faith during adolescence.

Over time the age range thought to encompass adolescence has widened. For some time the term was equivalent to the teenage years (13–19), but over the past century physical maturity has occurred earlier and earlier, and most youth have delayed entering the full-time workforce and getting married until at least their mid-20s. Research also suggests that brain development and maturation extend into the mid-20s.[5] For these reasons it makes more sense to conceptualize adolescence as roughly the period of life stretching from about age 10 to 20, or the second decade of life.

Scholars have made finer distinctions within adolescence, referring to ages 10–13 as *early adolescence*, 14–17 as *middle adolescence*, and 18–22 as *late adolescence* or *emerging adulthood*.[6] These distinctions in age help scholars focus on the key life transitions that occur in each segment of adolescence, such as the freedom that often comes with getting a driver's license in middle adolescence and the transition out of high school occurring in late adolescence. In this book we focus on how the religious and spiritual lives or identities of youth evolve during the transition from middle to late adolescence. The data we use as evidence were collected from a group of American youth who were between 13 and 17 when they were first surveyed in 2002 and between 16 and 21 when they were interviewed again three years later.

It is important to study religion and spirituality during adolescence for two reasons. First, the confluence of dramatic biological, psychological, social, and economic changes in adolescence suggests that this is a prime time for religious or spiritual change and development.[7] Youth in this age range are becoming more autonomous in many realms of life, discovering themselves, and forging their own identity based on what they have learned from family, friends, and the institutions in which they have been socialized.[8] How the myriad changes that adolescence brings shape the religious beliefs, practices, and salience of youth is one focus of this book.

A second motivating factor for the study of religious and spiritual trajectories in adolescence is that many studies have found religiosity and spirituality to be related to positive adolescent outcomes such as higher self esteem, better physical health, and higher educational aspirations, as well as protecting against early initiation of sexual activity, delinquency, and alcohol and drug use.[9] Examining how and why dimensions of religiosity and spirituality change in adolescence helps us better understand and support youth in their journeys of self-discovery and identity development.

This book is based on findings from the first and second waves of the National Study of Youth and Religion, a comprehensive multi-method research project examining the religious and spiritual lives of American youth. Findings from the first wave of this study, a baseline for the religious and spiritual lives of middle adolescents (ages 13–17) in the United States, were reported in the book *Soul Searching: The Religious and Spiritual Lives of American Teenagers* by Smith and Denton. That book revealed that in the early twenty-first century religion is a significant presence in the lives of American teenagers.[10] Most are involved in the religious congregations in which they were raised and profess that religion is an important part of their lives, and even though they are not particularly articulate about their specific beliefs, the vast majority embrace some religious identity. Further, the character of adolescent religiosity in the United States is highly conventional. Most follow the religious beliefs and practices of their parents, and although they are highly supportive of others choosing religious beliefs from among numerous faiths, even outside Jewish or Christian boundaries, they themselves rarely do.

Smith and Denton also find that at the level of subjective consciousness, adolescent religious and spiritual understanding and concern seem to be generally very weak. Most American adolescents have difficulty explaining what it is they believe, what it means, and what the implications of their beliefs are for their lives. So even though religion is very much a part of their lives, it seems to be unfocused, implicit, and just part of the background of life. In fact Smith and Denton label the particular religious outlook most represented among youth *Moralistic Therapeutic Deism*, which they define as a belief in a creator God who watches over human life on earth, wants people to be good, nice, and fair to each other, but does not need to be particularly involved in one's life except when needed to resolve a problem. Regardless of the fact that most adolescents cannot clearly articulate the meaning or influence of religion in their lives, however, religion is strongly related to other life outcomes and seems to have a largely positive influence in youths' lives. Smith and Denton provide a much needed description and analysis of the place of religion and spirituality in the lives of middle adolescents.

Armed with this baseline understanding of the general shape and form of religion and spirituality among American adolescents, the National Study of Youth and Religion then began to address a new set of questions: What happens to the religious and spiritual lives of these same adolescents over time? How do their beliefs and practices and the meaning of religion in their lives evolve? What does repeated measurement of religious beliefs, practice, and salience among these same youth show, and how do they themselves describe the changes in their lives during adolescence? What social contexts or life experiences facilitate or pose barriers to religious and spiritual development? These are all questions we tackle in this book.

The National Study of Youth and Religion (NSYR) started as a nationally representative telephone survey of U.S. households containing at least one teenager age 13 to 17. One parent and one teenager from each of these households were interviewed over the phone for about 30 and 50 minutes, respectively, between July 2002 and March 2003. In the spring and summer of 2003, seventeen trained project researchers conducted 267 in-person interviews in forty-five states. The second wave of the NSYR took place in 2005 and involved a telephone survey to reinterview our adolescent respondents and then follow-up in-person interviews with 122 of the youth who were interviewed in person in 2003.[11] At both waves of the study our interview participants were sampled to capture a range of American youth representing different religions and religious denominations, races and ethnicities, genders, socioeconomic statuses, residences (rural, suburban, urban), and regions of the country.[12]

To our knowledge the NSYR remains the most comprehensive study of the religious and spiritual lives of American youth to date. The survey and semistructured interview data coming from two points in time allow us to provide a reliable and representative description and analysis of the shape and content of religion and spirituality on the journey through adolescence at the start of the twenty-first century in America. Our data come from a nationally representative sample that is not limited to particular religious groups. Included in our study are nonreligious youth as well as a wide variety of religious youth from all types of backgrounds. However, because our sample represents the population of youth at this age in the United States, religious groups that make up a small percentage of the U.S. population—Latter Day Saints, Jews, Jehovah's Witnesses, Muslims, and others—also make up a small proportion of our survey respondents. Thus larger generalizations that we make are often most reliable for the majority religious groups in the United States: Protestants and Catholics. Other members of the NSYR research team are writing books and articles more focused on youth involved in some of the minority religious traditions within the United States.[13]

Here is what to expect in the coming chapters. Chapter 1 lays out our conceptualization of religiosity and spirituality and how it is experienced and refined throughout adolescence. We critique the fit between prior theoretical definitions or conceptualizations of individual religiosity and spirituality and how scholars tend to use surveys to measure religiosity across time. In other words, although scholars long ago identified the multidimensional nature of religiosity and the seeming inconsistencies across the dimensions within individuals (e.g., strong beliefs but low involvement or high involvement but a lack of salience), research involving survey data has been slow to incorporate methods that allow for a more holistic measurement of religiosity in its unique forms and their changes over time. We recommend an analytic approach that allows for seeming incongruities across components of religiosity (i.e., belief, practice, salience) that reflect the complexity with which humans experience their religiosity in daily life. We then situate our conceptualization of religious profiles in key contexts of adolescence—cognitive development, family socialization, peer interaction, and norms and roles—to better understand what we might expect in terms of the character, dynamics, and correlates of religiosity in adolescence. Although chapter 1 is primarily aimed at social scientists who study religiosity among youth and other age groups, our conclusions also encourage youth practitioners, religious institutions, parents, and the general public to more carefully consider what we mean when we say someone is *really religious, not religious,* or *becoming more* or *less religious.* Oversimplification of these concepts may lead to misunderstanding adolescents and the guidance they need and desire in working out their religious and spiritual identities.

In chapter 2 we describe in depth the five profiles of religiosity, called the five *A*s, apparent in the youth population of the United States. We introduce a prototypical youth from each of the five categories to help illustrate the profiles. Their lives demonstrate the range of religious and spiritual beliefs, practices, and salience in adolescents and how these dimensions of religiosity shift over time in protean packages of religious identity that we term *religious profiles.* They also illuminate the relatively constant feedback between religiosity, cognitive development, family socialization, peer involvement, and the norms and roles characteristic of adolescent life. We refer back to these youth, as well as others, throughout the book to demonstrate key points and findings with real-life examples.

We further develop the five general profiles of religiosity by showing other characteristics of youth that relate to membership in a given profile in chapter 3. These findings give a sense of individual, family, peer, and community factors that may be related to living out a particular profile of religiosity.

In chapter 4 we look at change over time in the dimensions of religiosity comprising a person's religious profile as well as change over time in the profiles to which adolescents belong. Although there are some interesting differences in magnitude, over time most dimensions of religiosity show slight downturns in the aggregate for adolescents. We present the probabilities of shifting between the main profiles of religiosity over the three years of our study. This chapter helps us understand the various types of religiosity that exist in the adolescent population and how often adolescents switch types.

We continue with our examination of forms of religious change in chapter 5 by presenting the discourses youth themselves use to summarize their religious or spiritual development over time. This analysis enriches our understanding of how youth themselves view the unfolding of religiosity in adolescence, clarifies our interpretation of the survey results, and suggests courses of action for engaging adolescents in religious or other identity-developing enterprises.

In chapter 6 we examine features of youth's lives that seem to promote either stability or change in their religious profiles. We find that parents, peers, and religious institutions have the potential to serve as social scaffolding that supports and encourages youth to make occasional refinements to the content, conduct, and centrality of their religious faith. The lack of these sources of social scaffolding or overscaffolding, both of which result from others not understanding an adolescent's needs and desires well, hampers youth's efforts to refine their faith, making it their own.

1

A Holistic Model of Religiosity and Its Contexts in Adolescence

I absolutely believe in God. He has a good sense of humor about things, and he is really understanding and forgiving. Religion is, um, definitely like a cornerstone, you know, a foundation for my life. There are other things that influence me, outside of religion, but that's the main factor. Over the past couple of years I have become more religious even though I have not been to church as much. I pray and think about God every day. (17-year-old white Lutheran boy)

Setting out to write this book about trends in religiosity during adolescence, we expected to identify a relatively common pattern of decreased religiosity during this life period, with stability in levels of religiosity for some and the occasional increase for others. We hoped to be able to describe when and how these journeys unfolded for youth. It sounded relatively straightforward, but our initial survey results quickly revealed what a challenge this project would be. Looking at specific measures of religiosity (e.g., prayer, religious service attendance, specific beliefs) revealed little change over time. Where change was identifiable it was minimal. For example, the number of youth who reported belief in God was just 6 percent lower in 2005 than it had been in 2003. Viewed from this angle, it seemed as though there was not much to report about *change* in religiosity through adolescence. To further complicate matters, when we asked youth themselves if they had gotten more or less religious between the two surveys, most of them said they had stayed the same. Even more interesting, the second most common response was that they had become *more* religious, and a minority of youth claim to have become less religious during adolescence. Finally, our preliminary analysis of the semistructured, in-person interviews more than once revealed both high and low dimensions of religiosity at the same time. There were also youth who scored off the charts on any question of religious intensity we could ask, alongside a small minority of youth who were consistently irreligious. However, many young people fell in between these two extremes, and in a variety of unique ways.

These results led us to closely reevaluate our own conceptualization of religiosity and how well our strategies of measuring religiosity matched that conceptualization. Our struggles reflect a key dilemma of social science: How do we capture the complexities of human action and identity while still summarizing enough to be able to draw conclusions and understand generalities in life? This book is our attempt to strike this balance and challenge scientists, practitioners, parents, and youth to think more carefully about what religiosity means, how we evaluate the religiosity of others, and the implications that various forms of religiosity and changes in religious identity have in adolescence. To consider these questions productively we must first examine how others have conceptualized religiosity in the past, where there is progress to be made in our conceptions of religiosity, and specific modifications that must be made to these models of religiosity during the specific life period of adolescence.

What follows is a description of the social scientific theories that have been used to understand what religiosity is, how well these theories mesh with the use of quantitative and qualitative data as methods of understanding religiosity, and what we know about religiosity in adolescence in particular. This chapter is heavy on the sociology of religion and the theories and methods used therein, but we hope it will also be useful to those in the general public who are interested in enriching their own understanding of religiosity, and that it will help readers think about religiosity in their own life, as well as in the lives of young people around them.

Theorizing Religiosity

What makes someone religious? Some dimensions of religion are more central than others in personal definitions of what it means to be religious. Sociologists and psychologists who study religion have worked for years to sort out and name the various dimensions of religion. An influential comprehensive sociological framework for understanding the multiple dimensions of religion was developed by Glock and Stark.[1] In the final articulation of this scheme there are five dimensions of religious commitment, or how religion is manifested around the world: belief, practice, knowledge, experience, and consequences.[2] The most frequent criticism of this conceptualization is that there is no dimension that accounts for the centrality of religion is in a person's life.[3] There have been several other frameworks offered for further elaborating multidimensional religiosity.[4]

Instead of selecting one prior framework on which to rely, we integrate the similarities and strengths of perspectives across these models to focus on what are generally agreed upon as three main dimensions of religiosity. We call these dimensions the three Cs of religiosity: the *content* of religious belief, the *conduct* of religious activity, and the *centrality* of religion to life. Understanding what a person believes, how he practices his religion, and the extent to which religion is an important part of his identity provides a comprehensive sense of a person's religiosity. The three Cs allow us to capture the nuances that define the impact of religion on daily life.

The *content* dimension of religiosity is in line with Stark and Glock's "belief" dimension, Lenski's "doctrinal orthodoxy" dimension, King's category of "dogmatism," Verbit's dimension of "doctrine," and Cornwall et al.'s dimension of "belief."[5] The *content* of belief is the specific ideas or doctrine that characterizes an individual's religiosity. Some religious beliefs are more distinguishing than others. Belief in God, or some divine being, is common among people who define themselves as religious. But there are other beliefs that are characterized by more variance, such as how literal one's sacred scriptures are or whether there is truth in multiple religions or only one. Such differences define religious content.

Content of religious belief is one area that highlights the difficulty of capturing nuance in individual belief using standard methods. For example, the content of individual beliefs is often, but not always, closely related to the particular theologies of a person's religion or denomination.[6] Yet in survey analyses, when specific questions about religious beliefs are not available religious affiliation is often used as a proxy for the content of an individual's religious beliefs. Knowing the types of religious beliefs an individual actually holds gives us more information about the kind of religiosity she practices and how her religiosity may relate to other attitudes and behaviors in life.

However, knowing the content of a person's religious beliefs does not tell us how she practices her beliefs or how strongly she holds these beliefs. How do people apply their beliefs in their daily lives? Do they engage in activities that hold religious meaning or significance? To answer such questions we turn to religious *conduct*, the practices that express and embody a person's religiosity. Stark and Glock label this dimension of religiosity the "ritualistic" aspect. Lenski distinguishes between public and private conduct, writing of the "associational" dimension, which includes public practices such as religious worship and prayer services, and "devotionalism," representing private religious practices such as prayer and meditation.[7] King has multiple categories for religious practice: "participation in congregational activities," "financial behavior," and "talking and reading about religion."[8] Verbit has a category called "ritual," and Cornwall et al. use the label "behavior."[9] In every classification of the dimensions of religiosity there exists one or more categories to describe religious actions, and most, like Lenski, divide actions into public (or social) and private (or personal) realms. Usually this dimension of practice refers to explicitly religious behavior such as attending services or praying. Others call for more consideration of practices that are a part of one's religious identity but not immediately recognizable as religious practices, such as voluntary service or involvement in social justice activities, a move we concur with as it acknowledges the practice of religion outside of formal religious institutions.[10] In sum, there are actions people participate in to conduct their religion; the frequency of these practices reveals part of a person's religious identity, but does not tell us the content of belief or the relevance or centrality of these practices in the entirety of a person's religious identity.

The *centrality* of a person's religiosity, or what Wimberley terms "salience," Cornwall et al. refer to as "affect," and Davidson and Knudsen call "religious consciousness," is the degree of importance religion has in a person's life.[11] People can hold similar religious beliefs or participate in the same religious rituals, but the extent to which they prioritize and integrate their religious identity with other role identities (e.g., student, friend, daughter, employee) adds another layer of complexity to religiosity as a whole.

Altogether we view religiosity as made up of unique and dynamic compositions of content, conduct, and centrality. Although each of the parts is unique, they are often overlapping and serve to reinforce each other. So, for example, the content of beliefs can be expressed through particular practices, and particular forms or frequency of religious conduct may reflect the centrality of religiosity in one's life. These dimensions also can operate separately, or even in contradiction to each other. People may participate in religious worship services where they do not agree with every message being taught. They may not belong to any religious institution but still consider religion to be a central system of guidance in their life. As a result, to gain a fuller picture of the dynamics of religiosity in adolescence we must examine not only all three dimensions of religiosity, but also how they coalesce over time.

How Does Spirituality Fit with the Dimensions of Religiosity?

Before discussing how to theorize religiosity as a sum of its parts, we would like to comment on how spirituality fits into our conceptualization of religion and religiosity. Spirituality is particularly difficult to define because it has multiple meanings across different types of groups in society and its meaning has changed over time.[12] Upon hearing the word *spirituality* some people think of Buddhist forms of meditation or chanting, some remember a book or website promoting spiritual growth outside a religious tradition, and some think of the recent sermon they heard in their Evangelical church encouraging them to be more spiritual (i.e., to seek a close personal relationship with Jesus) and less religious (i.e., going through the motions of religious rituals without meaning). Yet all of these perceptions of spirituality have a common element: each involves the personal search and desire for a meaningful connection to something or someone sacred.[13]

Wuthnow calls this exploration and constant search for epiphanies "seeking," as opposed to more conventional religious participation and practice, which he calls "dwelling." He writes that dwelling and seeking are not in opposition to each other, but people switch between them or allow them to overlap in creative, protean ways.[14] Roof writes that in its current forms spirituality seems to refer to "the inner life that is bound up with, and embedded within, religious forms, or much more loosely in keeping with humanistic psychology as a search on the part of an individual for reaching, through some regimen of self-transformation, one's greatest potential."[15] Whether a person practices spirituality within or outside a religious tradition, we can rely on a general definition of spirituality as the quest for personal, meaningful connection to something sacred, whether that is a major religious divine figure or another form.

In this book, when we talk about religiosity we are referring to a combination of the content of beliefs, religious conduct, and the centrality of religion in a person's life. Spirituality may come into play in any of these dimensions of religiosity. When we mention spirituality we are specifically referring to the personal quest to achieve and/or maintain a connection with some aspect of the sacred. Oftentimes when we mean to represent the full gamut of manifestations of religion and spirituality we use the terms together to be comprehensive and recognize their overlap.

Religiosity as a Dynamic Composite

As demonstrated in our review of prior work, what sociologists and psychologists of religion have been particularly good at is pulling apart religiosity to understand its various dimensions. What has been more challenging is developing theoretical models that represent the complexities of how people piece together the various dimensions of religiosity in their own lives.[16] One important advance in this direction is the first chapter of Hammond and Johnson's edited volume *American Mosaic: Social Patterns of Religion in the United States*. The chapter, titled "Locating the Idea of Religion," includes essays by Niebuhr, White, and Verbit and is motivated by the idea that to study and discuss religion or religiosity we need a concept or definition of religiosity on which scholars can generally agree. All three essays grapple with two complicated dualities of religiosity: the dynamic versus the static (or the variability over time in different dimensions of religiosity versus the essence, or some underlying consistency in the expression of religion and spirituality) and the individualistic (allowing for each person's unique package of religious identity) versus the more easily summarized psychologically consonant model that rarely fits individuals neatly.

There is no doubt that a person's religiosity and spirituality are dynamic and constantly unfolding. Everyday experiences react to and inform the content, conduct, and centrality of our religiosity. The challenge is how to observe and measure such a dynamic entity. Although religiosity is protean, meaning it can assume a variety of complicated shapes and forms that are versatile and readily changeable, we argue that dramatic change is uncommon and rarely instantaneous. There can also be somewhat of an essence behind religiosity. Therefore taking a snapshot of the dimensions of a person's religiosity at one point in time gives us a general sense of his religiosity around that time. Taking multiple snapshots gives us an estimate of patterns and directions of change over time as well as the essence that remains intact. This is how we use survey data to study religiosity. In this study we also use semistructured interviews in which adolescents describe to us the ongoing nature of their religious lives, and we can compare these narratives at two points in time. These qualitative data shed a bit more light on the dynamics of religiosity as lived and narrated. In-person observations of these youth's lives could provide an even better window on religiosity as it unfolds, but even then it is impossible to observe the inner workings of youth's minds, and it would be our interpretations of their religiosity as manifest on the outside. In other words, as social scientists we tend to theorize religiosity as very dynamic and protean but are less able to demonstrate this with data given the methods we have to study the process. We remain cognizant of this as we work through the book and present our findings in light of the difficulty of exactly matching theory and evidence in this realm.

There is more promise for overcoming the second dualism, individualistic versus psychologically consonant views of religiosity. Until recently most empirical researchers used data and methods to study religiosity that imposed an assumption of consonance on the subjects. Representing religiosity as a variable ranging from low to high using either one measure or an index of measures implies that you can reduce religiosity down to one dimension. This also implies that a person is consistent across the various dimensions of religiosity or that the dimensions are interchangeable, so that someone who reports very frequent religious service attendance and low importance of religion is the same as someone who reports very low attendance and high importance (because their average scores would be the same). In reality these are not good assumptions. People are notoriously inconsistent, and we should not ascribe a consistent level of religiosity to them.[17] We rely on a relatively new set of statistical methods, called latent class methods, to study religiosity. These methods allow us to uncover a set of religious profiles with varied composites of high, medium, and low religious content, conduct, and centrality, to more accurately reflect where most of the adolescent population falls in terms of religious profiles. Some youth are consistently high, medium, or low on religious content, conduct, and centrality. However, a large proportion does not fit neatly into these categories. The first book from this project demonstrated that; when defining ideal types of religiosity among adolescents a full 37 percent were not able to be categorized.[18] Therefore in this book we have sought to explain and describe religiosity in such a way that we understand how all youth operate and how a variety of youth are processing religiosity in connection with the many other aspects of their lives.

The most recent advances in trying to manage the dynamic and multidimensional nature of religiosity come from scholars utilizing the "lived religion" approach, designed to recognize the limitations of studying only institutionally based, and therefore psychologically consonant, forms of religiosity that are reduced to the one-dimensional scale from high to low. Instead the lived religion perspective argues that not everyone fully commits to or enacts an institutionally defined package of religious content, conduct, and centrality.[19] Rather than try to fit people into prearranged packages, McGuire argues, scholars must study religion as it is actually lived and experienced in peoples' everyday lives.[20] Her fieldwork brought to light examples of the complexity of lived religious experience, such as the Latina schoolteacher who considers herself a good Catholic, rarely attends Mass, but meditates daily at her home altar (where she mixes images of the Virgin of Guadalupe with those of Frida Kahlo, and traditional votive candles with healing crystals). Other scholars have demonstrated how people express themselves religiously and spiritually in ways that do not always fit neatly into the categories developed by social scientists.[21] Proponents of the lived religion perspective often point to the limitations of studying religiosity from survey data.[22] Surveys typically ask respondents to self-identify by denominational or other broad religious categories and measure religiosity according to how well individuals conform to the official religious standards, such as frequency of religious service attendance, scripture reading, or prayer on low to high scales. We agree that this is a valid criticism of surveys, but posit that there are now survey methods that can help mitigate some of these challenges. Using latent class methods we explore the data for patterns in how individuals package their religious content (or beliefs), conduct (or behavior), and centrality (or salience). Common forms in the population emerge, and then we present how well youth fit into these organic forms over time.

Personal Religious Mosaics

Based on the idea that religiosity is multidimensional, dynamic and essential, consonant and discrepant, we conceptualize individuals as having a protean package or composite of the three Cs of religiosity:

content, conduct, and centrality. The metaphor we use to help describe this composite is a tile mosaic. Individuals have a personal religious mosaic that they create and modify over time using colored tiles representing the different dimensions and aspects of religiosity. The different shades of the colors represent the intensity of those dimensions or aspects of religiosity in one's life. So, for example, believing in a personal God could be represented by teal tiles. The more intense or dark the teal, the more strongly a person believes in a personal God. The number of a certain color of tiles represented in the mosaic shows the degree to which an individual considers that dimension of religiosity to define her religious identity. If a person defines herself as religious primarily because she believes in a personal God, and not because of religious conduct such as attending religious services (possibly represented by purple tiles), then there will be more teal tiles in the mosaic than purple tiles.

The balance of certain colors of tiles is not only the result of individual choice or agency. Different people may have different colors of tiles, or different dimensions of religion, available to them. For example, if an adolescent has grown up in a home characterized by instability due to one or more parental breakups or frequent residential moves, her family is less likely to be rooted in a religious congregation, so she will have less exposure to and opportunity for regular involvement in public religious worship.[23] Therefore it may not be the youth's own agency that is determining how prevalent the purple tiles are in her personal religious mosaic; it may be that those particular tiles have not been available to her. As another example, an adolescent who is raised in a Jewish home will probably not have been socialized to see public religious service attendance as essential to religious identity, in contrast to an adolescent who is raised by Evangelical Protestant parents. Therefore the Jewish adolescent may have fewer purple tiles at his disposal than the Evangelical Protestant adolescent.

Thus based on the various tiles that are available to adolescents and their own decisions about the intensity of the color on those tiles and the balance of tiles in the mosaic, they are continually modifying their personal religious profiles. Of course some do more adjusting than others, and we explore these dynamics later. But the general point is that youth, like people of all ages, have these personal religious profiles or mosaics, and the goal of this book is to identify the most common forms of these profiles in the population, the personal characteristics of adolescents that tend to go along with each of these profiles of religiosity, and how these profiles adjust throughout adolescence and why.

Contextualizing Personal Religious Mosaics in Adolescence

Because we are studying the religious lives of adolescents in particular, we are especially interested in understanding the key social contexts of adolescents' lives: families, peers, religious institutions and congregations, and larger social and cultural groups, such as age (middle or late adolescence), gender, race or ethnicity, and region of the country. We look at how these contexts might shape the personal religious mosaics they develop. We also take into account specific individual characteristics and experiences of adolescents, such as personality features and cognitive development, that influence the type of religious mosaics they craft.

To ground our examination of this complicated web of social contexts and individual processes, we rely on the theoretical orientation of a life course perspective.[24] This perspective helps us to understand the temporal nature of a person's life. From birth until death a person's life unfolds as an interactive process shaped by the human aging and development process, but in the context of historical events and social contexts such as family, peers, and social institutions such as schools, religious institutions, and governments. Individuals' lives take certain trajectories made up of a set of transitions shaped by history and life circumstances. The life course orientation helps us understand religiosity by seeing it as a feature of an individual's life that unfolds along with other aspects of life. It is dynamic. Religiosity responds to other changes in life such as moving out of one's parental home or having a baby; at the same time religiosity likely shapes other aspects of life such as educational and career choices and ideas about who or when to marry. The key point is that religiosity is continually changing over time, usually only in subtle ways, but sometimes in dramatic ways such as conversion or complete apostasy. Many have argued that these changes are especially likely to occur during adolescence, so we investigate three years in the lives of a sample of American adolescents to try to understand any observed differences, how youth understand these changes, and other factors in life that seem to predict or go along with changes in religiosity during adolescence. Although there are many social, psychological, and even biological forces that may contribute to how religiosity unfolds in individuals' lives, we focus on a few of the arguably most important factors: the *social contexts* of *family*, *peers*, and *religious institutions* and the *personal characteristics* of *sociodemographics*, *temperament*, and *life experiences*.

Social Contexts

Family Background

Three key aspects of family life from birth through adolescence shape religiosity: the socioeconomic resources or well-being of a family or household, the stability of the home environment, and the religious characteristics of parents.

Two of the most important indicators of family socioeconomic resources are the level of education that parent figures have and household income. These indicators are related to the types of work adults in the household undertake, the social status a family or household has, and the opportunities that may or may not come to adolescents that reside in the household. We consider how family socioeconomic status might be related to the three dimensions of religiosity examined in this book (content, conduct, and centrality). When it comes to adult religiosity, research has tended to show that economic status is more closely related to the content than to the conduct or centrality of one's religiosity. Adults with less education and lower income are more likely to belong to more orthodox, conservative, or strict religious groups.[25] This research suggests that youth who have grown up in lower income households are more likely to have been exposed to religious principles characterized by a strong belief in a personal and involved God and a relatively black-and-white view of religion that is monotheistic and exclusive to one faith.

Few studies have closely examined the relationship between family socioeconomic status and adolescent religious conduct or centrality. In theorizing these relationships a number of competing ideas rise to mind. Throughout time and context, to varying degrees, religious involvement has been somewhat of a status symbol, a piece of the American middle-class identity.[26] Particularly families with young children may think it is normative and desirable to be involved in a mainstream religious congregation.[27] Parents with more education and income may strive to bolster their middle- or upper-class family identity with regular religious involvement and strong public expression of the importance of religion to everyday life. Economically challenged families who strive for middle-class status may see regular family involvement in a religious institution and the expressed importance of religion as one route to this status. Studies have also shown that many rely on religious involvement to cope with challenges in life.[28] The most economically disadvantaged families may rely on religion and its formal institutions to deal with the stress of making ends meet. A potential challenge to the religious involvement of these families, however, may come in the form of logistical difficulties that poverty imposes. Families in which parents have less education and lower income face a variety of difficult circumstances, such as long, irregular, and inflexible work schedules, which make participation in religious activities difficult. Church activities are often scheduled around a 9-to-5 weekday work schedule for men and a stay-at-home-mom schedule for women.[29] Because religious participation usually involves transportation and many poorer families do not have functional personal transportation, making the trip to religious institutions is that much more of a challenge. These factors may contribute to reduced religious involvement among youth from economically disadvantaged homes.

Features of the home environment may also pose a challenge to the conduct and centrality of religiosity in the lives of youth. Youth who are raised with both biological parents in the home are more likely to be religiously engaged.[30] When parents split up one or both of them may feel too embarrassed to maintain participation in their religious congregation, or they may not want to see each other there, so the parents may choose to let the family's involvement lapse. There is evidence that adult religious participation wanes following divorce, on average, and this has implications for resident children of divorcing parent figures. For children who were born into one-parent households or whose parents separated before the family ever attended religious services, it is less likely their families will take up religious involvement, compared to households with two biological parents, because of societal and religious norms that dictate that marriage should precede births and divorce is undesirable.[31] Of course many religious institutions recognize the challenges to the diverse family forms in the population, and even design special programs to welcome and support all types of families. On average, however, religious institutions are not as inviting to those outside the idealized middle-class family with two married parents.[32]

Frequent residential moves, which are often related to family socio-economic status, have been found to decrease social integration among adults.[33] Residential moves of a reasonable distance may also impose difficulty remaining integrated and involved in a religious institution. Searching for a new religious institution, forming new connections to people there, and learning the norms and styles of that institution are all time-consuming and often uncomfortable. Families who move a great deal are more likely to decrease their religious participation over time. This may be another mechanism through which family socioeconomic status shapes the level of religious practice in the lives of adolescents and therefore the style of their overall religiosity.

Another important feature of the home environment is the emotional quality of family life. Studies have documented the deleterious effects of poor parental mental health on family functioning and youth well-being.[34] Parents who are more stressed or depressed may be less likely to help youth maintain involvement at a religious institution. This may be explained by a general lack of planning, action, or follow-through in these households, but possibly also an aversion these parents feel toward a social institution where they will need to interact with other, more positively functioning parents and families. It may be true that some parents who struggle with stress or depression may turn to religious institutions for help and support, and in that case it would increase family religious involvement, but we expect that on average poor parental mental health will pose a barrier to family and youth religious participation.

The relationship between a parent and child has also been linked to offspring religiosity.[35] It seems that there are reciprocal forces at work. Parent-child closeness seems to encourage religious practice and salience, and families involved in religious practice and for whom religion is very important report higher quality parent-child relationships. In general, because religious involvement in adolescence is so closely connected to the way a family has practiced religion since the child's birth, we argue that close ties between a parent and child will serve to reinforce any shared religious practice and salience within a family. Stated another way, when there is tension and strife between parent and child they are less likely to want to spend time together, so any religious participation that existed earlier is at risk of falling apart in these circumstances.

Finally, many scholars have reasonably argued that the most important family characteristic in the shaping of adolescent religiosity is parent religiosity.[36] Previous research with the youth from the National Study of Youth and Religion supports this.[37] Although some research suggests that the parental influence declines as adolescents age, Myers finds that parental religiosity during childhood and adolescence continues to be an important predictor of religiosity even into adult-hood.[38] Parent religiosity provides an important role model for youth and determines to a large extent the type of religious exposure they experience during their childhood and adolescent years.

Peer Influence

Following the influence of parents, the second most emphasized factor shaping the religiosity of youth is peers.[39] De Vaus discovered substantially more parent influence than peer influence on the beliefs of high school students, but peers influenced religious involvement almost as much as parents did.[40] Parents' religious beliefs and practices were the most important influence on the high school students in Hoge and Petrillo's study, but peer pressure was significantly related to participation in a religious youth group.[41] Peer influence on religious participation seems to intensify in late adolescence.[42] However, similarity of religious beliefs does not seem critical in the choice of friends, except for members of very strict, conservative, or cult-like religious groups.[43] Ozorak found that peers do influence adolescent religiosity, though the relationship is complex.[44] In general, feeling connected to peers is related to higher religiosity, but there was no measure of peer religiosity in this study. King, Furrow, and Roth confirm the importance of peers, and Regnerus, Smith, and Smith find that the more friends and schoolmates report attending religious services, the more an adolescent herself reports attending services.[45] Thus the beliefs and practices of close friends are likely to play some role in the contours and dynamics of adolescent religiosity.

Religious Institutions

Applying the life course perspective, we expect that the religious institutions or congregations that a youth is exposed to during adolescence will shape the type of religiosity he practices and any changes in religiosity over time. Some evidence from other studies supports the connection between institutions attended in adolescence and the life-long shape of religiosity. In a study of three churches known to have large numbers of high school adherents, Lytch details the characteristics of the churches that seem to attract and retain adolescent participation.[46] Religious institutions that are successful seem to provide a sense of belonging, a sense of meaning, and a challenge to develop competence useful to becoming good adults (i.e., leadership skills, ability to set and achieve goals, etc.). She argues that by fulfilling these needs religious institutions can "catch" youth and engage them in self-transcendent states as their emotional and cognitive development unfolds. Dahl argues that adolescence is a time of "igniting passions," and if adolescent attention and potential can be directed toward positive social institutions and behaviors, such as religious involvement, this will be more protective than the often deleterious influence of substance use, delinquency, and other risk behaviors common to adolescence.[47] In chapters 3 and 5 we examine characteristics of religious institutions that promote various types and paths of religiosity in adolescence.

Personal Characteristics Related to Unfolding Religiosity

The lives of adolescents are also shaped by their relationships to groups with whom they share sociodemographic characteristics such as age, gender, and race or ethnicity. There are other personal characteristics that help define personality and how individuals respond to the social contexts and experiences that come with the journey through adolescence. We call these characteristics of youth temperament; they include mental or emotional traits of a person or her disposition, such as how temperamental she is and to what extent she feels the need to fit in with those around her. There are also a host of life experiences common to adolescence that may be related to the type of religiosity a youth lives over time: decisions about whether or not to remain living with one's parents, schooling transitions, employment schedules, social interactions involving romantic relationships, sexual behavior, substance use, and delinquency. Any number of traumatic events may also occur (e.g., death in the family) that could alter religiosity in a variety of ways.

Sociodemographics

As humans age through childhood and adolescence a process of cognitive development results in very different thinking about religion over time.[48] A variety of stage theories have been posited based mainly on Piaget's, Kohlberg's, and Erickson's general theories of cognitive, moral, and identity development across the life course. The most cited of these stage theories is Fowler's seven stages of faith development.[49] He and his colleagues argue that people usually move from a stage of "mythical/literal faith" in childhood to a "synthetic/conventional faith" in early adolescence, meaning that the Piagetian shift from more concrete to abstract thinking is occurring. Fowler argues that adolescents increasingly desire a more personal relationship with God and that reflections on the past combined with concerns about the future and personal relationships contribute to the shaping of one's world-view and values. A shift to the "individuative/reflective faith" stage occurs in late adolescence or young adulthood; this involves a critical examination and reconstitution of values and beliefs and a shift from relying on external authority to establishing authority within the self, or an "executive ego." As with any stage theory of cognitive development, Fowler's work draws criticism for assuming that a universal linear trajectory applies to individuals with complicated lives across a range of cultural and historical settings.[50] Still it is important to recognize that age will likely correlate with some change in a person's religiosity given the changes in how a person thinks about religion at key points in adolescence.

There are also social implications associated with age when it comes to religiosity. Society and social institutions (including religious ones) set expectations for the types of activities and concerns people at different ages should be preoccupied with. Early adolescents are often expected to be involved in age-based training and rites of passage within religious institutions (e.g., bar or bat mitzvah, confirmation, baptism). Middle to late adolescents, however, are often viewed as having received the necessary religious training and perhaps are excused from active religious involvement to focus on educational, career, or other life goals until they begin to form families, when they are expected to reintegrate into religious communities.[51] Not every religious organization has diminished expectations of adolescents, but this view of emerging adulthood may help explain an overall trend of middle to late adolescents being less involved in religious institutions than those who are younger or older. Of course reduced involvement among older adolescents is not completely about religious institutions lowering their expectations of these youth. There are many other age-specific life experiences competing for their attention and devotion, such as the increased importance of peer-only social interaction, sometimes involving behaviors not sanctioned by religious institutions, such as drinking, smoking, drug use, criminal activity, and sexual behavior.[52]

Gender may also have implications for religiosity in adolescence. Repeated studies have found females to be more religiously inclined than males, and biological and social arguments for these findings are regularly debated.[53] We expect to see comparable gender differences in the adolescents we study. Gender modifies the experience youth have within the important social contexts described earlier, so there may be unique gender patterns in how religiosity unfolds during adolescence.

Racial or ethnic identity is another sociodemographic factor known to be associated with differences in religiosity. Taylor and colleagues find that African American adults have higher levels of both public and private religiosity and are more likely to endorse positive statements or attitudes concerning the strength of their religious commitments compared to European Americans.[54] Yancey finds evidence to support these findings as well as showing that African American adults are also more religious across a variety of domains than either Hispanic Americans or Asian Americans.[55] Members of these two minority groups are more likely than European Americans to declare that religion is personally important but do not differ in other dimensions of religiosity. Some scholars have argued that economic disadvantage associated with minority status accounts for the higher rates of religiosity among African Americans.[56] However, Yancey convincingly argues that the uniqueness of African American religiosity probably has more to do with issues of oppositional identity; historically African Americans needed to develop alternative social institutions when opportunities to join existing majority institutions were denied them, and involvement in the black church (especially in rural areas) was so widespread and normative that it was hardly an individual choice.[57] In any case, the unique culture of many ethnically based religious communities will likely show up in varying patterns of religiosity in adolescence across different racial and ethnic groups.

Even a space as large as a geographic region, such as the American South, becomes a feature of one's identity and can influence religious content, conduct, and centrality in one's life. Regional concentrations of denominations have led to some characteristic patterns in the United States, generally described as a more devoted South and a relatively irreligious West.[58] Youth growing up in an area with a particular religious identity may come to experience, practice, or discuss religiosity in a manner shaped by their region of residence.

Youth Temperament

Some characteristics of youth themselves jointly shape their religious beliefs, practices, and salience, especially mental or emotional characteristics.[59] Cognitive abilities partially explain understandings of religion and decisions about personal religiosity and spirituality. Individual personality characteristics might be in operation as well.[60] People who are more conformist, risk-aversive, or strategic or who tend to join social groups are probably more likely to become and remain religiously engaged and involved.[61] It is very difficult to disentangle whether these observed features of individuals stem more from biological differences or come from variance in social environments as children, but it is important to consider how characteristics of youth themselves relate to the type of religiosity they live and any changes in religiosity over time.

Life Experiences

Another set of personal characteristics that likely relate to religiosity in adolescence includes events and activities youth experience. Strict or exclusive content in religious beliefs, regular religious conduct, and a strong centrality of religion don't typically co-occur with certain risk behaviors such as alcohol, tobacco, or drug use, delinquency, and early and promiscuous sexual behavior. Such activities are typically denounced in religious organizations, especially in youth-centered programs, which discourage religiously involved youth from participation. Youth who decide to experiment in these areas will likely feel a diminished sense of belonging within a religious community where these behaviors are openly denounced.

Other life events during adolescence are education, training, and employment. Youth are setting a career trajectory of sorts in this period of life, so they are often expected to focus on the development of human capital more than religious development. Educational and employment activities consume many hours during this stage of life and may squeeze out time for thinking about or participating in religious activities.

Adolescents, like other age groups, can experience traumatic and life-altering events, such as a parental divorce or a death or severe illness in the family or of a friend. These experiences can shake one's foundation and bring to light ultimate concerns such as the meaning or value of life, the existence of God, and the purpose of religion.[62] Marcia argues that identity development of all types, not just religious identity, is a recurring process between crisis points and commitments.[63] As adolescents mature they are likely to bump into crises, sometimes of the traumatic kind we mention here, that lead to a reevaluation of their values and choices.

Summary

This chapter has examined some of the issues that social scientists encounter in their efforts to conceptualize and measure religion in a way that accurately reflects the complex lived experiences of the people we study, while at the same revealing general patterns in personal characteristics and social circumstances that seem related to the types of religiosity in which people engage. Throughout the remainder of this book we hope to contribute to a growing body of literature that reexamines how scholars have measured religion and takes seriously a person-centered approach to understanding the religious lives of young people.

Taking a life course perspective, we recognize that adolescence is a unique period of life. In addition to the complexities of measuring religion, we must also consider the social contexts and personal characteristics of adolescents that interact with their religious experiences and commitments. These mechanisms of life alter each other in recursive ways. How a person's social contexts, personal characteristics, and religious or spiritual identity unfold over time are linked in ways that are often difficult to disentangle but informative to explore. In future chapters we build on the theoretical arguments presented here by examining the ways family, peers, religious institutions, sociodemographics, youth temperament, and life experiences are both influential and reactive to the religious lives of youth.

While acknowledging the theoretical complexities of measuring and modeling religiosity among adolescents, we turn in the next chapter to this very task. We employ a method that allows us to account for the myriad variations of lived religion while at the same time uncovering clear patterns among the religious lives of adolescents.

2

Profiles of Religiosity in Adolescence

Religiosity is a personal characteristic that is difficult to measure in generalities. Indeed a single measure of religiosity, such as how often someone attends religious services, can prove misleading in characterizing religiosity. For example, if you hear that a person attends church every week, you might assume he is very religious on a variety of dimensions. Yet his church attendance may be driven by nonreligious motivations, such as a desire to maintain social networks or to fulfill expectations from family members. In these cases attendance may not be accompanied by other types of personal religiosity, such as frequent personal prayer, strong beliefs, or a reliance on religious principles in everyday life. Furthermore the scales or indices of religiosity that many researchers use, averaging or summing levels of practice with levels of importance or levels of belief, can obscure important configurations of the multiple dimensions of religiosity in people's lives. Is a person who has strong religious beliefs and personal religious salience but never attends religious services really that similar to someone with strong beliefs who attends religious services every week but does not feel close to God or consider religious ideas very relevant to other aspects of life? Focusing on beliefs alone or an average of all three aspects of religiosity results in an assumption that these two people are very similar. However, a focus on religious practice or salience suggests they are very different religiously.

Consider Diego and Jared, two young men from Catholic families. Diego rarely attends any sort of religious worship service, but he tells us religion is "very central" in his life. Jared attends Mass once or twice a month, but says he is "not, like, deep into the faith." Diego is more religious in a private manner and less involved in public practice, and Jared is more involved in a public sense but less concerned about having his beliefs and religious identity be front and center when it comes to the rest of his life. Using a multi-item, low-to-high index to measure religiosity as a variable that describes Diego and Jared would result in two very similar scores (if calculated using a sum or average of the various dimensions of their religiosity). Yet their religious identities are qualitatively different, with clear implications for how they live their lives and for their systems of meaning. For a complete characterization of the role of religion in adolescents' lives we need to carefully profile those who do not necessarily have consistently high, medium, or low levels of religiosity on every dimension.

Our approach is to identify and describe the most common profiles of religiosity among adolescents in the United States using a person-centered approach as opposed to a variable-centered approach. The variable-centered approach suggests that we can categorize people as falling along a continuum of degrees of some variable such as religiosity. A person-centered approach, in contrast, begins with the idea that there are various types of people, or discrete and mutually exclusive profiles in the population, best captured with a typology. Taking a person-centered approach provides a fresh perspective on the contours of religious life among youth. We use this approach to examine common patterns in how youth combine the various dimensions of religiosity in order to identify a set of religious profiles that accurately captures adolescent religious lives.

To accomplish this goal we use a statistical method called latent class analysis (LCA), a statistical technique that takes all possible combinations of responses to a set of survey questions and identifies which response patterns are most common in the population.[1] We use eight measures of religiosity from the NSYR survey data: two measures of religious content (belief in God and attitudes toward religious exclusivism), three measures of religious conduct (the frequency of individual prayer, religious service attendance, and helping others outside of organized volunteer work), and three measures of centrality (importance of religion, closeness to God, and frequency of thinking about the meaning of life). All of the survey questions were asked in both waves of the survey, in 2002 and 2005. These eight measures are used to jointly characterize the classes (or religious profiles) that exist in the lives of adolescents in the United States.

Primarily we rely on survey measures of religiosity often applied in Western contexts: belief in God, exclusivism, prayer, attendance, importance of religion, and closeness to God. However, we also incorporate two less standard and less obviously religious measures. The first is the question about how often youth think about the meaning of life. This measure is included to tap spirituality, or the drive to connect to that which is sacred, in a way that does not directly reference organized religion. The second is a question about how often the respondent helps those who are needy, outside of organized volunteer work. This measure is an attempt to leverage a measure of religious or spiritual conduct that has no direct reference to organized religion. Clearly not everyone thinking about the meaning of life or helping others is doing so with religious or spiritual intentions, but we do consider these traits to be markers that might help delineate types of religiosity or spirituality that are a bit more individual and less connected with Christian language and ritual. Although by themselves they are imperfect measures of religiosity or spirituality, we expect that combined with the other measures they will help to delineate the types of religious and spiritual youth living in the United States.[2]

The results from LCA provide a parsimonious categorization of the youth population into the five latent classes or profiles of religiosity introduced in the introduction: the Abiders, the Adapters, the Assenters, the Avoiders, and the Atheists. The selection of the five As based on the statistical analysis was also consistent with the general types of religiosity that emerged from our analysis of the semistructured interviews. The categorization of five profiles of religiosity is stable, meaning that the same five classes provide the best fit to our survey data at both time points (2002 and 2005). The same five profiles appear among men and women, across racial and ethnic groups, and across religious affiliation. In other words, the five As describe the religious lives of virtually all American adolescents. Except for the Atheists (a small group of between 3 and 5 percent of the population), the other four groups are spread relatively evenly throughout the population at both time points, ranging from between 17 and 31 percent of the population (see figure 2.1). For a detailed description of the latent class methods we use, please see Latent Class Analysis, appendix B.

Two Consistent Profiles

The easiest youth to categorize religiously are those who provide us with consistent answers across the eight measures of religiosity. We tend to assume that the responses of most youth will be congruent or

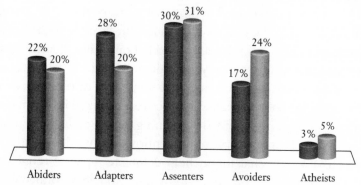

■ Wave 1: 2002 (AGES 13-17)
■ Wave 2: 2005 (AGES 16-21)

Figure 2.1 Distribution of the five religious profiles at Wave 1 and Wave 2.
Source: National Surveys of Youth and Religion, 2002, 2005.

consistent across the eight religion questions. Congruence is unique, however, to two profiles of religiosity that represent only about a quarter of American youth: the Abiders and the Atheists. Though seemingly at opposite ends of what most consider a religiosity continuum, these two groups share a level of consistency in their religiosity unmatched by the rest of the youth in our study. Not surprisingly Abiders' survey answers reflect consistently high levels of each dimension of religiosity; Atheists are also consistent in their reported disconnect from religion on all dimensions.

The Abiders

The first profile of religiosity we describe is one whose members are highly religious on almost every component we consider. Abiders are those youth who report consistent involvement in religious practices, belief in a personal God, and a high level of religious importance in their own lives. Ashley's story provides a good example of a youth who is characterized as an Abider.

Ashley

At the time of our first interview with her Ashley was 15 years old and about to enter eleventh grade. She was living in the Northwest with her mother, father, and a twin sister. She is a white girl with curly brown hair, a few freckles, and braces. Ashley was a straight-A student who described herself as shy yet not bothered by having different, "more conservative" political views than her friends. Her parents knew all her friends (and their parents) well, and they carefully monitored her activities. When bringing Ashley to the first interview, her mother made a point of introducing herself and inquiring about the purpose of the interview and how the findings from the project would be disseminated. Once her mother left and the interview started, Ashley talked about getting along with her parents well and having the same personality as her mother. She has a different personality than her "type A" father, but the two of them share a love for science fiction. She reported feeling comfortable talking about most things with her parents, except when she held back the occasional fact, such as having watched an R-rated movie at a friend's house a few nights earlier, which was against her parents' rules.

When asked how she was raised religiously, Ashley said, "I was raised as a Christian, since I was little." While she was growing up her family moved twice. Though they moved within the same state, the moves were far enough to need to switch churches each time. In each place they lived they were involved in church: a Baptist church, then an Evangelical Covenant church, then another Baptist church. In the interviews we did as a part of this study, it was common for families to exhibit a drop-off in religious service attendance following a residential move that required finding a new place of worship in order to stay involved. That Ashley's parents twice sought new congregations is evidence of their strong commitment to regular religious involvement. Ashley told us that she and her parents' religious beliefs are "super similar, like identical." When commenting on what religion does for her family relationships she said, "I think that since we . . . we do things, like at church together, that's like another area that we're, we can be unified and that helps, just to keep us more connected. [Believing the same things] gives us a lot more in common, and it gives us like the same goals in life. And the same like backgrounds and basis for the way we act."

In that first interview Ashley described herself as a religious and spiritual person whose outlook on life is influenced by what she believes. She talked about believing in a powerful and just but loving God who judges right and wrong but is merciful and personally involved in her life. When asked to summarize her personal religious beliefs, Ashley responded much more specifically than most of our study participants: "Um, well I believe in like God the father, Jesus Christ, the Holy Spirit, three in one, like Jesus rose from the dead and that, like his act, um, it's like personal salvation for those who believe in him. That enables us to be able to go be in heaven and like be in unity, like kinda, like know God." Her beliefs reflect classic Evangelical views, including the idea that Christianity is the one true religion and that people should accept all of the teachings of their religion, not pick and choose.

At the time of this first interview Ashley was very involved in her family's large Baptist church. They attended every Sunday morning, both a main service and Sunday school. She attended the youth group class on Sundays, where a sermon for young people was given. She also was involved in youth choir on Sunday afternoons. She went to a youth group meeting at the church almost every Tuesday night; describing these meetings she said, "I get strengthened in my religious beliefs and I also get kind of a community of people who are there to support me." She had attended summer camps and youth retreats and had recently gone on a mission trip to Central America with her youth group. She appreciated the exposure to another culture, but more important, she believed that the trip had strengthened her faith in God. Ashley talked about praying throughout the day every day and knowing that God answers prayers. She believed God responded to her prayers about everything from feeling less anxious and passing a quiz to not missing a flight home from Central America when they were delayed getting to the airport. She described catching her flight as a miracle from God. Ashley said the size of her church made it difficult to get to know very many people, especially church leaders such as the minister and head youth minister. She felt close, however, to her Bible study leader and a youth ministry helper who led the mission trip. She described the youth leaders as good role models for how to live "a Godly life."

Religion seemed highly salient to Ashley. She discussed extensively how religion influenced her actions and feelings and said that her faith was integrated into her life. Religion, she said, served as the basis for how she lived. She described feeling very close to God, except for occasional times when she was not focused on him and what he wanted for her. She talked about being both religious and spiritual, explaining that it is her spirit that connects and communicates with God. Ashley seemed very thoughtful about life, religion, and her purpose. She wanted to help people in general and give them joy, but she thought there is also a religious purpose in life, "to help people come closer to God and like to bring them in spiritually, like to support people spiritually."

Even though all seemed to be going well in Ashley's life at the time of this first interview, she had recently been diagnosed with clinical depression. It was especially bad when it was dark, during the winter, and when she was at school. She talked about dealing with short bouts of depression about once a day or so, during which she would experience a particularly negative outlook on the world around her. She had just started therapy and medication to manage the depression. When we revisited Ashley about two years later she was still dealing with her depression through medication and therapy and had since learned that some of her relatives also suffered from depression; in fact an aunt had committed suicide just after our first interview with her. Ashley's parents were very supportive of her treatment and very invested in helping her manage her illness.

Much had changed for Ashley over the two years between interviews. She'd bleached her bangs blonde (but left the rest of her hair brown), had three piercings in both ears, and wore a lot of black. She grew out of being a "band geek" into an "artist type" who spent a lot of time writing for the high school literary magazine. She had slipped and earned a couple of Bs in her senior year, but that was fine with her. Ashley was headed to a regional state university a couple of months after the interview, the only college to which she applied. She passed two AP exams to give her a head start. Ashley now had a boyfriend of eighteen months whom she adored and said she could see a future with him. She met him at church. Over the two years she had experimented with marijuana, cigarettes, and alcohol but was not particularly interested in any of them. She was physically intimate with her boyfriend ("everything up to sex"), but they were planning to wait until they were married to have sexual intercourse.

Over the two years between interviews religion remained very important to Ashley, despite some significant life changes. Her boyfriend and parents still attended the large Baptist church, but Ashley had an encounter at that church with a peer who despised her and made life difficult for her. As a result she began attending a different church with a friend, a Nazarene church that she described as being very similar to her Baptist church. Her parents understood and supported her decision. She attended the Nazarene church weekly and participated in youth group there until graduating from high school and getting ready to depart for college. She still believed in a personal and involved God, felt close to him, and prayed regularly. She thought she may have gotten a little less religious because she was involved in fewer activities at church, but she went to some kind of religious service or meeting at least once a week. She said that between work, school, and other activities it became difficult to go to as many church functions as she had in the past.

Asked to sum up what the major changes were in her life over the past couple of years she said, "I became more who I wanted to be and less what I thought others wanted me to be." Ashley's reflections on her life conveyed the sense that she had been working to establish her own identity, all the while facing her depression issues and keeping religion central in her life.

Although there have definitely been challenges and changes in Ashley's life, she is fairly typical of the group of youth in our study who are consistently high on most dimensions of religiosity and spirituality across the period of the study. Their lives are not entirely predictable or stereotypical, but religion continues to be a salient and central feature of their lives. The Abiders are the group most likely to attend religious services weekly or more. They are also most likely to pray on their own regularly; none of the Abiders reported that they never pray. On the whole the Abiders are incorporating both public and private religious practice into their life almost every week, if not every day. Members of this religious profile also score relatively high on our alternate indicator of religious practice: the frequency of helping others outside of organized volunteer activities. Abiders score the second highest in reporting this type of helping behavior, following just behind the profile of religiosity we describe as the Adapters. Altogether, high levels of religious conduct, in both public and private, define Abiders.

The Abiders' highly engaged religious conduct is combined with equally high levels of religious centrality. These adolescents are most likely to report that religion is either extremely or very important in their daily life. In addition they more often say that they are extremely or very close to God, compared to the other religious profiles, and very few Abiders report feeling distant from God. Abiders think about the meaning of life more than the average adolescent; as a group they are the second most likely to report thinking about it very often. The Abiders feel close to God and value religion and its guidance in their lives.

The content of the religious beliefs reported by Abiders sets them apart from other religious profiles. All Abiders report belief in God and are the most likely to express this belief in terms of a personal God involved in their everyday lives. Although it may surprise some, adolescents in the United States are on average not very likely to report exclusivist views of religion, such as believing that only one religion is true or that one should accept all the teachings of a religion. However, Abiders have the highest likelihood of having an exclusivist view of religion and are more likely than the other profiles to believe that only one religion is true and that people should accept all teachings of the religion they follow.

The reason we label this group "Abiders" is because they seem to be living a rather conventional, institutional form of religiosity with standard expressions of organized religions that are mainstream in the United States. Ashley epitomizes the characteristics of an Abider, and as a member of this group she is among the minority of adolescents who talk about how religion shapes their actions.

> *Interviewer*: Do you think that [your religious practices] influence how you think or believe or live?
>
> *Ashley*: I think so because, like, I can't really believe in God and his truths without it having that effect, like on how I act and how I live. I think it helps me to love people because it gives me . . . It's like the world's a fallen world type of thing, and so since I'm a part of that, it's like wow, you know, since God loves us, then I should probably love others.

The Atheists

An important characteristic of the Atheist profile, as with Abiders, is the relative congruence of their religious identity. Membership in the Atheists profile is perfectly predicted by not believing in God. Only a small proportion of people in the United States are willing to declare that they definitely do not believe in God. In our study about 3 percent of 13- to 17-year-olds in 2002 fit this category, matching closely what Edgell, Gerteis, and Hartmann find for adults in the United States.[3] Although a small group, the Atheists are interestingly different from youth who are simply passively disengaged from religion, and thus it is important to characterize this group separately.

Samantha

At the time of our first interview Samantha was 15 years old and living in her grandmother's house in the Northwest with her two parents, a younger sister, and her grandmother. Since her mother and father married they have lived there to help care for her grandmother, who was widowed long ago and has always had health issues. Her mother runs a day care center in the home and her father works as a handyman. Samantha, a white girl who is short and overweight with light brown hair, green eyes, and some trouble with acne, revealed her introversion and uniqueness at the very start of the interview.

Interviewer: What kind of people are you friends with?
Samantha: Mm, I don't really have a lot of friends.
Interviewer: Why would you say that is?
Samantha: Just because I'm not really the average teenager.

When the interviewer asked what she meant by not being an average teenager, Samantha responded that she dropped out of school when she was in the seventh grade because it was not a challenge to her and her teachers gave up trying. She attended high school online from home for a while, but lost interest in that as well. By age 15, however, she started taking college courses at a nearby commuter college. By the time of the second interview, when she was 17, she had completed two years of college courses and expected to have an associate's degree, probably in criminal justice, by age 18.

Samantha reported great relationships with both of her parents and is especially close to her father, who enjoys discussing books with her and stories they have heard on National Public Radio. Although her grandmother attends church every Sunday, neither parent has attended since Samantha was born, and religion is not a subject they discuss. Asked how she felt about religion during the first interview, Samantha said, "Well, I, I always sort of thought that religion was just something that people used to just cope with the way things are. And my mechanism of coping with the way things are is . . . I just have sort of an innate sense. I mean, it's just not something that I really feel that I need. I use logic and the rationale that I just can't do anything about what has happened."

Samantha did not believe in God, and her lack of belief did not change at all by the time of the second interview. In fact at the second interview her life was pretty similar to when we first met her, although there were two significant changes in her life: she had moved into her own apartment in town and found a new best friend who thinks just like her and works with her part time at a public library. When Samantha was asked if she considers herself either agnostic or atheist, she said, "probably atheist": "It just is what it is. . . . [Religion] just isn't on my radar."

Samantha closely resembles the other youth in our study who are not religious at all. She grew up in a family and network of friends where religion simply was not a part of daily life. The youth who are outright atheist and completely unengaged with any religious tradition (only 3 percent of the youth in our nationally representative survey sample) usually have had almost no exposure to religion from their families. Invitations to church from neighbors and friends found them uninterested. Another striking feature of this very small group of Atheists in our study is that they overwhelmingly stand out from other youth their age in confidence and intellectual ability, and they seem relatively immune from or at least irresponsive to peer pressure. Identifying the causal process here is difficult. Do these youth self-identify as "different" in general and as a result find embracing an atheist identity easier? Or do they feel different from others because of their lack of religious socialization or disbelief, and then craft a larger identity of not fitting in with those around them?

In either case, even though Samantha is not a typical teenager, she is happy, has a great sense of humor, is able to think critically, and is nearly self-sufficient at age 17. She has taken a unique path through adolescence but seems to be doing well.

Unsurprisingly Atheists like Samantha are extremely unlikely to pray every day or attend religious services regularly (weekly or more). However, there is still a small probability that Atheists attend religious services at least sporadically (see appendix table B.3). One explanation for this attendance at religious services may be that a majority of these youth still live at home and some may be required to attend religious services with their parents. Having been raised in a nonreligious home Samantha has never attended religious services, nor does she engage in any religious practices such as prayer. Atheists are also very unlikely to hold exclusivist views about religion. They do not believe there is one true religion, and they do not think that people need to believe in every aspect of the religion they follow.

On the question of how important religion is to daily life the Atheists have a very high probability of being in either the somewhat important or not at all important category. The Atheists have the highest likelihood of all the religious profiles of never thinking about the meaning of life. Questions of existence or ultimate reality seem relatively uninteresting or unimportant to these youth. As for Samantha, she is confident in her position on religion and does not express any doubt or hesitation about her atheistic views. She is not hostile toward people who are religious, but rather takes a "whatever works for them" attitude. For herself, she has chosen to depend on "logic" rather than any religious ideas.

Making Sense of Inconsistency

Increasingly scholars who study the meaning and practice of religion in everyday life recognize that most people do not fit neatly within the boundaries of classification.[4] Pinpointing and describing those who do have consistent packages of religious identity, either very religious in all dimensions or completely irreligious, is relatively easy. More challenging is identifying those whose religious lives are not characterized by uniformity and recognizing key differences among them. We now turn our attention to this challenge as we describe the remaining three religious profiles revealed by our analysis. The nuances within styles of religiosity have key implications for understanding the religious lives of youth and understanding how religiosity in adolescence affects the emerging adult life course.

The Assenters

The Assenters represent the image that might come to mind for many people when thinking about religiously middle-of-the-road youth. They are likely to say they believe in God and engage in some level of religious practice; however, religion does not appear to be very central to their lives. They are not particularly strong on measures of personal salience, spirituality, or service to others.

Jared

Our first interview with Jared, an African American boy, took place when he was 16. He lived with both parents in a very poor neighborhood of a large city on the East Coast and is the youngest of four children. Jared was popular and made many friends through sports. He said he chose to hang out with them because they are "good people." He actively avoided fights and interactions with kids his age involved in gang activity and selling drugs. He was hoping to get a master's degree in computer engineering and was focused on his schoolwork, but he had also started to get distracted by partying, drinking, and getting in the occasional fight.

Jared's mother attended Mass weekly at a Catholic church, but his father never went. Though his father usually worked long hours, Jared doubted that he would attend services if he were not working. Jared used to go regularly with his mother when he was a child but said that he currently only goes to Mass about once a month. Religion was not discussed in the home. Jared considered himself Catholic and believed in God, but said, "That is about as deep as it goes. . . . I'm not a hundred percent but I do attend church on occasion." Jared's view of God was of "an almighty black person controlling our lives." He looked to God for hope, he said.

Two years later Jared was doing well. He said that in between interviews he had really scared himself by passing out drunk and waking up in the emergency room next to a bag of his own stomach contents. After this incident he had "calmed down" and now was doing really well in school, getting along with his parents, and had a girlfriend he adored. Jared was very close to his girlfriend's parents and said they were like second parents to him. They were easier to talk to than his own mother and father. His girlfriend and her parents pushed him to attend religious services regularly (with them or his mother), and they encouraged him to read the Bible daily. He felt good about his increased church attendance and said it made his mother happy. Here is what he said about his own religiosity at the second interview:

> Um, I would say that, as a Christian, I'm not like, deep into the faith. Like I believe and I agree with the Bible to an extent you know but, I'm not the type to go Sunday, Monday, Wednesday, and Friday. I go to Bible study every once in a while and I don't, I personally, I haven't even read the whole Bible like, I know people my age that, even my girl, she could quote scriptures, not me.

Jared believed his faith had strengthened somewhat over the past couple of years.

> Well, before, I didn't believe, because I used to pray all the time but it felt like my prayers was never answered, and it's been within these last two years that I've realized that God is good because I'm healthy, like I've outgrown my asthma and I have no enemies. Um, my girl is like everything that I ever wanted in life and like she's what makes me happy. You know, she came in my life at the right time, when I was finished with all the nonsense I was doing and I was getting focused on school. I think it's cool, I definitely believe that God is a good guy, he [is] always on time.

Even though he believed more strongly in God and felt God answered his prayers and provided for him, he believed he could be still more religious. Although he said he could probably do more to actually live like God would want him to he added, "I don't think much about what I'm doing, I just do it." His biggest struggle was over having sex with his girlfriend: "It's like, once you start it's hard to stop, and especially when you're in a relationship, and it's like, neither one of you all are virgins. So, it makes it even harder. It's like, and you know you're both attracted to each other, so that's the really, really difficult part. And, yeah, I haven't been doing too good with that."

Jared had his beliefs and he attended religious services and prayed often. He felt close to God, but unlike Ashley did not describe religion as central or driving all of his actions.

Jared's religious life is typical of the Assenters. When it comes to religious content they are likely to believe in a personal God, although they rarely have exclusivist views on religion (i.e., that only one religion is true or that all teachings of religion must be accepted). Assenters are most likely to fall in the middle of the spectrum on personal prayer and religious service attendance. They have not abandoned either practice, but neither are they regularly engaged like Abiders. The centrality of religion is relatively low for this group. When it comes to religious salience they are much more likely to say religion is somewhat or not important than they are to say it is very or extremely important. Although a sizable proportion report being somewhat close to God, Assenters are very unlikely to report feeling very or extremely close to God. They may participate in public and private displays of religion, but religion is not integrated into their lives as it is for Abiders and that seems fine with them.

Recall that when Jared was asked about the importance of religion in his life he said, "Um, I would say that, as a Christian, I'm not like, deep into the faith." Asked whether or not religion is the basis for how he lives his life, he said, "Um, no, but I could, I do, sometimes I think about it, when I'm making the important decision that I think might have a negative effect, but if it's nothing major, I don't even, I don't think about it at all, I just do it."

For many Assenters like Jared, God and religion are recognized and acknowledged, but not in a central or essential way, which is why we call them Assenters. They typically assent to the religious beliefs with which they were raised, but religion seems tangential to the rest of life, and that is generally fine with them. When considering alternative measures of religious expression Assenters are the least likely of the five religious profiles to report that they help other people or that they often think about the meaning of life. They are open to the idea of religion and see its value, yet they also seem content to maintain a loose connection to religion. As Jared put it, "I do pray. Before I didn't, so I guess you could say I have become more [religious], but it's not to an extreme; it's not an extreme difference." Talking again about the role of religion in his life, he said, "I mean, it's there but I wouldn't say, I wouldn't say I fine-tune my life to make sure that I live by the Bible."

The Adapters

The Adapters would probably score moderately on any overall scale of religiosity. In fact on an aggregate scale they might look very similar to the Assenters, with average or middle-of-the-road religiosity. However, latent class analysis allows us to explicate specific dimensions of religiosity and highlight some important distinctions between the Assenters and the Adapters. Earlier we introduced Diego and the problems that might arise when comparing him with Jared on scales of religiosity. Diego's story provides a good example of why it is important to consider the varying dimensions of religiosity found among the Adapters.

Diego

At the time of our first interview with him, Diego was 18. He is Latino and lived on the West Coast with his mother and father, who had been married for thirty-six years. A much older brother (by seventeen years) lived nearby. Diego felt very close to his mother and described his relationship with his father as "okay." The family had recently experienced a rough patch in their lives due to the alcoholism of Diego's father. His father had quit drinking before the interview, however, and Diego reported that his family life had been much better since. Diego described his parents as sporadically religious in his childhood years. He went to a Catholic school for kindergarten and first grade, and during that time his parents attended Mass. After he left Catholic school his parents stopped attending Mass. When Diego was 16 he began attending youth group and Mass with his cousin and decided to go through first communion and confirmation just a year before our first interview. Eventually Diego's parents began attending Mass again with him. Diego described a significant increase in his religious feelings in the year before the interview.

When asked if he saw himself as religious or spiritual, he said, "Religious, yeah." He believed in a personal God, "a sort of father figure who is always there for [him]." He prayed every night and tried to attend Mass weekly, though other commitments, such as schoolwork, often got in the way. He stopped going to youth group because "life was too crazy with trying to graduate and all." After his cousin stopped attending youth group or Mass regularly he felt less inclined to go.

In talking about how important religion was in his life, he said it was "very central." He said that religion definitely influenced what he did and provided him with a "moral system," even if he did not regularly attend Mass. When he prays he feels "very close to God, like he is right there listening." He believed prayer to be so important that he prayed every night, even when he was so tired that he would like to just go to sleep. He never missed a night.

The recent resurgence of religiosity and spirituality in Diego's life made him happy. Even though he had been unable to keep up the public practice component of his religiosity, there was no sense that his beliefs or the importance of religion in his life had dropped off as his attendance had. Instead Diego adapted the various dimensions of religiosity to create a religious practice that worked for him. Two years later his description of his level of commitment to religion was much the same. When asked how he saw himself religiously or spiritually, he said:

> Um, well I know I'm Catholic. But I think I'm, you know, I think like a lot of Catholics, I don't adopt everything they say. I take it for what it is. I don't try to follow it to the core. And I think God understands me like that. And spiritually-wise, I pray every day. Sometimes I go to church, sometimes I don't. . . . I think, I would like to go to church more, but I don't know if it's like necessarily like the first thing on my list. I'm okay with like the place I am right now. I pray every day. I got, you know, I have everything I want, you know. I try to, you know, to be good, as whatever good is, but I try to be it. And uh, I think I'm satisfied with it. I think I'm okay with it.

He still believed in God, prayed regularly, and found that religion had a big impact in his life. He said things always "pop into" his head about what is right or wrong, and that would not happen without his being so close to God. He believed God kept him safe and supported him.

Diego didn't talk to any of his friends, or even his parents, about his beliefs, frequent prayers, or answers to prayer. He kept it to himself; it was his own personal faith. Although he had occasional doubts, especially when he thought God was not answering his prayers, he remained pretty consistently connected to God on his own.

As is evident in Diego's story, the Adapters share some similarities with the Abiders, including a consistently reported belief in God. Unlike the Abiders, however, a minority of Adapters also reported belief in a less personal, uninvolved version of God. Another trait that distinguishes these two profiles is that Adapters are much less likely to have an exclusivist view of religion compared to Abiders, instead resembling Assenters on this question. Adapters are more pluralistic and generally accepting of whatever religion or version of religious beliefs people choose for themselves. In addition these nonexclusive beliefs are often applied to their own faith; they report being free to pick and choose for themselves which constellation of religious beliefs and practices best suits them. Recall how Diego described his Catholic faith: "I know I'm Catholic. But I think I'm, you know, I think like a lot of Catholics, I don't adopt everything they say, I take it for what it is. I don't try to follow it to the core. And I think God understands me like that."

Later in the interview he talked about having read some parts of the Old Testament that were difficult to understand and accept: "But that's one thing that threw me off. And it kind of made me go, you know. But all it did was it reiterated the fact that I should pick and choose what I believe, you know? That I don't have to take the whole thing for what it is. That I can take parts and pieces, you know? And I know a lot of people say, well you have to take the whole thing. And I don't think you should, you know?"

Diego's nonexclusive views of religion extend beyond the particularities of his own Catholic faith to people of other religions as well.

Interviewer: Do you think other people who don't have a religious faith should have one?
Diego: I, it's up to them, to the person in charge, and I'm sort of indifferent. I don't, if they don't have one, then I don't think they should have one.
Interviewer: And why is that?
Diego: 'Cause it is a personal choice, you know some people need the support, I need the support, other people just don't.
Interviewer: Do you think it is okay for someone of one religion to also practice other religions, or should people only practice one religion?
Diego: I think it's, I think it's up to that person whether they want to take, you know, I wouldn't do that, but . . .
Interviewer: It's up to them? Why is that?
Diego: Because this is a personal choice, and it's, no one can make that choice except them.

When it comes to religious conduct the Adapters are an interesting group. They are much less likely than the Abiders to attend religious services once a week or more. In fact their answers to questions about religious service attendance are very similar to those for the Assenter religious profile. Though the Adapters are the most evenly spread across the three response categories (regularly, sporadically, and never), both Adapters and Assenters are most likely to fall in the middle category of attendance. Thus membership in the Adapter versus Assenter profiles is not necessarily distinguished by levels of attendance, making it difficult to predict who will be in the Adapter profile by looking at religious service attendance alone. Looking at prayer, we see a somewhat different picture. On this indicator the Adapters look a little more like the Abiders than the Assenters. Like Abiders, the highest probability is that Adapters will pray at least once a day, and they are unlikely to report that they never pray. However, they are much more likely than the Abiders to fall somewhere between daily and never praying.

With regards to our alternative measure of religious practice, the Adapters are the most likely of all five profiles to regularly help others in need outside of organized volunteer opportunities. So although the Adapters might not be as involved in religious institutions or pray quite as much as the Abiders, they do serve others more frequently. Whether or not this always takes on a religious or spiritual connotation can be debated. Surely helping others is not always consciously motivated by religiosity or viewed as religious practice per se, but increasingly scholars are calling for new analysis strategies that take into account the ways people practice their faith and spirituality that do not take institutional forms legitimized by organized religion and religious elites.[5]

The Adapters also exhibit relatively high levels of religious centrality, less than Abiders but more than Assenters. They have a high probability of reporting that religion is extremely or very important to them. Of all the indicators we use the Adapters are most similar to the Abiders when it comes to the closeness they feel to God. The majority of Adapters report feeling extremely or very close to God, in contrast to the Assenters, who were very unlikely to report this level of closeness to God.

The complex relationship between religious conduct and religious centrality found among Adapters is illustrated once again in Diego's story. In spite of his recent decline in attendance at Mass and youth group, he still professes to be religious, saying that religion is part of his everyday life and has a significant impact on his life. His primary connection to religion is that he believes in God and prays regularly.

Diego: I pray every night and I, whenever I need support, I, you know, I pray to God and ask for it.

Interviewer: So you believe in God?

Diego: Yeah.

Interviewer: And when you think about God, who or what is God to you?

Diego: I don't know, I sort of think like, sort of like a father figure, like a person that, but like the perfect father figure, like the person that will love me no matter what the personal situation I'm in. The person that's gonna stand by you no matter what, and that's what I think, that's what I see in him.

Interviewer: Do you tend to think of God as personal or impersonal?

Diego: Tend to think of him as personal.

Interviewer: Do you tend to think of God as active in human life or removed from human life?

Diego: I think he's active.

Interviewer: Do you think of God as more loving and forgiving or demanding and judging or something else?

Diego: I think he's more loving and forgiving.

In both interviews Diego frequently described how God supported him and helped him through life. He recounted several examples suggesting that the help he received was in response to his prayers. In one such example he lost his wallet, prayed extensively, and gave up meat and sweets for Lent. Shortly thereafter he found the wallet. Finding his wallet, he said, was God's response to his prayers and Lenten sacrifices.

Like other Adapters, Diego reported engaging in service to others. In his first interview he talked about volunteering at the local hospital. He started out volunteering through a class at school, but he continued after the class was over and ended up volunteering at the hospital for about a year and a half. He said that he stayed because he liked it and because it felt good to be helping people. Diego believed that helping others was important. Although he did not believe that people should be forced to do volunteer work, he did think it was something that people should do.

In addition to specific volunteer work Diego talked about trying to help others around him. He told a story about sticking up for someone whom he did not know well. His friends were spreading rumors about this person, and Diego called them out on it, asking them to stop spreading the rumors. Later in the interview he talked more about this impulse to help other people:

I think, I think people do have a moral obligation to help others. I don't know. I don't want to impose anything, but like, I think that people do have maybe a sense of, or they should have a drive to maybe stick out their hand and help somebody up, you know. I don't think that letting somebody fall and then just turning a blind eye to them is the right thing to do at all. You know, you can't, you can't let somebody go out the window and die there, you know, or to just let somebody stay on the course of self-destruction. You can't do that. You have to stick out a hand.

Another feature of the Adapters that distinguishes them from other groups is that they are the most likely of the religious profiles to say they think about the meaning of life very often. Thinking about the meaning of life is not a typical measure of religiosity, and we are not arguing that this is a purely religious measure. However, when coupled in a latent class analysis with other, more standard measures of religiosity, this question reveals a unique group of personally religious youth who practice and express religion in adaptive ways.

Taking all of the survey measures together, we see that Adapters are a group of youth for whom religion is important, though they may be living it out in ways that are not as conventional as the Abiders'. On the one hand, they tend to feel very close to God, pray somewhat regularly, help others, and think relatively often about the meaning of life. However, they may or may not regularly attend church and are not very likely to hold exclusivist views about religion.

For some of the Adapters their religiosity may reflect an aversion to involvement in particular religious communities. For example, one of our interview participants classified as an Adapter was raised by her Pentecostal grandmother and great-grandmother. However, she grew frustrated with the expectations of how she had to dress and present herself and stopped attending despite expressing deep salience of religion in her life. She said, "I was raised Pentecostal . . . and I would have to go to church. I still do once in a while. But, it was just like I felt . . . like I am religious, but I just don't like that you have to wear skirts all the time and can't wear pants. And, it's just like you gotta be plain, like you can't wear no kind of jewelry, nothing, no earrings, just skirts and dresses."

Another reason some youth are adaptive in the ways they live their religion is that they or their families may have faced barriers to becoming or staying religiously involved over time. One example of this type of situation comes from a Latina we interviewed whose parents divorced when she was 1 year old. When she was 10 her mother was put in jail for drug possession. She moved in with her father and stepmother, but they divorced when she was 15. Her mother took her to church occasionally when she was young, and she attended another church with a neighbor for a while in her early teens, but regular attendance had never been a part of her life. Her interview responses suggested that her parents were uninterested in religious involvement. However, they also may have felt they did not belong in a religious institutional setting, or at least did not have the time and energy to engage in this way, given the family's struggles and illegal activities. Trying to sort out the causal ordering of why this family and young woman never consistently engaged in a religious institution and institutional forms of religious practice is difficult, but it likely has a connection with various social and structural barriers. Still, this young woman prays every night, says, "God is on my side," and believes that he is a father figure to her. There are many youth like this in our study, whose family situation is such that getting involved and staying involved in a religious institution is a challenge. For many Americans the ability to find a religious institution that meets their needs within a reasonable distance (walking distance for many with no personal transportation), to find the time to attend (working around inflexible work schedules with brief opportunities for sleep), and to feel accepted for who they are (alternative family forms, addictions, depression) is extremely difficult and sometimes impossible. When maintaining a profile of religiosity in which every component is at the highest level is too challenging, individuals adapt. The Adapters tend to keep their personal or affective religiosity higher despite lower levels of institutionally based practice. This unique and adaptive packaging of religious conduct, content, and centrality sets the Adapters apart from groups like the Assenters. Although both groups might appear average on a traditional scale of religiosity, a closer examination of their religious mosaics reveals important differences in their lived religious experiences.

The Avoiders

Avoiders tend to score very low on all measures of religiosity. They do express belief in God, however, and on rare occasions they pray or attend a religious service. We call this group the Avoiders because it seems as if they are avoiding being either religious or irreligious. They are not Atheists nor dismissive of religion in their discussion of it, but they are uninterested in having religion be a part of their life. They acknowledge religion and believe in a set of basic tenets, but they do not engage with religion at all.

Brandon

Brandon was 16 when we first interviewed him. He is white and lived in the Northwest with his mother, to whom he was very close. His parents divorced when he was in the eighth grade. His dad still lived nearby, and they saw each other about three times a week. Brandon felt a little closer to his mother than his father, whom Brandon described as the strict parent. Brandon's older sister was away at college. Brandon spent a lot of time hanging out with friends, watching *The Simpsons*, and listening to rap music.

Brandon said that his family was never religious; he wasn't raised that way. In the past few years he had been invited to some Christian youth groups a few times by friends, and he learned something about God there. He used to not believe in God, but at these youth group meetings he learned that "God does exist," and now he believed in a God who "just sort of stands back and watches out for you." He attended the youth groups, which he recalls as Catholic and Unitarian, only a few times, but the ideas stayed with him. He said he was "not really that into it" when explaining why he chose not to go to the meetings anymore, adding that people can be religious and spiritual without having to be a part of a congregation or go to religious services. Brandon was quite happy with his situation; he had some degree of belief but did not engage in any religious practices or otherwise act on these beliefs. He kept busy with school, where he was satisfied with the Bs and Cs he received, and he played a lot of sports. Hanging out with his friends, especially at parties where they drink, was fun for him.

He started off the second interview by announcing that a lot had changed in two years: "I was probably doing a whole bunch of dumb stuff. Smoking and not caring about school, and now I'm working thirty hours a week and going to college." He said he got his life "back on track." He had his own apartment and his girlfriend "sort of" lived with him. She stayed there three or four nights a week.

Much had happened in those two years between interviews. His mother's Parkinson's disease, which he had not even mentioned in the first interview, had gotten so bad that she had to move into an assisted living home. Then Brandon developed a blood clot in his leg and ended up in the hospital for two months. He considered his life-threatening medical emergency a major turning point in how he thought about life and how he lived it, and said that it brought his family closer together. His parents now got along much better.

In spite of all of the changes in his life, his views on religion remained essentially the same between interviews. When asked about his own religiosity in the second interview he said, "I'm hardly religious. I believe in God and stuff, but I don't really live my life like that." He denied being agnostic or atheist, saying only "I'm not religious." He believed in God and said, "Maybe I prayed a couple of times in the hospital." He still had a couple of friends who attend religious services often and were what he called "really religious," but that did not interest him. He had nothing against it; religion just wasn't his thing.

Brandon was also quite happy with how his life was going generally. He was attending community college with high hopes of being a police officer. He was proud of himself for turning his life around and his new self-sufficiency.

Like Brandon, Avoiders as a group report a belief in the existence of God. However, they are most likely to say that God is impersonal or uninvolved in daily life. They are very pluralistic and are extremely unlikely to report exclusivist views of religion. When it comes to religious conduct, there is about a 50–50 chance they will report never praying or praying moderately. Their reports of religious service attendance look similar to their reports of prayer: they are unlikely to attend once a week or more and most likely to never attend. With regard to religious centrality, they are very unlikely to say that religion is very or extremely important and similarly unlikely to report being very or extremely close to God. The Avoiders' most common answer to the question about closeness to God is that God is either somewhat or extremely distant. Overall this group seems nearly detached from religion, though they do still express a belief in God and at times some practice or connection to God.

Brandon's story illustrates well the Avoider profile. In many ways his life looks similar to those youth who are categorized as Atheists: he does not engage in any religious practices or consider religion to be at all a part of his life. However, Avoiders like Brandon differ from Atheists in at least one significant way. Although Brandon describes himself as "not religious," he does not seem ready to reject the idea of religion altogether. He believes that there is a God and does not have any particular opposition to religion. Religion just does not have a role in his own life. When asked why, he says he has just never been interested in religion. He summarizes his religious beliefs by saying, "I believe in

God and I believe there are religions or there is religion, but I just don't choose to go down that path."

Summary

Taking eight survey items representing three core components of religiosity—content, conduct, and centrality—we have used latent class methods to map the patterns and dynamics in adolescent religiosity in the contemporary United States. Our results suggest there are five main profiles of religiosity for adolescents: Abiders, Adapters, Assenters, Avoiders, and Atheists. What is most interesting and new about our results is that they can be used to characterize different profiles within a larger group of youth who are normally considered to be moderately or nominally religious. We are able to separate the Adapters from the Assenters and the Avoiders from the Atheists and better understand how different these groups may be. For a summary of all five latent classes and the characteristics of each of them, see figure 2.2.

Descriptive analyses or studies of either predictors or consequences of religiosity usually conceptualize or operationalize religiosity as unidimensional, a construct that ranges from low to high in individuals. This requires using a single measure of religiosity or averaging across a set of measures. Either of these approaches eliminates interesting information about the ways youth package the various dimensions of religiosity within their religious identity. In the study of religiosity there have been increased calls for a better understanding of lived religion, or the ways individuals creatively enact the beliefs, practices, and salience of religiosity and spirituality in their own lives.[6] Typically those arguing for a lived religion approach emphasize the usefulness of less structured or ethnographic methods to capture religiosity in its own forms and not impose a set of measurements that reflect institutional involvement and preference for Evangelical Christian forms of belief and practice. We concur with the value of such an approach and these research methods. We would add that there are new methods for the analysis of survey data that may also move us toward a better operationalization of lived religion. One such option is the method we have used: latent class analysis.

Latent class methods allow us to retain information about the interesting ways individuals combine the various dimensions of religiosity, some at higher levels than others. We return here to the image of adolescents crafting mosaics that represent their religious and spiritual

The Five *As*

Abiders	• Have highest probability of giving most religious response to each of the standard measures of religion:
	   o Belief in God, exclusivism, prayer, attendance, importance of faith, close to God
	• Second highest response to alternative measures of religion:
	   o Helping others and thinking about the meaning of life

Adapters	• Believe in a personal and involved God • High personal religious practice and centrality • High service to others and thinking about life • Not very exclusivist • Variance in public religious practice
Assenters	• Tend to believe in a personal God • Feel somewhat close to God • Faith not likely to be very important in life • Not exclusivist • Practice occasionally
Avoiders	• Express some belief in God, but often a distant impersonal God • Low levels of religious conduct and centrality
Atheists	• Do not believe in God • Highest probability of giving the least religious response to every question

Figure 2.2 Summary of religious characteristics of the five religious profiles. *Source: National Surveys of Youth and Religion, 2002, 2005.*

lives. Using the colored tiles of religious conduct, religious content, and religious centrality, adolescents balance the various colors and patterns of their mosaics. Although each individual mosaic is unique, when we step back we can begin to recognize patterns among these youth, shared strategies for creating the mosaics of their religious lives.

Several stakeholders can learn from the results we present in this chapter. For social scientists who study the influence of religiosity on other aspects of life, especially among adolescents, it may be important to consider these profiles of religiosity and how studying their causal influence may improve our understanding of the role of religion in adolescence. Are there significant differences in the risk behaviors or well-being of the Adapters and the Assenters? Which group's form of lived religion is more protective? It could be that the high religious salience of the Adapters helps them cope with life's challenges better than the Assenters, but the Assenters' higher likelihood of institutional engagement may link them to more adult supervision, higher expectations, and greater social capital than the Adapters. In addition this typological approach to religiosity may help us better understand how Atheists fare when it comes to well-being and risk behaviors. In an analytic model in which religiosity runs from low to high, the minority of Atheists are likely swamped by the experiences of the Avoiders, thus obscuring our understanding of how Atheists compare to the Abiders and others. Given that Atheist youth are willing to state unpopular beliefs, they may have a particularly strong sense of self that protects them against other struggles in adolescence. We explore some of these issues in chapter 3.

The implications of viewing religiosity in a typology framework as opposed to a low-to-high framework extend to religious institutions and leaders, parents, and those who work with youth in a variety of settings. Religiosity is complex and multidimensional, so programs for youth (and likely adults as well) should be designed to address this. Youth could be better understood by knowing the profiles of religiosity into which they tend to fit. Programs could be designed around the types of profiles we identified. Youth who do not attend services or youth group meetings regularly should not be assumed to have reduced commitment to their beliefs. Nor should anyone assume that lower religious involvement necessarily equates to lower affective religiosity or salience. Alternatively youth who are regularly involved in religious activities should not be assumed to have high levels of affective religiosity or feel particularly close to God.

We hope this chapter inspires readers to rethink their own definitions of religiosity and how they apply them. We have tried to offer a more nuanced understanding of what religiosity is and how its multiple components are packaged in the real world.

3

Roots and Ramifications of the Five *A*s of Religiosity

My ideas about God come from my parents. Um, that's where they all originate[d]. Before my grandma passed away, she was a big influence. She was very religious. She kind of taught me how to pray—the right way to pray. And she was the one that really pushed, you know, the whole religion thing. And, being Catholic is something my parents taught me through church. (Diego, an Adapter)

Religion affects the way I treat people, um, it gives me like criteria to look at things through. I mean, it colors like my world view, I think. . . . It's important 'cause it gives people goals and I mean, not really goals, it gives them a purpose and it gives them hope and like it gives them something larger than themselves to belong to. (Ashley, an Abider)

Religion is just really not my thing. I always sort of thought that religion was just something that people used to just cope with the way things are. And my mechanism of coping with the way things are is I just have sort of an innate sense. I mean it's just not something that I really feel that I need. (Samantha, an Atheist)

As suggested by the variety of experience within the religious profiles we designate the five *A*s, adolescents have a wide range of religious expression. Approaches to religion are shaped by individual agency, but many other factors, such as socioeconomic characteristics, ethnic and gender identity, and family religious background, are likely pulling adolescents in particular directions. Are Abiders and Atheists from totally different worlds, or do they share any social characteristics? Are males and females drawn to different forms of religiousness? Are differing economic backgrounds related to which form of religion young people embrace? How does family background affect the types of mosaics youth create in the refinement of their religious lives? In other words, what personal characteristics and experiences may be related to particular expressions of religiosity?

As part of the larger project of this book, we are also very interested in how the form one's religiosity takes is related to a range of life outcomes. How do youth behaviors and well-being vary, on average, across the five religious profiles? Are certain religious profiles associated with less risky behavior? higher ambitions? fewer instances of depression?

At the time of our first survey, when respondents were 13 to 17 years old, we found that demographic characteristics, family background, and youth temperament were related to the adolescents' religious profiles. We also found that membership in a given profile at the time of the first survey was related to life outcomes measured at the time of our second survey, when the youth were 16 to 21. Who is struggling or satisfied, at risk or healthy, and how have their religious practices shaped their decisions and their accomplishments? Exploring the nonreligious characteristics of youth in relation to the religious profile they best fit allows us to see how youth become religious in certain ways. Looking at adolescent faith in this larger context also reveals how particular styles of religiosity may affect the general well-being of young people.

In the sections that follow we present and describe a series of tables showing results from bivariate analyses conducted using our first wave of survey data (2002) to explore the relationships between membership in each of the five *A*s and demographic characteristics, several aspects of family background, and youth temperament. For example, table 3.1 shows the relationship between demographic characteristics (race or ethnicity, gender, and age) and membership in each of the five *A*s. As in all the tables, one can look at the first column of numbers to see the percentage of the total population meeting the characteristic represented in that row; the next five columns show the percentage of each of the five religious profile groups that meets the characteristic represented by that row.[1]

Race and Ethnicity

Religious institutions are among the most racially and ethnically segregated social institutions in the United States.[2] Racial and

Table 3.1 Youth Personal Demographic Characteristics by Religious Profile, Ages 13–17 (Percentages)

	U.S.	Religious Profile				
		Abiders	Adapters	Assenters	Avoiders	Atheists
Race/ethnicity						
White	68	74	55[ab]	69	77[a]	80
African American	15	15	24[ab]	13	7[a]	3
Latino	11	7	14	12	9	7
Female	51	56[b]	59[b]	47[a]	40[a]	36[a]
Age 13–15	60	63[b]	62	61	55[a]	45[a]
Age 16–17	40	37[b]	38	39	45[a]	55[a]

Source: National Survey of Youth and Religion, 2002.

Note: Female and age percentages may not add to 100 due to rounding. Not all race/ethnicity categories presented.

[a] Difference from the Abider profile is statistically significant ($p < 0.05$) in a multivariate model.

[b] Difference from the Atheist profile is statistically significant ($p < 0.05$) in a multivariate model.

ethnic identities involve aspects of cultural and often religious identity. Therefore, as other research has shown, the content, conduct, and centrality of religion vary along racial and ethnic lines. There is a stronger emphasis on religiosity in African American communities than others, leading to higher levels of religiosity among African Americans than among whites, Latinos, and Asian Americans.[3]

Our study is no exception to these general findings. African American youth are more likely to be found among the Abiders and Adapters, the groups characterized by higher levels of religious centrality, than they are among the Avoiders and Atheists, groups characterized by little if any religious centrality. African American youth account for only 7 percent of the Avoiders and 3 percent of the Atheists. Latinos are similarly unlikely to be Atheists and more likely to be Adapters or Assenters. Unlike African American youth, however, Latinos are underrepresented among the Abiders.

Although the majority of Adapters are white (55 percent), comparing this to the representation of whites in the general population (68 percent) actually suggests that white adolescents are the racial group least likely to identify as Adapters.[4] Compared to their representation in the U.S. population, white adolescents are found at similar rates among the Assenters, but are overrepresented among the Abiders, Avoiders, and Atheists.

Gender

Across ages, races, and a wide range of religious traditions, female adolescents report higher levels of religious engagement than males.[5] As Miller and colleagues argue, girls are socialized from an early age and may also have some biological predisposition to be more risk-averse, on average, than boys. Young women are more likely to follow in the footsteps of their grandmothers, mothers, sisters, and female friends and less likely to risk perceived social or supernatural judgment by stepping away from religion. Abiders and Adapters are more likely to be young women: 56 percent of Abiders and 59 percent of Adapters in our analysis were female. Atheists and Avoiders, in contrast, are made up of more males than females; adolescent boys compose roughly 60 percent of these groups.

Age

Conventional wisdom suggests that as youth get older, the social context of their lives may create distance from religious engagement. Autonomy from parents; increased time commitments such as for work, school, and extracurricular activities; and cognitive developments that may facilitate a critical reexamination of faith are all features of late adolescence that might be correlated with lower levels of consistent religious commitment. In our study we also find that, although the differences are not large, older adolescents are less likely than younger to identify with religious profiles characterized by high levels of public or private religious engagement. In table 3.1 we see that the younger age group (13–15) is slightly overrepresented among Abiders and Adapters. The older age group (16–17) is overrepresented among the Avoiders and Atheists, the two religious profiles that are most distant from public and private religious engagement.

Family Background

In chapter 1 we explained the importance of understanding not just the personal characteristics of the adolescents, but also the significance of the larger social contexts within which adolescents live out their lives, specifically their religious lives. Table 3.2 examines the family

Table 3.2 Family Background Characteristics by Religious Profile, Ages 13–17 (Percentages)

	U.S.	Religious Profile				
		Abiders	Adapters	Assenters	Avoiders	Atheists
Parent education						
High school or less	22	16	31	21	20	11
Some college	34	30	36[a]	34[a]	33	35
College or graduate degree	44	54	33[a]	45[a]	47	54
Parent income						
Income more than $50,000	51	60	39[ab]	53	52	70
Income less than $50,000	43	35	56[ab]	39	42	28
Living with both parents	57	68	49	60	53	56
Parents in same home whole life	19	25	14[a]	18[a]	18	17
Parental depression[c]	2.7	1.8[b]	2.6[b]	2.8[b]	3.3[b]	5.1[a]
Extremely close to parent	42	52[b]	51[b]	33[ab]	35[ab]	27[a]

Source: National Survey of Youth and Religion, 2002.
Note: Percentages may not add to 100 due to rounding and missing income data.
[a] Difference from the Abider profile is statistically significant ($p < 0.05$) in a multivariate model.
[b] Difference from the Atheist profile is statistically significant ($p < 0.05$) in a multivariate model.
[c] Parental depression represents the mean number of depressive episodes experienced in the previous 6 months, on a scale of 0-30, rather than percentages.

background characteristics of the youth in our study. These character-istics represent the family contexts and resources available to youth as they move through adolescence.

Most adolescents in the United States have one parent with at least some college-level education. Forty-four percent of adoles-cents in the United States have at least one parent with a bachelor's degree or higher. Another 34 percent have at least one parent who has some college but no residential parent with a college degree.

Only 22 percent of adolescents have parents with no education past high school.

Atheists and Abiders, the religious groups with the most consistently aligned dimensions of religiosity (all low or all high), have the most educated parents. In contrast adolescents whose parents have a high school diploma (or less) are highly overrepresented among the Adapters, making up 31 percent of this group compared with 22 percent of the general population.

Examining household income reveals a similar pattern. Fifty-one percent of adolescents in the United States live in households that earn more than $50,000 a year, but only 39 percent of the Adapters fall into this income category. In contrast 70 percent of Atheist youth and 60 percent of Abider youth have parents who earn more than $50,000 a year.

The majority of American adolescents live with both of their parents. When correlating that fact with religious profiles, however, we see that youth who live with both parents are overrepresented among the Abiders and to a lesser extent among the Assenters. In contrast youth living with both parents make up a smaller than average percentage of the Adapters and Avoiders. In addition to asking which parents are in the household, we also asked about the length of time that the parents had lived in the same home. This measure represents a level of stability and continuity in the living situations of youth. Table 3.2 shows the percentage of youth in the United States and within each profile whose parents have lived in the same home for all of the youth's life. Only 19 percent of the population of adolescents have parents who have lived in the same house during the entirety of the youth's life, yet 25 percent of Abiders have parents who report this level of residential stability. Assenters and Avoiders are close to the national average, and Atheists are slightly below average. Adapters, however, report the lowest rates of residential stability, only 14 percent.

Parental well-being was measured by asking parents to report how many times in the previous six months they had felt sad or depressed for at least three days in a row. The answers ranged from 0 to 30 with a mean of 2.7. The means within each religious profile provide insight into the potential relationship between parental well-being and the religious lives of youth. Parents of Abiders report the lowest levels of depression, with a mean of just 1.8 experiences of depression in the previous six months. Parents of Atheist youth reported the highest number, with a mean of 5.1. Parents of youth in the other three religious profiles fall in the middle, with reported averages ranging from 2.6 to 3.3.

Youth were asked how close they feel to the parents with whom they live. Forty-two percent report feeling extremely close to at least one of their parents. The remaining 58 percent gave answers ranging from not close at all to very close. When looking across the religious profiles, however, we see that more than 50 percent of all Abiders and Adapters report extremely close relationships with their parents. In contrast, Assenters, Avoiders, and Atheists are all less likely than the national average to report having an extremely close relationship with at least one parent.

Family Religious Context

Of all of the family background characteristics we examine, the one that we expect to be most closely associated with adolescent religiosity is the religious lives of their parents. Table 3.3 shows the relationships between the religiousness of parents and the five religious profiles. Various religious traditions emphasize different elements of religious expression, and how parents practice religion affects the religious lives of their children. The emphasis on personal religiosity and religious centrality found among Abiders and Adapters appears to be consistent with the form of religiosity that is common among conservative Protestants. Abiders are most likely to have parents associated with the conservative Protestant tradition, compared to all of the other religious traditions. Youth with conservative Protestant parents are also overrepresented in the Adapter profile. Mainline Protestant and Catholic parents are represented among the Assenters and Avoiders at rates higher than the national averages. Youth with Jewish parents are overrepresented among Avoiders and Atheists.

Parental reports about attendance at religious services appear in all of our analyses to be highly correlated with the religious profiles of adolescents. In table 3.3 we see a distinct relationship between parental attendance and the five religious profiles. Abiders stand apart, as 86 percent of these youth have parents who report attending religious services regularly, compared to the national average of 47 percent. Parents of Adapters and Assenters have attendance patterns that are much more consistent with the national averages, with Adapters being slightly below and Assenters slightly above the average for regular attendance. Avoiders and Atheists are the least likely to have parents

Table 3.3 Family Religious Background by Religious Profile,
Ages 13–17 (Percentages)

	U.S.	Religious Profile				
		Abiders	Adapters	Assenters	Avoiders	Atheists
Religious tradition of parent						
Conservative Protestant	43	64[b]	51[ab]	35[ab]	22[a]	15[a]
Mainline Protestant	16	11[b]	14[a]	18[a]	20[a]	23[a]
Catholic	26	13	26[a]	34[a]	29[a]	18
Jewish	2	0	1	2	6[a]	4
Unaffiliated	7	1	4[b]	6[b]	15	31
Parent attendance						
Weekly or more	47	86[b]	41[ab]	43[ab]	20[a]	8[a]
Sporadically	38	14[b]	48[ab]	42[ab]	47[a]	39[a]
Never	15	1[b]	11[ab]	16[ab]	33[a]	52[a]
Parents prays for youth daily	61	79[b]	69[b]	55[a]	40[a]	26[a]

Source: National Survey of Youth and Religion, 2002.
Note: Percentages may not add to 100 due to rounding and minority religious groups not in the table.
[a] Difference from the Abider profile is statistically significant ($p < 0.05$) in a multivariate model.
[b] Difference from the Atheist profile is statistically significant ($p < 0.05$) in a multivariate model.

who attend regularly; parents who never attend compose 33 and 52 percent of these two religious profiles, respectively.

Attendance at religious services tells us something about the public religious practices of the parents of adolescents, but we also measured parents' private religious expression by asking parents how often they pray for their child. Abiders and Adapters are most likely to have parents who report praying for them daily. Parents who report praying daily for their children are underrepresented among the other three profiles when compared with the average for all of the parents in the study. This suggests that youth who have a parent with a higher level of private religious practice (especially a parent who makes children the focus of her prayers) may follow the religious example of their parent.

Peers

Families are the most important social factor in shaping the religious lives of adolescents, but peers are also a defining aspect of the social context of the lives of youth. Adolescent peer groups can significantly influence the religious lives of youth, as our findings suggest. Table 3.4 presents responses to questions about the religious lives of our respondents' closest friends.[6] On average American adolescents reported that 77 percent of their five closest friends are religious.[7] As we would expect, however, the percentage of religious friends varies across our five religious profiles. At the high end Assenters, Adapters, and Abiders report that 80 to 90 percent of their closest friends are religious.

Table 3.4 Religious Characteristics of Five Closest Friends by Religious Profile, Ages 13–17 (Percentages)

	U.S.	Religious Profile				
		Abiders	Adapters	Assenters	Avoiders	Atheists
Average (mean) percentage of close friends who are religious	77	91[b]	83[ab]	80[a]	52[ab]	35[a]
Average (mean) percentage of close friends with whom the youth talks about religious belief and experience	39	59[b]	44[a]	29[a]	22[a]	33[a]
Average (mean) percentage of close friends involved in a religious youth group	32	56[b]	31[a]	25[a]	15[ab]	23[a]

Source: National Survey of Youth and Religion, 2002.
[a] Difference from the Abider profile is statistically significant ($p < 0.05$) in a multivariate model.
[b] Difference from the Atheist profile is statistically significant ($p < 0.05$) in a multivariate model.

Avoiders report that 52 percent of their friends are religious, and only 35 percent of Atheists' friends are religious.

Our interviews with youth also reveal, however, that young people don't often talk about religion with their friends. We asked youth how many of their friends they talk with about matters of religious belief and experience, and they responded that, on average, they discuss matters of faith with only two of their five closest friends. Once again the likelihood of having friends with whom one talks about religion varies across the profiles. Abiders and Adapters report the highest averages, 59 and 44 percent, of their friends being people with whom they talk about religion. In a change from previous patterns, the Avoiders—not the Atheists—are the least likely to have friends with whom they talk about religion. Atheists report talking about religion with 33 percent of their friends, compared with 22 percent for Avoiders and 29 percent for Assenters.

Looking at how many peers are involved in religious youth groups reveals a similar pattern across the five As. Avoiders report the lowest percentage of friends involved in a religious youth group, 15 percent. Atheist and Assenter youth are also below average, with 23 and 25 percent of their friends involved in youth groups. Adapters are close to the national average at 31 percent, and Abiders are far above the average, at 56 percent.

Youth Temperament

Individual characteristics are often related to a young person's form of religious belief and expression. Youth who are more conformist and risk-aversive or who tend to join social groups are probably more likely to become and remain religiously engaged and involved.[8] In table 3.5 we examine two characteristics of youth temperament that may relate to the type of religious profile an adolescent adopts. We asked parents to report whether or not their child has a bad temper, and on average, 42 percent of parents reported that their adolescent child has a somewhat bad or very bad temper. Youth perceived as bad-tempered are overrepresented among the Avoider profile, at 50 percent. In contrast youth with a bad temper are underrepresented among the Abiders; only 34 percent of Abiders are reported by parents to have a somewhat or very bad temper.

We then asked youth how important it is to fit in with what other teens think is cool. Answers to this question revealed a striking

Table 3.5 Youth Temperament by Religious Profile,
Ages 13–17 (Percentages)

	U.S.	Religious Profile				
		Abiders	Adapters	Assenters	Avoiders	Atheists
Parent reports that youth has a somewhat bad or very bad temper	42	34	44	41	50	46
Youth says it is not important to fit in with what teens think is cool	21	19[b]	23[b]	15[b]	24[b]	44[a]

Source: National Survey of Youth and Religion, 2002.

[a] Difference from the Abider profile is statistically significant ($p < 0.05$) in a multivariate model.

[b] Difference from the Atheist profile is statistically significant ($p < 0.05$) in a multivariate model.

difference between youth in the Atheist profile and the rest of the youth in our study. Forty-four percent of Atheists say that fitting in with what is considered cool is not important at all. Overall only 21 percent of adolescents give this answer. As was suggested in chapter 2, it seems that youth with a nonconformist identity are more likely to fit a religious profile that requires some level of nonconformity to the mainstream religious ideals of our culture. In contrast very few Assenters appear to be nonconformists; only 15 percent report being uninterested in fitting in with what is cool.

Religious Institutions

In chapter 1 we identified religious congregations as social institutions that have the potential to shape the religiosity of young people. To explore this issue further we limited our analysis to those youth who reported having some level of affiliation with a religious congregation. Sixty-nine percent of the adolescent population in the United States attends religious services more than a few times a year, and in this analysis we consider these youth to be affiliated with a religious congregation. Unsurprisingly nearly all Abiders are affiliated with a religious congregation, and a majority of Adapters and Assenters also have an affiliation. Avoiders are unlikely to be regularly connected to a religious congregation. We asked those adolescents connected to a religious congregation to describe the various characteristics of these congregations. Their responses are reflected in table 3.6.

Table 3.6 Congregational Evaluations by Religious Profile, Ages 13–17 (Percentages)

	U.S.	Religious Profile			
		Abiders	Adapters	Assenters	Avoiders[c]
Affiliated with a religious congregation[b]	69	99	80	70	22
Religious congregation is usually warm and welcoming	77	86	79[a]	68[a]	57[a]
Religious congregation usually makes respondent think	64	79	69[a]	50[a]	34[a]
Religious congregation is rarely or never boring	47	60	54	32[a]	20[a]
Opportunities for youth to be involved in religious services	84	88	85	81	72[a]
Adults in congregation who talk with or encourage respondent	81	91	83	73[a]	58[a]
Ministry to youth is a very important priority (parent report)	66	78	71	60	45

Source: National Survey of Youth and Religion, 2002.
[a] Difference from the Abider profile is statistically significant ($p < 0.05$) in a multivariate model.
[b] The first row reflects the percentage of each profile affiliated with a religious congregation. The remaining rows are limited to those youth within each profile who attend religious service more than a few times a year. The numbers in these rows reflect the percentage of this subgroup who responds to each question listed.
[c] Only a very small number of Atheists report being part of a religious congregation. The small sample makes the percentages difficult to interpret, and they are therefore not reported here.

Among youth who are affiliated with a religious congregation 77 percent say their congregation is usually a warm and welcoming place, 64 percent report that their congregation usually makes them think, and 47 percent say that their congregation is rarely or never boring. The religious congregations of most youth in our study provide opportunities for youth involvement in services, and the large majority of youth involved in a congregation report having encouraging adults in their congregation.

Examining these responses across the religious profiles reveals a clear and consistent pattern. Abiders and Adapters provide more positive assessments of their religious congregations and are the most likely to report opportunities for engagement, either during religious services or through interactions with adults in the congregation. Assenters and Avoiders are less likely to describe their congregations as welcoming, challenging, and engaging. Not surprisingly it is the Avoiders, the group in this analysis that is the most disengaged from religion, who are the least likely to report that they have adults in their congregations with whom they can talk.

Parents of religiously affiliated adolescents were asked to assess the extent to which ministry to teens was important in their religious congregations. Among these parents 66 percent reported that ministry to teens is a very important priority in their congregation. Parents of Abiders were the most likely to say this is an important priority, and parents of Avoiders were the least likely.

There are surely real variations across congregations with respect to their ability to reach and engage adolescents. It may be that congregations that welcome, challenge, and integrate youth encourage religious practices and commitments that are consistent with Abider or Adapter religious profiles. Congregations that don't engage the youth in their midst may foster religious practices and commitments more consistent with the Assenter and Avoider profiles. It is also likely that those youth and parents who are invested in a particular version of religious expression may be more proactive in seeking out religious congregations that encourage and support their religious identity and commitments, leading to a match between the religious profiles of youth and the characteristics of their congregations.

The pattern we see in the congregational assessments of these adolescents may also reflect differences in how youth view and describe their religious social contexts rather than (or in addition to) objective differences across congregations. Religiously engaged youth may be more predisposed to see their religious congregations in a positive light. Adolescents who are more disengaged from religion may be less favorable in describing their congregations or have less exposure to these congregations on which to base their assessments. The true relationship between religious profiles and congregational characteristics is likely some combination of these pathways of influence. Parents—who tend to produce children who resemble them religiously—likely seek out congregations that support their religious identities. And religiously engaged youth are probably more likely to view religious communities in a positive light. On the other hand, adolescents who are affiliated with a congregation that is not welcoming or challenging may be more likely to disengage from these religious communities. Whatever the case, among those youth who are affiliated with a religious congregation, the characteristics of the congregation appear to be an important element of the social context surrounding the path through adolescent religiosity.

Characterizing the Five *As*

Drawing on the data just described, we have developed portraits of each of the five *As*. These portraits are presented in a way that enriches our understanding of each group as a whole and the kinds of youth who are most likely to live their religiosity in certain ways.

Abiders

The religious mosaics of Abiders reflect high levels of conventional measures of religiosity: high levels of religious service attendance, of personal prayer, and of closeness to God. So what are the personal characteristics and social contexts that are correlated with being a highly religious Abider? Characteristics that have been linked in previous research to high levels of religiosity also correlated with Abiders in our study. The Abiders include a higher than average number of females, younger adolescents, and white and black youth. Abiders are also connected to religious social networks; parents of Abiders typically attend church regularly, pray daily for their child, and are more likely to be conservative Protestants than any other religious tradition. Compared to other youth Abiders also report the highest levels of religiosity among their close friends. Almost all Abiders are affiliated with a religious congregation and the majority report that these congregations provide a welcoming, challenging atmosphere that values and integrates youth. Ashley, the Abider from chapter 2, is a good example. She has a close religious social network with very religious parents and friends. Although she changed religious congregations several times during her adolescence she made it a priority to remain engaged with a religious community.

Abiders' lives outside of religion are also characterized by a certain measure of social stability. Their parents have higher than average levels of education and income and lower than average levels of depression. Abiders are the youth most likely to live with both parents and to have lived in the same home for their entire life. More than 50 percent of all Abiders report being extremely close to at least one parent, and another 46 percent report being fairly or very close to a parent.

In terms of the mosaic metaphor introduced earlier in the book Abiders have access to a wide variety of religious tiles, but their mosaics are typically constructed from traditionally recognized "religious colors," with a high level of religiosity resulting in vivid, saturated color schemes. The mosaics they create have recognizable patterns, suggesting some level of religious uniformity or stability. The traditional, uniform nature of their mosaics reflects elements of stability in other areas of their lives as well. Youth with an intact family, moderate to high family income, and well-educated parents are more likely to be Abiders than are youth from alternative family arrangements with lower levels of income or parents with lower levels of education. This latter group of youth may encounter structural constraints that could limit their access to the range and intensity of religious colored tiles seen among the Abiders. Abiders live in worlds that are more patterned and predictable than many of their peers, and this coherence seems to permeate their religious lives as well.

Atheists

As the only religious profile to completely reject religion Atheists are a unique group. They are predominantly white, male, and at the older end of the age range in our study. Like Abiders, Atheists display a high level of coherence in their religious lives; they are consistently nonreligious across all of the measures in our analysis, and this coherence is reflected in some other areas of their lives. Their family socioeconomic status tends to be above average. Atheists and Abiders share the highest percentage of parents with at least a college degree. Atheists have an even larger percentage of parents in the higher income category. Atheists do not differ significantly from the rest of the youth in our study in their living situation; the rate at which they live with both parents and the years of residential stability are similar to the rates of the whole population of American adolescents.

In contrast to the stability of their living situations, family functioning in the households of Atheists might suffer in comparison to other groups. Parents of Atheists report much higher levels of depression than any of the other groups. In addition Atheists have the lowest percentage of youth reporting that they are extremely close to at least one parent.

The social networks of youth who are categorized in the Atheist profile also tend to be nonreligious. Their parents are far more likely than other parents to be unaffiliated with any particular religious tradition; 52 percent say they never attend any kind of religious services, and just 26 percent say they pray daily for their child. The friendship networks of Atheist youth include few religious friends compared to the rest of the youth in our study. Another feature of this small group is that they seem less sensitive to the opinions of their peers. When asked how important it is to fit in with what their peers think is cool, Atheists are the most likely to say that it is not at all important. As we indicated in chapter 2, Atheists seem to share some level of social isolation and nonconformist identity that is reflected in their attitudes about their peers. Recall that Samantha began her interview by describing this very phenomenon, quickly volunteering that she doesn't "have a lot of friends" because she is "not really the average teenager."

The social contexts of Atheists in our study include very little if any exposure to religion. Religion just doesn't appear to be a part of their life experience. This may significantly limit the kinds of tiles that are available to them or that appeal to them in the creation of their mosaic-like religious profile.

Assenters

Assenters reflect the typical American adolescent in many ways, including gender, race, and age distributions. Parental income, education, family structure, and parental levels of depression are also in line with trends for the entire population of adolescents. However, a lower than average proportion of Assenters report being extremely close to their parents. Examining the religious backgrounds of Assenters, we see that they fall in the middle of all of the religious profiles in terms of parental attendance and prayer. Conservative Protestants are underrepresented among Assenters, and mainline Protestants and Catholics are overrepresented. Jared, the Assenter we met in chapter 2, was connected to a Catholic parish through his mother, though he himself attended only sporadically. Similarly the majority of Assenters are affiliated with religious congregations, but they do not appear to be engaged by these congregations to the same extent as the Abiders. In general, stable families with adequate resources characterize Assenters' lives, but their parents are not as religiously engaged as those of Abiders.

Assenters have a higher than average percentage of friends who are religious, but the percentages of these friends who are involved in a youth group or with whom they discuss religion are lower than average. In fact Assenters display the largest discrepancy of all the religious profiles between having religious friends and talking with their friends about religion. In addition Assenters are the group most likely to report that fitting in with what is cool among their peers is important to them, suggesting that this group may be more influenced than other groups by the opinions of their peers.

When we examine the types of mosaics that Assenters are crafting, we recognize that they are not particularly close to their moderately religious parents, and they value the opinions of their peers but do not talk with their friends about religion. This combination of characteristics raises questions about the extent to which the religious mosaics of Assenters may be shaped in part by their perceptions of what is considered cool among their peers. Given the limited religious expression of their parents and their heightened concern with the opinions of their peers, it is not surprising that Assenters do not consistently include active expressions of religion as tiles in their mosaics.

Avoiders

Avoiders are nearly disengaged from religion. As a group they are more likely to be male and at the older end of adolescence. Like the Assenters, parental income, education, and residential stability are all consistent with the averages for the households of American adolescents. Our findings show that like the Assenters and the Atheists, family dynamics among the Avoiders appear strained. Parental depression is higher than average, and only 35 percent of Avoiders report being extremely close to a parent.

Avoiders have little exposure to religion through their social networks; 33 percent of their parents report that they never attend religious services, and the percentage of Avoiders whose parents are unaffiliated with any religious tradition is twice the national average. As would be expected given the level of religiosity found among their parents, only a small proportion of Avoiders claim affiliation with a religious congregation. Of those who are connected to a congregation, less than 60 percent feel welcomed or engaged by the adults there. Though the lives of Avoiders are largely characterized by distance from religion, most do have some level of exposure to religion in their lives.[9] Such was the case for Brandon. He had little exposure to religion through his parents, but he did have a few religious friends whose invitations to youth group meetings exposed him to ideas about God. These limited connections to religion may make it difficult for Avoiders to eschew religious tiles entirely as they create their mosaics.

Adapters

Adapters live their religious lives with certain dimensions of religion more engaged than others. They typically report high levels of personal religiosity—prayer, importance of faith, closeness to God—but more sporadic involvement in religious practices such as religious service attendance. Responses from their parents indicate similar patterns; these parents are less likely than parents of Abiders and Assenters to report regular attendance at religious services, but are second only to Abiders in reporting daily prayer for their child. Most Adapters' parents are conservative Protestants, a religious tradition that emphasizes personal religious commitment. The large majority of Adapters are connected to a religious congregation and report relatively positive evaluations of the congregation.

Adapters look similar to the Abiders on several of the variables presented in this chapter. Females and younger adolescents make up a higher than average percentage of this group. Like Abiders, they report being close to their parents and have higher than average numbers of religious friends with whom they discuss religion. Their friends are not very likely to be involved in a youth group, however, which could suggest some level of adaptive religiosity among their peers, in that their friends are religious but not involved in organized religious youth groups.

Adapters diverge from the Abiders and other religious profiles in other important ways as well. This religious profile has the highest percentage of minority youth; both black and Latino youth are more likely to be Adapters than any of the other religious profiles, even when we control in our analyses for socioeconomic differences between members of these different racial and ethnic groups.[10] We also find that being an Adapter is correlated with lower than average levels of family stability and resources; parents of Adapters report the lowest levels of both parental education and income. Adapters are also least likely to be living with both parents, or to have parents who have lived in the same home throughout their child's life.

As we noted earlier, there are several possible reasons for an adaptive approach to religion. The correlation between race and an adaptive religious approach suggests that there may be cultural differences to consider, and that religion may operate differently among different subcultures of youth.[11] In a separate book using these same NSYR data, Christerson, Edwards, and Flory explain how the religious cultures in which white, black, and Latino youth are raised vary in distinct ways, leading to different forms of religiosity in adolescence and young adulthood across these groups.[12]

Another possible explanation for these adaptive religious practices is that some youth may face constraints in their daily lives that limit their ability to maintain institutionally based and congruent religious profiles. Whereas the social context of Abiders' lives was characterized by stability, on average the Adapters appear to be youth whose lives are characterized by some degree of instability and lack of resources. Consider Diego's story as an example. His parents remain married, but the family struggled to deal with an alcoholic father and the realities of living in a high-crime neighborhood. Diego and his parents have gone through periods of more regular attendance at Mass, but this has not been a consistent feature of their family life. Like Diego, many Adapters deal with realities in their lives that may create barriers to institutionally based religious practice, despite their personal commitment. If parents work late shifts or weekends, if a parent is unsupportive of a youth's interests, or if a parent is dealing with life stresses associated with low socioeconomic status it may be particularly difficult for any of the family members to be engaged in evening or weekend religious activities. Struggling families may not be able to afford the time or resources required for regular participation in religious services. As Adapters arrange their own religious mosaics, the tiles at their disposal may be more restricted as a result of family situations and limited resources.

The Five *A*s and Related Life Outcomes

A wealth of research demonstrates the myriad ways in which religion is related to life outcomes for young people. Adolescent religiosity is positively related to higher self-esteem, more positive life attitudes, and more constructive social behaviors, and inversely related to depression, suicide ideation, and suicide attempts.[13] The religious commitments of adolescents have also been found to protect youth from delinquency and risk behaviors.[14] Wallace and Forman discovered that religious youth are more likely to engage in activities that are beneficial to their health, such as exercising, eating properly, and getting enough rest.[15] In other research youth religiosity is often inversely related to early initiation of sexual activity and the frequency of sexual activity, and there is evidence that youth religious participation may improve educational outcomes.[16]

This body of work examining religion and life outcomes among youth is entirely based on analyses that conceptualize religiosity from low to high and finds that lower religiosity is risky and higher religiosity is protective. We compared these findings to what we learned from our person-based typological approach, which allows us to consider how membership in the religious profiles we have identified relates to other areas of life as these youth move through adolescence.

Determining causal direction (the proverbial chicken-and-egg dilemma) is notoriously difficult when examining the relationship between religiosity and other life outcomes. There are strong theoretical reasons to argue that religion will be protective for youth when it comes to risk behaviors, health, and subjective well-being (i.e., religion and religious involvement often provide youth with a moral order, learned competencies, and social capital or resources that protect and support them).[17] But youth with higher levels of social and physical well-being and a lower propensity for risky behaviors may also feel more comfortable joining and remaining involved in religious institutions.[18] Without a randomized controlled experiment we can never prove that religion has a causal influence on youth well-being, and it would be unethical and impossible for researchers to randomly assign religious identity, beliefs, practices, or salience to humans.[19] Therefore the best approach is to use a range of feasible methods (e.g., different sampling techniques, modes of data collection, and methods of analysis) to provide multiple forms of evidence.[20] Our contribution is to see how membership in each of the five *A*s relates to different outcomes and to compare this to what other methods have shown.

One way to increase our confidence in findings that contribute to understanding the causal influence of religion is to look at data that come from multiple points in time. Specifically, if we know and understand where youth are religiously at one point in time, we can then examine their life at a later point in time in order to see what kinds of outcomes follow our earlier assessment of their religious lives. This is an advantage over other studies that take a survey of current religious characteristics and ask in the same survey about prior experience with risk behaviors. Without accounting for the relationship between religion and risk behaviors over time it is more difficult to posit a causal effect of religion on decision making. For example, a 15-year-old who is religiously engaged and regularly attends a church where there is clear opposition to premarital sex would likely attend church less often if she became sexually active. She may feel uncomfortable being told to avoid sexual relationships when she herself has decided to become sexually active. In that case, if she participates in a survey on one day when she is 17 years old and reports that she does not currently attend religious services and that she is sexually active, she contributes to the finding of low religious service attendance being related to sexual activity. Many interpret this relationship to mean that those who are attending religious services regularly are less likely to have sex (a causal relationship). Our example illustrates, however, that it could also be the case that those who start to have sex are more likely to stop attending (a reverse causal explanation). Such a possibility changes our understanding of the relationship between religious service attendance and sexual behavior.

In the sections that follow we present and discuss tables showing bivariate relationships between being in one of the five *A*s at the time of the first NSYR survey (2002; ages 13–17) and youth outcomes ascertained about three years later, in the second NSYR survey (2005; ages 16–21). To increase our confidence in these bivariate results we also conducted multivariate analyses controlling for additional variables, including a lagged measure of the dependent variable when possible.[21] These results provide more conservative estimates of a causal relationship between profiles of religiosity and life outcomes. However, this evidence is not proof of a causal effect, and we remain cautious in the conclusions we draw. Footnotes in tables 3.7 and 3.8 indicate when a relationship between membership in one of the five *A*s at the time of the first survey and a given outcome at the time of the second survey is statistically significant ($p < .05$) in the more conservative multivariate regression models.[22]

Risk Behaviors

Of particular interest to many people who work with youth are questions surrounding the various risk behaviors in which youth may engage. Table 3.7 shows the relationships between religious profiles at the time of the first survey and the extent to which youth have engaged in selected risk behaviors at the time of the second survey. Across the first three measures in this table—smoking cigarettes, drinking alcohol, and having sexual intercourse—we see a very similar pattern. Youth who were Abiders at the time of the first survey stand apart from the other profiles, with much lower levels of reported risk behaviors at the time of the second survey. Youth who were classified as Atheist or

Table 3.7 NSYR Wave 2 Youth Risk Behaviors by Wave 1 Religious Profile (Percentages)

	U.S.	Religious Profile (2002)				
		Abiders	Adapters	Assenters	Avoiders	Atheists
Smokes daily	14	5	15[a]	15[a]	22[a]	21
Drinks weekly or more	20	9	18[a]	25[a]	29[a]	30
Had sexual intercourse						
Never	46	69[b]	41[a]	41[a]	38[a]	31[a]
By Wave 1 (2002)	19	9[b]	20[a]	20[a]	24[a]	33[a]
By Wave 2 (2005)[c]	35	22[b]	39[a]	39[a]	38[a]	35[a]
At least one friend in trouble	55	43	57[a]	61[a]	58[a]	52

Source: National Surveys of Youth and Religion, 2002, 2005.

Note: Percentages may not add to 100 due to rounding.

[a] Difference from the Abider profile is statistically significant ($p < 0.05$) in a multivariate model.

[b] Difference from the Atheist profile is statistically significant ($p < 0.05$) in a multivariate model.

[c] Sexual intercourse by Wave 2 reflects the percentage of youth who had first intercourse after the Wave 1 survey and prior to the Wave 2 survey.

Avoider at the time of the first survey have the highest rates of engaging in these behaviors at the time of the second survey. Assenters and Adapters report levels of these three risk behaviors that tend to be a little lower than the Atheists and Avoiders and noticeably higher than the Abiders. For example, just over 20 percent of Atheists and Avoiders smoke at least once a day, compared with only 5 percent of Abiders. Adapters and Assenters fall between these two groups but are closer to the upper range, with 15 percent reporting that they smoke daily. Similarly whereas only 9 percent of Abiders drink alcohol weekly or more, weekly drinking among the remaining four profiles ranges from 18 percent (Adapters) to 30 percent (Atheists).

The measure for sexual intercourse is divided into three categories: youth who had engaged in sexual intercourse at the time of the first survey, youth who had engaged in sexual intercourse at the time of the second survey (i.e., they first had sexual intercourse in the time between the two surveys), and youth who at the time of the second survey had never engaged in sexual intercourse. Abiders are the group most likely to have never engaged in sexual intercourse, at 69 percent. In contrast 30 to 40 percent of each of the four other religious profiles report that they have not had sex. Atheists are the most likely to have had sexual intercourse at the time of the first survey, though the proportion who have sex for the first time between the two surveys is similar to the rates for Adapters, Assenters, and Avoiders.[23] So although significant proportions of youth transition into sexual activity at some point between the ages of 13 and 21, Atheist youth are likely to make this transition sooner than those from other religious profiles.

The final variable included in table 3.7 asks the youth to identify how many of their five closest friends have been in trouble for cheating, fighting, or skipping school. This question serves as one gauge of the types of peer influences youth might encounter as they make decisions about their actions. The proportion of each religious profile that identified at least one friend who had been in trouble is shown in this table. As with the previous variables, Abiders are the least likely to report having a friend who got in trouble. However, youth who identified as Assenters at the first survey have the highest proportion, 61 percent. This finding is especially interesting since in some of our prior analyses the Assenters were particularly influenced by their peers and wanting to appear cool to them.

Abiders are associated with a significantly lower likelihood of engaging in risk behaviors through late adolescence. Adapters and Assenters experience some protective effects when compared with

Atheists and Avoiders, but not all of these differences remain in the multivariate analyses, where we control for additional factors such as gender, age, socioeconomic status and family structure.

Health and Well-being

In our analysis we found relationships between classifications in the five religious profiles at the time of the first survey and health and well-being at the time of the second survey (see table 3.8). Abiders report health and well-being outcomes that are slightly more positive than average, but they aren't alone in their positive outcomes. For this group of measures Atheists report levels of positive health and well-being that are similar to those of Abiders. Adapters and Avoiders tended toward the lower end of the well-being scales.

Table 3.8 NSYR Wave 2 Health and Well-being by Wave 1 Religious Profile (Means)

	U.S.	Religious Profile (2002)				
		Abiders	Adapters	Assenters	Avoiders	Atheists
Feels sad or depressed (1–5)	2.3	2.2	2.4[ab]	2.3[b]	2.3[b]	2.1
Overall health (1–5)	3.8	4.0	3.8	3.8[a]	3.7[a]	3.9
Body Mass Index	23.7	23.2	24.0	23.9	23.8	22.8
Life satisfaction scale (1–5)	3.6	3.7	3.5	3.5	3.5	3.5
Life mastery scale (1–5)	3.7	3.8	3.6[a]	3.6[a]	3.6[a]	3.7
Educational goals[c]						
College graduate	50	50	49[b]	52[b]	48[b]	37
Postgraduate or professional schooling	32	38	28[b]	31[b]	31[b]	51

Source: National Surveys of Youth and Religion, 2002, 2005.
[a] Difference from the Abider profile is statistically significant ($p < 0.05$) in a multivariate model.
[b] Difference from the Atheist profile is statistically significant ($p < 0.05$) in a multivariate model.
[c] Educational goals represent percentages instead of means.

We asked youth to report how often they feel sad or depressed using a scale from 1 (never) to 5 (always). The average level of depression for the late adolescent population in the United States was 2.3. Among Atheists and Abiders the average was 2.1 and 2.2, respectively. Adapters, however, had the highest average, 2.4 out of 5. Though these differences seem slight, multivariate regression models reveal statistically significant differences between the religious profiles.

Respondents were also asked to rate their overall health on a 5-point scale from poor to excellent because self-reported health has been shown to be a stable and reliable indicator of adolescents' physical and mental well-being.[24] In addition, we used a combination of questions about body height and weight to calculate the Body Mass Index (BMI) of each respondent. The results are illustrated in table 3.8. Abiders and Atheists have the highest reports of overall health. Avoiders report the lowest levels of overall health while Adapters and Assenters fall in the middle. In multivariate analysis both Abiders and Adapters report overall health that is better than the Assenters and Avoiders at statistically significant levels. The average BMI results shown in table 3.8 do not reveal large differences across the five religious profiles. However, Abiders and Atheists have the lowest average BMI scores, once again demonstrating the best health outcomes at the time of the second survey.[25]

The next two rows in table 3.8 reflect mean scores of a life satisfaction scale and a life mastery scale. Each of these scales was created by combining responses to a series of survey questions related to how satisfied youth are with their life and the extent to which they feel empowered and in control of their life and their decisions. Both scales range from 1 to 5, with 5 representing the highest level of satisfaction or life mastery. Life satisfaction scores are very similar across all of the religious profiles. There does not appear to be a significant association between one's religious profile at the time of the first survey and the extent to which one reports being satisfied with life at the time of the second survey. There are some notable differences, however, in the average mastery scores reported by each group. Abiders have the highest average score, followed closely by the Atheists. The remaining three religious profiles have lower scores that are all very similar to each other.[26]

Educational Goals

The final variable presented in table 3.8 represents the educational goals of the youth in our study. Youth were asked how far in school they would like to go. These results indicate that Atheist youth have the highest educational aspirations; 51 percent express a desire to receive some type of postgraduate or professional training. This is not surprising given that the parents of Atheists are also among the most highly educated parents in our study. However, the Atheists continue to stand out from the other religious profiles even when we control for or take into account the educational levels of their parents.

Summary

The religious lives of youth shape and are shaped by a whole host of social factors. We have explored the role of personal characteristics, family contexts, and peers, as well as life outcomes such as health and risk behaviors. Through this process we see that the religious lives of youth do not exist in a vacuum but are intricately tied to other areas of their lives.

Religion in Social Context

Religious expression is closely associated with family stability and socioeconomic resources. Family stability and access to higher than average levels of socioeconomic resources seem to allow or possibly encourage youth to craft consistently patterned religious mosaics. On average Abiders and Atheists come from the most advantaged family backgrounds. Although these two groups seem completely opposite from each other religiously, what they share is a highly congruent packaging of the various dimensions of religion, as either the most religious or the least religious on almost every measure. Among the Adapters low levels of family stability and resources emerge in the adaptive religious patterns of youth who appear to be personally committed to faith but not consistent in their public practices of religion.

Affective dynamics are also an important element of family context. Lower levels of parental depression and higher levels of closeness to parents are associated with the religious lives of Abiders and Adapters. While the public practices of these two groups differ somewhat, they share the internal component of religiosity (closeness to God, importance of faith, and personal prayer). There appears to be a connection between an adolescent's emotional access to his parents and his affective connection with faith. Those groups who have less emotional access to their parents—Assenters, Avoiders, and Atheists—also exhibit lower levels of religious affect and centrality.

Religiosity of parents continues to be profoundly important in shaping the religious profiles of youth.[27] Although Abiders and Atheists have some contextual factors in common, they differ significantly in how religious their parents are. Having a very religiously engaged parent means that Abiders have had greater access to religious tiles from which to draw in creating their personal religious mosaics. Conversely youth who grow up with parents who do not believe in God or participate in any religious practices are not as likely to even have certain tiles from which to draw in creating their personal religious mosaics. In addition the religiosity of parents may create a context in which the incorporation of religious tiles is considered normative, is modeled by parents, and is positively reinforced by family and friends. Adapters, Assenters, and Avoiders also demonstrate patterns of religiosity that reflect elements of the religious practices reported by their parents. In addition to the religiosity of parents, among youth affiliated with a religious congregation we find a clear link between their institutional engagement and their assessments of these congregations.

Religion and Life Outcomes

The patterns we found for religion's relationship to risk behaviors follows previous research in that those youth who are the most consistently engaged in religion (the Abiders) demonstrate what appear to be protective effects that reduce their likelihood of involvement with risk behaviors. Those youth who are consistently disengaged from religion (the Atheists, and to a lesser extent the Avoiders) are the most likely to be involved in risk behaviors such as smoking, drinking, and initiating sexual behavior earlier.

In *Soul Searching* Smith and Denton outline a set of theoretical mechanisms that help explain the significant relationships that are found between religious engagement and risk behaviors, highlighting the role of moral directives, role models, and network closure in the lives of religiously engaged youth. Smith and Denton argue that youth who are religiously engaged internalize the moral directives of religious communities that discourage smoking, drinking, and having nonmarital sex. In addition religious communities may provide youth with adult role models who reinforce these moral directives and monitor behavior related to them. When youth and parents are involved in the same religious community they are likely to share a social network, leading to network closure. In these cases parents have greater access to information about their child's behaviors and activities, they are likely to know the other youth and adults with whom their child interacts, and parents, youth and other members of their social networks are more likely to share a common set of values and worldviews discouraging substance use and sexual behavior. Of course Atheist youth are usually not embedded in these types of moral communities, and often these types of risk behaviors are not a threat to their moral order or social network. Many did tell us they have no interest in substance use or sexual behavior because of the risks to both physical and mental health. However, youth who are not engaged in religious communities (Atheists and Avoiders) are on average more likely to be involved in adolescent risk behaviors.

Interestingly, in a departure from previous research we find that on measures of overall health and well-being it is not the case that highly religious youth are doing significantly better than all nonreligious youth. It is true that the Abiders appear to have more positive outcomes than some of the other religious profiles; however, Atheists appear to be quite similar to Abiders on measures of health and well-being. In fact in the multivariate analysis there were no statistically significant differences between these two groups.

Our analysis diverges from previous research with respect to life outcomes partly because of the approach we take to conceptualizing and measuring religiosity. Rather than considering nonreligious youth to be a monolithic category, the latent class analysis separates nonreligious youth into the two groups of Avoiders and Atheists. In examining these as two distinct expressions of nonreligiosity we see differences between these two groups in terms of the social contexts of their lives as well as their future life outcomes. When we consider the differences in the social and religious contexts between these two groups it is not surprising that their life outcomes reflect differences as well. There is something different about youth who can clearly articulate their atheist identity and youth who are not religious but have not reached a point where they identify themselves as completely irreligious, either because they are not willing to do so or because they have just not thought much about it.

Because both Abiders and Atheists exhibit the highest levels of health and well-being it is important to think about what these two groups have in common. For one, they do tend to come from relatively well-to-do backgrounds in terms of parent education, income, and family stability. These advantages make it more likely that they have the time and parental encouragement to consider their own personal religious beliefs, identity, and practices and work to keep them in line with one another. However, the pattern of positive health and well-being outcomes remains even after controlling for their advantaged backgrounds in multivariate analyses. It is also likely that a coherent belief or meaning system (whether total engagement or disengagement with religion) serves to build confidence in youth and provides them something to fall back on when times are tough. In addition the relatively consistent belief systems may reduce potential experiences of cognitive dissonance that could threaten adolescent well-being.[28] In other words, although Atheists are engaging in more risk behaviors, these behaviors may not necessarily be in conflict with their moral order or the expectations of their social network.

The remaining three profiles—Adapters, Assenters, and Avoiders—exhibit some form of incongruence in their religious profiles. Adapters appear to be personally committed to religion but inconsistent in their religious practices. Assenters engage with religion on various dimensions but acknowledge that religion is not central to or salient in their everyday lives. Avoiders are personally disengaged from religion but continue to have some identification with religion in their life. The Avoiders' ties to religion, however distant, may sustain awareness of a disconnect between their life choices and religious norms and expectations. It seems plausible, then, that for these three profiles a lack of congruence in their particular mosaics might be associated with lower health and well-being outcomes. Stated differently, the more consistent mosaics of Abiders and Atheists might provide them with confidence, self-assurance, and cognitive harmony that is beneficial to their personal well-being and aspirations for the future.

Our results support the growing literature on how religion provides a set of moral guidelines and religious institutions provide social structure to discourage youth from participating in behaviors such as smoking, drinking, and having nonmarital sex, defined by many religious institutions as immoral or problematic. However, the usual interpretation from survey studies of the role of religion in the lives of youth is that more religion is better and less is bad for youth. This interpretation is challenged by our results. At this point in time Atheists are doing as well as Abiders on our measures of health and well-being, suggesting that a coherent worldview and meaning system supports adolescent well-being. We do not yet know, however, how this process will develop over time. Although Atheists report high levels of current health and well-being, they also report slightly lower than average numbers of close friends, are the least likely of all youth to be close to their parents, and have parents with the highest levels of depression.

These characteristics of their social networks, coupled with their non-conformist social identity, highlight potential sources of social isolation that may influence their future life outcomes in ways that are not yet apparent.

The results of our analysis can inform scholars as well as practitioners interested in the lives of youth. Future research should continue to explore the mechanisms by which religion is related to life outcomes. Our research highlights the need to consider not only the protective effects of religion, but also the importance of congruent religious identities and worldviews. The implementation of youth programs addressing religiosity or spirituality should also consider that youth seem to do very well when they are afforded the opportunity and social support to develop a personal identity that is congruent and integrated. In other words, it may be that youth who are most in need of religious or spiritual guidance, so that it will make a difference in their overall well-being, are those who have yet to integrate their various forms of identity in ways that they can articulate and gain confidence from.

4

Slightly Moving Parts of the Whole

Like I constantly am, you know, I follow God's will and I believe in him and that sort of thing, but like my practice has waned a little, probably because of high school, because I'm so busy I don't have time, or I forget to pray, you know, or stuff like that. But I think spiritually I am stronger because I've never waned on that. I've never denied it or anything. (16-year-old white, female Latter Day Saint)

I think I am the same religiously, but I just don't go to church, so according to the church I have become less religious, but I don't feel that way. (18-year-old Latina Catholic)

The reflections of these two young women, who participated in NSYR in-person, semi-structured interviews, illustrate recognition of the multiple dimensions of religion and the complex and sometimes loose connections between those dimensions that we described in previous chapters. Their words reveal the dynamic nature of religiosity and how the multiple dimensions of religion can increase, decrease, or stay the same in ways that are not always parallel or consonant with one another. This kaleidoscopic nature of religiosity makes tracking and explaining religious change very difficult. In chapters 2 and 3 we worked to convey the nature of religiosity, its components, and the ways the components are pieced together into mosaics by presenting snapshots of how these personal profiles of religiosity look at one point in time. However, religiosity is dynamic, especially in adolescence, when youth are discovering who they really are and making autonomous decisions about their beliefs, values, and religious identities. So it is important to look at religiosity across time, at levels of stability and change in content, conduct, and centrality, as well as how some youth shift to different profiles of religiosity as they age. Evidence from the survey and interview data also helps us understand how youth perceive and describe in their own words the dynamics of their religiosity during adolescence.

Stability in the Content of Religiosity during Adolescence

The content of individual religious belief is a key characteristic of a personal religious mosaic. Content is, however, one of the least studied areas of religiosity in adolescents. Clydesdale finds that youth in their first year out of high school usually place critical identities and beliefs in a "lockbox" of sorts, because they are spending more time on education and work in an effort to avoid downward social mobility.[1] Their fear of failing in this regard and their desire to fit into mainstream American culture discourage them from spending time cultivating, exploring, or expanding their values and beliefs. It is assumed that once youth transition into adulthood and form families they can open the lockbox of their beliefs and adjust their values to fit their lives and desires.

Arguably the most central component of most major religions is the belief in a supreme, sacred being, so a key piece of the content of religiosity is one's view of God. In our 2002 and 2005 NSYR surveys, we asked adolescents, "Do you believe in God, or not, or are you unsure?" In the 2002 survey 84 percent of 13- to 17-year-olds reported that they believe in God, and 3 percent reported that they do not (see figure 4.1). The remaining 13 percent responded that they do not know or are unsure about whether or not they believe in God. Thus the vast majority of teens believe in God or allow for the possibility that there is a God; definitive rejection of the idea of God is quite rare. About three years later, in the 2005 survey, the percentage of NSYR adolescent respondents who reported a definitive belief in God dropped from 84 percent to 78 percent. The percentage of youth who said that they do not believe in God went up slightly, from 3 percent to 5 percent. A larger increase was seen in the percentage of respondents who expressed uncertainty about belief in God. In 2005 this number had increased from 13 percent to 18 percent. During adolescence, youth as a group become slightly less sure of their belief in God.

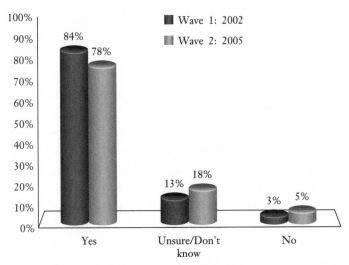

Figure 4.1 Belief in God at Wave 1 and Wave 2. *Source: National Surveys of Youth and Religion, 2002, 2005.*

The aggregate changes in each category across time provide us with some important information about total levels of belief in God among adolescents, and how beliefs shift as adolescents get older. However, examining individual-level trajectories of change and stability over the three years better contextualizes our understanding of the various dynamics of religious belief among our youth respondents. Overall belief in God remains very stable for these adolescents. A full 81 percent reported the same level of belief in God in 2005 as they did in 2002. An examination of the 19 percent of youth who changed their level of belief in God shows movement in a variety of directions. As the overall levels of change suggest, the larger amount of change is a decline in belief in God. In 2002 84 percent affirmed a belief in God. Of this group of youth, 86 percent continue to report belief in God in 2005. However, 12 percent of this group, who said they definitely believed in God in 2002, reported being unsure about God in 2005. Another 2 percent of the firm believers in 2002 report they do not believe in God at all in 2005. Uncertainty, not disbelief, accounts for most movement away from definite belief in God. As a percentage of the entire group of youth respondents, 11.5 percent of the youth in our survey believed in God in 2002 but report that they do not believe in God or are unsure whether they believe in God in 2005.

Fewer adolescents made the transition from disbelief or uncertainty to a firm belief in God. However, a nontrivial number of youth

(6 percent of the whole youth population) do report increased certainty of their belief in God during adolescence. During the 2005 survey only about 50 percent of the teens who were not believers in 2002 continue to say they do not believe in God; 34 percent of this group is now unsure about God, and 14 percent report that they now believe in God. The youth who were unsure whether they believed in God in 2002 demonstrate movement in both directions with respect to belief in God by 2005. About 50 percent of the teens who were unsure of their belief in 2002 remained unsure in 2005; 11 percent of this group now reports that they do not believe in God. However, 36 percent of those who were unsure in 2002 reported in 2005 that they do now believe in God. Among uncertain youth more move toward belief in God rather than away from it.

To keep the big picture in perspective, however, it is important to note that the majority of respondents express a belief in God at both time points. And while the majority of youth's belief in God remained stable over time, there was some change in both directions. During the three years between the surveys about 6 percent of the youth moved toward more certain belief in God. About 13 percent, however, reported declining belief in God.

Of youth who reported believing in God or being unsure of their belief in God, we asked "Which of the following comes closest to your own view of God? God is a personal being involved in the lives of people today; God created the world, but is not involved in the world now; or God is not personal, but something like a cosmic life force." As Smith and Denton show in *Soul Searching*, there is variance in the characteristics youth attribute to God, and there is also sometimes a shift in how God is viewed during adolescence. By 2005 fewer youth viewed God as a personal being; 67 percent expressed this view of God in 2002, compared to 63 percent in 2005. The number of respondents who view God as an uninvolved creator stayed about the same across time, just over 12 percent. The percentage of youth who agreed with the statement "God is not personal, but something like a cosmic life force" increased slightly, from 14.4 percent in 2002 to 16 percent in 2005. The small changes in overall percentages for each response category reflect more stability than change in adolescent views of God.

At first glance the majority of youth appear to continue to believe in a personal, involved God, and very few teens report holding a view of God that is not represented in the response options. But though the aggregate numbers hold steady, there is actually a fair amount of movement within these categories. Twenty-five percent of youth who believed in a personal God in 2002 no longer do in 2005. Most of these youth report believing in 2005 that God is either a creator who is not involved with the world now or an impersonal cosmic life force. On the other hand, of the youth who report believing in a personal God at the second survey, only 79 percent held this belief at the time of the first survey. The other 21 percent previously reported different views of God, most commonly of an uninvolved creator or a cosmic life force, but now claim belief in an involved and personal God. We find that the majority of youth (61.4 percent) report the same views of God in 2005 as they did in 2002. Among those whose views have changed there is movement in and out of all of the possible response categories. Given that viewing God as a personal, involved God was the most common response among youth, it is not surprising that this category also has the largest loss between 2002 and 2005. Approximately 16 percent of youth who answered this question believed in a personal God in 2002 but reported some other answer in 2005. In comparison, 12.5 percent of those who answered this question reported a different view of God in 2002, but in 2005 reported viewing God as personal and involved.

A final way to think about change in adolescent beliefs about God is to consider the likelihood of changing from having any kind of belief in God to no belief at all, and how this is related to the view of God one has initially. Exploring the two survey questions together, we gain insight into how a youth's view of God at a certain point in time relates to the chance that he will lose faith in God in the years that follow. Of the youth who in 2002 held a personal view of God, only 2 percent reported not believing in God at all in 2005. In contrast almost 5 percent of the youth who viewed God as an uninvolved creator and almost 9 percent of those who viewed God as a cosmic life force in 2002 no longer believed in God in 2005. Not surprisingly most of the youth who report no belief in God in 2005 were those who were unsure of their belief in 2002 and answered "none of the above" to the question about how they view God. The more personally involved a youth perceives God to be, the less likely he is to lose faith in God over time.

Another distinguishing feature of the content of religious belief, especially in the context of the United States, is the extent to which a person accepts religious particularity (that only one religion is true) versus pluralism (that there may be truth in more than one religion). Although there have been increases in religious diversity and pluralism over time in the United States, a central component of American

Christianity has always been a claim of exclusive truth.[2] In the NSYR telephone survey youth are asked two questions about exclusivist belief:

Which of the following statements comes closest to your own views about religion?

- *Only one religion is true*
- *Many religions may be true*
- *There is very little truth in any religion*

Some people think that it is okay to pick and choose their religious beliefs without having to accept the teachings of their religious faith as a whole. Do you agree or disagree?

Trinitapoli outlines the distribution of these beliefs for the NSYR survey sample in 2002 and supplements these analyses with examples of how youth talk about exclusivism and pluralism in the semistructured in-person interviews.[3] She finds that 29 percent of 13- to 17-year-olds in 2002 believe that only one religion is true, 51 percent believe you must accept all teachings of a religion, and 20 percent believe both that one religion is true and that believers of that religion should accept all its teachings. In other words, about 20 percent of the adolescent population in the United States holds exclusivist religious beliefs.

About three years later, when we resurveyed these youth in 2005, we find that the percentage of young people who believe that only one religion is true remained the same (see figure 4.2). Although there appears to be no change in the aggregate percentage believing one religion is true, looking at individual-level change between surveys shows that about 30 percent of the NSYR respondents gave a different response to this question at each of the two time points. The change, however, was slight. The majority of respondents (all but about 2 percent) changed to an adjacent answer category. Dramatic change, either from only one religion is true to there is very little truth in any religion or vice versa, was uncommon (1.4 percent and 0.7 percent of the whole population, respectively).

Acceptance of picking and choosing religious beliefs from within a religious faith increased from 47 percent to 49 percent. The overall change was small, but the change among individual youth respondents was more substantial. Just over 38 percent of respondents reported a different answer in 2005 than they did in 2002. In the first survey 53 percent of youth said that it is not okay to pick and choose beliefs from a religious tradition; only 37 percent of these youth (20 percent of the total sample) still agreed with this statement in 2005. The change in

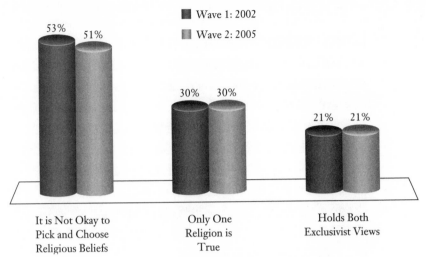

Figure 4.2 Exclusivist views at Wave 1 and Wave 2. *Source: National Surveys of Youth and Religion, 2002, 2005.*

their responses seems to indicate a shift toward greater acceptance of individualized religious beliefs. However, we also find a comparable shift in the opposite direction: 36 percent of the respondents who agreed with this statement in 2002 reported in 2005 that they no longer think it is okay to pick and choose beliefs from a religious tradition (17 percent of the total sample). A sizable number of youth have become more individualistic regarding acceptance of religious teachings, but an almost equal number have come to believe that one should accept the entirety of a religious tradition's teachings.

Putting both of these measures together we assess what happens to a combined measure of exclusivism over time among these youth: the percentage of those who believe both that only one religion is true and that one should not pick and choose religious teachings from within one faith. We find a fair amount of stability, with 82 percent remaining in the same category across time (70 percent remained nonexclusive and 12 percent remained exclusive). Interestingly among the 18 percent of youth who report different views on exclusivism in 2002 and 2005, half switched from exclusivism to nonexclusivism and half changed in the other direction. In other words, there is no strong trend in one direction or the other.

The overriding story of belief in adolescence is one of stability: for the most part adolescents are not making radical changes in their beliefs across these three years. When there is individual-level change there is not a strong trend in any particular direction. There

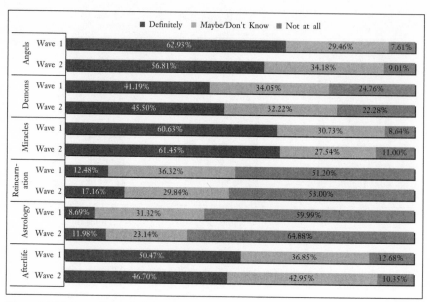

Legend: ■ Definitely ■ Maybe/Don't Know ■ Not at all

		Definitely	Maybe/Don't Know	Not at all
Angels	Wave 1	62.93%	29.46%	7.61%
	Wave 2	56.81%	34.18%	9.01%
Demons	Wave 1	41.19%	34.05%	24.76%
	Wave 2	45.50%	32.22%	22.28%
Miracles	Wave 1	60.63%	30.73%	8.64%
	Wave 2	61.45%	27.54%	11.00%
Reincarnation	Wave 1	12.48%	36.32%	51.20%
	Wave 2	17.16%	29.84%	53.00%
Astrology	Wave 1	8.69%	31.32%	59.99%
	Wave 2	11.98%	23.14%	64.88%
Afterlife	Wave 1	50.47%	36.85%	12.68%
	Wave 2	46.70%	42.95%	10.35%

Figure 4.3 Various religious beliefs at Wave 1 and Wave 2. *Source: National Surveys of Youth and Religion, 2002, 2005.*

is not a radical upswing in atheism, nor is there a rapid increase in pluralism over these years of adolescence. A decent amount of individual change between response categories over time suggests that youth are adjusting beliefs to some degree, but usually in small increments.[4] These patterns also hold when we look at a variety of other religious beliefs in our data, including belief in angels, demons, miracles, reincarnation, astrology, and an afterlife. Figure 4.3 shows the distribution of these beliefs in our sample of youth over time.

An aspect of religious identity that is closely related to the content of one's religious beliefs is the religion or religious group with which one identifies. In the NSYR surveys we asked respondents at both points in time (2002 and 2005) to tell us the religion with which they generally affiliate. Table 4.1 shows what percentage of youth identified with each religious affiliation, including those who reported having no religious affiliation, in the 2002 and 2005 surveys.

Overall there is very little change in the religious affiliations of these youth three years later. The most significant changes in religious affiliation are found in the decrease in those who report a Protestant affiliation and the increase in those who do not claim any religious affiliation, resulting in an overall change of around 7 percent

Table 4.1 Religious Affiliation (percentages)

	2002 NSYR Survey Ages 13–17	2005 NSYR Survey Ages 16–21
Protestant	53.30	46.62
Catholic	23.27	22.86
LDS/Mormon	2.74	2.65
Jewish	1.50	1.29
Jehovah's Witness	0.63	0.76
Pagan or Wiccan	0.41	0.13
Muslim	0.36	0.39
Buddhist	0.34	0.19
Eastern Orthodox	0.29	0.45
Hindu	0.13	0.18
Native American	0.12	0.04
Other affiliations[a]	0.33	1.81
No affiliation	15.00	21.88
Don't know /Refused to give affiliation	1.57	0.76
N		2,530

Source: National Surveys of Youth and Religion, 2002, 2005.
Note: Percentages may not add to 100 due to rounding.
[a]Other affiliations include groups representing less than 0.10 percent of the population in Wave 1, such as Christian Science, Unitarian Universalist, Baha'i, and Satanist.

for each category. Most of the youth who changed their affiliation from a Protestant denomination to "no affiliation" were not very actively practicing their Protestant faith (in terms of religious service attendance or prayer) in 2002, so the move does not represent a radical change in religious participation.

When it comes to non-Protestant religious affiliations, identification remained remarkably stable between the two surveys. Despite recent reports in popular news outlets, our data do not reveal any radical movement of American youth into (or out of) more conservative or Evangelical Protestant groups or Eastern or pagan religions. Previous findings from this study showed that youth living in the United States in 2002 were highly likely to affiliate with the same religion or religious group as one or both of their parents. Our 2005 survey suggests that three years later the situation is much the same.

Shifts in Religious Conduct during Adolescence

Another very important aspect of the religious lives of youth is the degree to which they engage in religious practices (publicly or privately), or what we term religious conduct. From 2002 to 2005 there were noticeable declines in aggregate levels of the religious conduct of adolescents in our study. Several studies have detected average declines in religious service attendance during adolescence in the United States.[5]

Comparing the frequency of religious service attendance in 2002 and 2005 reveals an overall trend of declining participation in public religious practice. Figure 4.4 shows that the percentage of youth who reported that they attend religious services once a week or more declined by just over 13 percent during this time, from 42 percent to 29 percent of all youth attending weekly or more often. The percentage of youth who reported that they never attend increased by 10 percent, from 18 percent to 28 percent. The trend is clearly toward reduced religious service attendance over time in adolescence, but again, few youth made dramatic changes. The majority of youth reported similar or only slightly lower attendance patterns in 2002 as compared to 2005. Over 66 percent of the 2005 survey respondents stayed within one category of their 2002 survey responses. Twenty-four percent of respondents reported a decrease in attendance of two or more answer categories, and only 7 percent went from attending weekly or more often to never attending three years later. In contrast a sizable minority (15 percent) reported increasing their level of religious service attendance by one or more categories.

Not surprisingly, when looking at other forms of public religious practice, such as religious education (e.g., Sunday School) or youth group participation, we find similar patterns of decrease. In general as adolescents age they become a little less involved in religious institutions than they had been before. Some youth do make radical changes, but these cases are few and far between.

We use the frequency of religious service attendance to measure public practice and personal prayer to measure private religious practice. Because adolescence is a time of increasing but still limited autonomy, public religious practices such as religious service attendance do not necessarily indicate a youth's personal desires regarding religious conduct. The public religious practices of many youth may still be influenced by demands or expectations from family and peers as adolescents transition to adulthood. Private religious practices, however, are

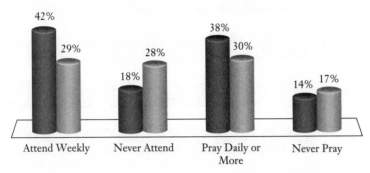

Figure 4.4 Religious service attendance and prayer at Wave 1 and Wave 2.
Source: National Surveys of Youth and Religion, 2002, 2005.

presumably activities over which youth have significant autonomy. Adolescent reports about their private religious practices, in this case how often they pray, reveal something unique about the way they conduct their religious lives and the role of religion in their lives.[6]

At the time of the 2005 survey respondents reported lower levels of overall private prayer than had been reported in the 2002 survey. For example, 38 percent of youth said they pray at least daily in the 2002 survey; that rate fell to 30 percent in 2005. In 2002 14 percent said they never pray; that rate rose to 17 percent by 2005. Only 31 percent of youth reported praying with the same frequency in 2005 as they did in 2002. If youth who change their response by only one category are considered stable, however, then the percentage of youth with relatively stable levels of prayer increases to 64 percent. Only 13 percent of youth responded to the question about frequency of prayer with answers that were two or more categories above their 2002 responses, indicating that they pray more frequently than they did three years prior. However, over 23 percent of youth decreased their frequency of prayer by two or more response categories by 2005. So again responses suggest a fair amount of fluidity in how often adolescents pray, and on average this change trends downward over time, but there are certainly some adolescents who pray more often as they get older.

Other private forms of religious conduct that we ask about in our surveys include practicing a day of rest, fasting, and meditating. As shown in figure 4.5 the average decrease over time in practicing a day of rest looks similar to other forms of religious practice, whereas fasting

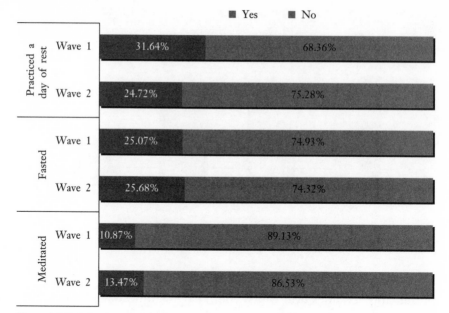

■ Yes   ■ No

Figure 4.5 Religious practices in the past year at Wave 1 and Wave 2. *Source: National Surveys of Youth and Religion, 2002, 2005.*

and meditating remain rather stable and are practices in which a small proportion of the youth population ever engage.

The Centrality of Religion over Time in Adolescence

The third dimension of religiosity we consider is the centrality of religion, or the importance that youth accord to religion and spirituality in their lives. Evidence regarding how this dimension of religiosity changes in adolescence is mixed, with some studies finding stability during adolescence and some showing average declines.[7] We asked questions such as the following to measure religious salience in the NSYR telephone surveys: "How important or unimportant is religious faith in shaping how you live your daily life: extremely important, very, somewhat, not very important, or not important at all?" Answers to this question suggest a slight overall decrease in the importance of religious faith (see figure 4.6). Fewer young people considered religion to be in an important category, either extremely, very or somewhat, in 2005; more young people felt that religion was not important. In the overall distribution there was

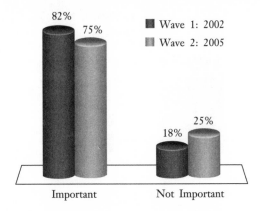

Figure 4.6 Importance of faith at Wave 1 and Wave 2. *Source: National Surveys of Youth and Religion, 2002, 2005.*

82%
75%
18%
25%

Wave 1: 2002
Wave 2: 2005

Important   Not Important

a shift of about 7 percent from the important to not important answer categories.

Analyzing the importance of faith to individuals reveals that once again there was movement in both directions. In the total sample of youth respondents 21 percent indicated that their faith was more important to them than it had been three years earlier. In contrast 34 percent gave an answer that was lower on the importance scale. Although over 50 percent provided responses that changed between 2002 and 2005, this change at the individual level was typically slight rather than dramatic; nearly 88 percent gave answers that were the same or within one response category at both surveys. The minor adjustments in both directions provide evidence that youth are a little more likely to experience decreases than increases in faith. However, there is a fair amount of revising the importance of faith in both directions.

Other questions that indicate the centrality of religion reflect a similar pattern. For example, we asked, "How distant or close do you feel to God most of the time? Would you say extremely distant, very distant, somewhat distant, somewhat close, very close, or extremely close?" All of the close responses decreased in 2005, and all of the distant responses increased (see figure 4.7). As with the importance of faith question, however, changes at the individual level are slight rather than dramatic. About 79 percent of youth reported answers in 2005 that were the same or within one category of their answers in 2002; a change from extremely close to any of the distant categories was very rare. To keep these changes in perspective, it is important to note that even though there have been overall declines in reported closeness to God, the majority of youth continue to say they are at least somewhat close to God.

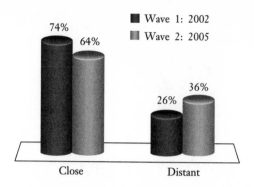

Figure 4.7 Closeness to God at Wave 1 and Wave 2. *Source: National Surveys of Youth and Religion, 2002, 2005.*

The individual variables we have examined to this point reveal few dramatic changes in the content of religious beliefs, religious conduct, or the centrality of religion in the lives of this group of 13- to 17-year-olds that became 16- to 21-year-olds in 2005. Their religious lives seem fairly stable, yet there is a fair amount of minor adjustment in this period, mostly in the extent to which these youth publicly practice religion. These small changes are not surprising, as adolescence is a time in which youth gain independence and often spend increasing amounts of time devoted to education, work, and socializing in peer-only environments, all of which compete for time spent in religious institutions.[8] Another common theme that emerges when looking at the three dimensions together is that individual-level change occurs in both directions. The autonomy that comes with adolescent development does not necessarily encourage a separation from or debiting of religious belief, practice, or salience. A fair amount of youth showed increases by 2005 in belief in God or exclusivist views, religious practice, or religious salience. The overall stability of religiosity during adolescence must also be acknowledged if we are to fully understand the religious beliefs and expression of young people.

Transitions between Religious Profiles in Adolescence

Because religiosity is multidimensional, dynamic, and not always congruent across dimensions it is important to move beyond an examination of individual religious measures. We need to also study religious change in ways that account for its multidimensional complexities. In chapter 2 we presented the five most typical profiles of religiosity found at any one point in time among adolescents. We use another set of latent class methods called latent transition analysis (LTA) to assess how likely youth were to shift between these five profiles of religiosity, or the five *A*s, between 2002 and 2005. LTA allows us to estimate the probability that members of one profile at the first time point will remain in that profile or move to any of the four other profiles by the second time point.[9] This allows us to see what type of movement there is between religious profiles as youth mature and move through adolescence.

Building on the LTA results we examine the religious profile or profiles that best fit each youth at each wave of the survey. Table 4.2 shows what percentage of youth from each profile best matched that profile three years later and what percentage of youth transitioned to fit a different profile three years later. For example, among the youth who fit the category of Abiders at the time of the first survey, 85 percent remained best characterized as Abiders three years later. In fact for every group the majority of individuals fit the same religious profile over time. This suggests that there are not large-scale changes in the contours of religious life for those moving from middle to late adolescence. The religious profiles of youth remain fairly constant during this period of life.

When there is change or transition from one religious profile to another, the change is usually to a class that is similar but characterized by less religious conduct or centrality. Studying transitions across religious profiles yields similar results to what we found studying each component of religiosity separately: slight decreases in most forms of religiosity during adolescence.

Table 4.2 Transition between Religious Profiles from 2002 to 2005 (percentages)

NSYR Survey Wave 1, 2002	NSYR Survey Wave 2, 2005				
	Abiders	Adapters	Assenters	Avoiders	Atheists
Abiders	**85**	<1	15	0	0
Adapters	01	**65**	28	05	01
Assenters	03	04	**67**	23	03
Avoiders	00	05	<1	**84**	11
Atheists	00	02	01	45	**52**

Source: National Surveys of Youth and Religion, 2002, 2005.

Although Abiders were very likely to stay Abiders, those few who did transition usually moved into the profile of Assenters. According to our results, original Abiders had very little chance of becoming an Adapter, Avoider, or Atheist during the three years covered by our surveys. Kayla's story illustrates the typical transition from Abider to Assenter.

Kayla

Kayla, a 14-year-old African American, met us at the public library in an East Coast state for our first interview. Her 73-year-old foster mother, with whom she has lived since she was two days old and whom she calls "Mother," dropped her off. Kayla doesn't know her biological mother well and doesn't know her father at all. Her biological mother, she was told, is a crack addict. Kayla was extremely easy to talk to and polite, thoughtful, and mature. She described her foster siblings, who came in and out of their home and with whom she was very close. She said that she had a lot of friends at school.

When the interviewer asked how she had been raised religiously, she said:

> My mother is a sucker about God. Oh my goodness. She . . . everything you say . . . "Take it to God, Kayla. Take it to Jesus," and I do it, and it works. Um, I'm a Christian. She is a Christian. She has raised me right. She is very . . . everything you say . . . "That's what God wants you to do, then you do it Kayla. If that's what you have in your heart to do, you do it." She wants me to be the best I can be, but she wants me to know that the way you live has to be the way a Christian lives.

When asked if she has religious beliefs similar to or different from her mother's, Kayla said:

> I don't think we have any different beliefs. And the only reason I say this is because I'm not, I don't want to say, I'm not in that mind-set to think on my own yet. I think that she has the . . . she paves the way for what I think. Just because she'll like, she'll say something and to me it doesn't make sense, but as I get older, it starts making sense, and then I start to listen to what she has to say more often than I'll listen to what somebody else has to say. You know, I just think she . . . everything that has to do with Christians, I think she's right about, in my opinion. You could tell me something, she could tell me something, and I'll think she's right. Even if you're right, I'll think she's right, just because I'm just biased when it comes to her, you know what I mean, so I just I stick with her.

Kayla seemed keenly aware that her religious beliefs and practices come from her mother and was quite happy learning from her and receiving encouragement from her. She feels that she is not yet at the point to independently reason about her personal beliefs.

In this first interview Kayla expressed strong belief in God, "a higher power who has control, but also loves people and does things." She also expressed high levels of practice and salience, but like many others did not want to be seen as a religious zealot: "I don't get down on my knees or light candles or anything. . . .. I try to do my best by people, but I don't, you know, go around putting fliers about Jesus on people's cars or anything." She did say that Christianity is the one true religion and people should follow only one religion.

Kayla and her mother attended religious services almost weekly at their nondenominational Protestant church. She liked the people at her church, especially the pastor, who had a good sense of humor. Kayla prayed every morning upon waking up and other times during the day and believed God answers her prayers. She told a story of praying to God to figure out her purpose in life, and he encouraged her to sing. Now she sings a lot, and everyone tells her what a beautiful voice she has. Kayla described herself as very close to God: "He's my father. He's the daddy I never had."

By the time of our second interview with Kayla, when she was 16, her life had seen dramatic and painful changes. Her mother's 45-year-old biological daughter had moved in and was butting heads with Kayla. Kayla thought this woman was using her mother for a place to sleep and had taken out a very large loan that she probably could not pay back. Their struggles had led to Kayla's running away for a time, after which she was transferred to an alternative high school for at-risk students. She had also started seeing a doctor for mood-stabilizing medication. Now, even though she was living back with her mother, whenever she got angry and started yelling her mother would call the police. It seemed to be a tense and unstable situation, often leading Kayla to escape to her 21-year-old boyfriend's home.

Kayla's religious life changed as well. Kayla went from describing herself as religious on every dimension during our first interview (at age 14) to being moderately religious on every dimension at the time of the second interview (at age 16). She still expressed belief in God, but she was less exclusive about her beliefs, feeling that people should believe and do what makes the most sense to them. She continued to identify herself as a Christian, saying that her purpose in life was to serve God and Jesus, but she had stopped attending religious services because people there were "so phony." In addition to dialing back her attendance, Kayla's praying decreased over time. In the first interview she said that she prayed multiple times a day; in the second interview she said, "I try to pray every day and I would like to think I pray every day but, I don't know, maybe every other day." When asked if religion is still the basis for how she lives her life and makes decisions Kayla acknowledged, "No, it's not; it should be, but it's not." After learning that Kayla goes to church less often, prays less often, and is less reliant on religion in her life, the interviewer asks how she feels about the changes in her religiosity. Kayla says, "I'm okay with it." She explained, "I know how I feel about God, I know what I believe in, I think that's all that should matter. I pray all the time, not all the time, I pray when I can, when I remember. And I do a lot of things and I feel like I shouldn't have to go to church to prove to anybody that I'm a Christian, you see what I'm saying. So I don't really like going to church like that."

Another feature of Kayla's religious identity that had changed was her new sense of autonomy and a decline in how much religion underlies her sense of wrong and right. At the time of the first interview, she explained where her ideas about right and wrong come from with a response that illustrates how central religion was to her:

> They come from my religion. Really my religion and how I feel. I'm a very independent person. . . . You know, when it comes to ideas, I have really . . . I can stand on my own feet. I don't lean on anybody. I think it really comes from my religion, though. I think it comes from the fact that it tells you in the Bible about what's wrong and what's right. And you have to . . . people base their lives on their religion, or if you don't have religion, you base your life on that, but mine comes from my religion and it comes from the way I've been raised, which was by my religion.

Kayla expresses personal independence but ultimately claims that her sense of right and wrong comes from her religion. In the first interview Kayla was almost entirely accepting of whatever the Bible said, or at least her mother's interpretation of it. Recall that she said that even if the interviewer told her something that was right and her mother told her something that was wrong, she would believe her mother. When asked in the second interview if she still shared the same religious beliefs as her mother, she said, "They're still the same. Um, we're Christians. We, I believe, we believe that Jesus came and died on the cross for our sins." At this point she was struggling with whether to still say "we" or "I" in reference to her beliefs, a change from when she completely relied on what her mother said as the truth. When the interviewer asked Kayla whether people should adjust their views of what is right or wrong based on the world changing, here is what she said:

> I know in the Bible it says you're not supposed to have sex outside of marriage, and that's what my mother goes on, and I understand that. That's real. You shouldn't. I know I shouldn't, but once you taste the fruit you gonna want some more, you see what I'm saying? And when the kids are that young, they gonna wanna do it for so many reasons. And the only thing you can really tell them is, "Protect yourself, make sure you wear protection, and get checked out every six months." You know what I'm saying? I don't know, that's, that's my view. I think people should change as the world goes on, for real, that.

Kayla is developing autonomy and trying to make sense of what she was taught as a child. In the first interview she admitted to completely and totally relying on what her mother or the Bible said, but now she is altering these ideas to match her own experiences and observations of the world.

During the years between our interviews, Kayla moved from religious and spiritual engagement on all dimensions to less involvement in all domains. She still considers herself a Christian, however, and defended her current constellation of beliefs and practices as her own, and as just enough for her. Instead of abiding by regular, institutionally encouraged beliefs and levels of religious conduct, she was assenting to a moderate level of religious content, conduct, and centrality in her life.

Although Kayla's story is unique, it contains many elements shared by other Abiders who transitioned to the Assenter category. The fact that Abiders were unlikely to transition to any of the other profiles suggests that when those who are highly religious become less religious, they tend to do so across the board (not just in public religious practice), but not drastically. They do *not* tend to switch to an adaptive religious profile in which their attendance lowers but their levels of prayer and religious salience remain very similar. Instead they tend to fall into a group (the Assenters) where their practices (attendance, prayer, and helping others) and salience (importance of religion, closeness to God, and thinking about the meaning of life) both decline somewhat. This combination of declining in most aspects of religiosity and being "okay with it" characterizes the shift from Abider to Assenter.

One puzzle resulting from our analysis is why we find almost no Abiders that shift into the Adapter group.[10] Doing so would involve a small decrease in prayer and religious service attendance, but very little to no decrease in the importance of religion and closeness to God. It seems that if a person starts adolescence in the generally consistent profile of the Abiders, being highly religious on all domains, any lessening of religiosity means a lessening across the board. Perhaps the Abiders are socialized into believing that religious practice and salience go hand in hand, so that when one wanes the other does as well. Some (most commonly Evangelical Christians) view religion, or their own faith, as akin to a brick wall, where the bricks are different dimensions of religiosity, so that when one brick is removed, the entire wall falls.[11] They are encouraged to keep all dimensions of religiosity high. Perhaps this emphasis on consonance in religiosity leads to more consonant change as well. This pattern of congruent change among Abiders is consistent with the findings of Smith and Snell.[12] Comparing data from NSYR surveys of the youth when they were 13 to 17 and again when they were 18 to 23, they find that it is not common for youth who start out very religious to maintain a strong personal and private side to their faith despite a significant decline in their religious service attendance over time. The analysis of Smith and Snell and our analysis in this book indicate that for youth whose religious lives are a consistent package of engaged religiosity, religious decline is most likely to also come in a coherent package.

Adapter to Assenter

The 28 percent of adolescents who were most likely to be Adapters at the time of our first survey shrank to 20 percent by our second survey. Although there is at least a slight probability that youth would move to any of the other four classes in those three years, the most likely transition was from being an Adapter to being an Assenter. Doing so involved some mix of the following: praying less often, helping others less often, finding religion to be less important in daily life, feeling less close to God, and thinking about the meaning of life less often. Michael experienced this type of transition.

Michael

At the time of our first interview with Michael, who is white and from a small northwestern town, he was a 16-year-old just beginning to discover his talents as a linebacker on the local high school football team.

He perceived himself to be smarter than most kids his age and a little odd for how much he liked to read and ponder science, philosophy, and world history. But football had recently given him a new pastime and an entrée into teen life and peer acceptance. Michael is the third of four children and lived with his mother, father, and sister. His older brother was away at college, one sister was on her way to college the following year, and Michael himself planned to go to college and become either a geneticist or a historian. If he could change one thing about himself, he said, it would be his bad temper. He felt very close to his mother and was grateful that she helped him manage his temper.

Michael's family is Catholic; he was baptized at age 7 and confirmed at 13. He explained that he and his parents had pretty much the same beliefs, but he saw evil as the collection of all bad will on earth rather than something demonic. Michael viewed himself as religious and spiritual, but added that he is pretty independent in how he thinks about it all. He described his belief in God by saying, "I think God is kind of . . . an all-powerful entity of goodness, and the reason why we don't have the goodness on earth is that we rejected him initially, and the only way that we can actually get it back is by working for it. I think it's kind of like a torn relationship, a strained relationship that he has with us."

He explained that his beliefs had changed over time, in that he used to accept the teachings of the church, but now he thought about everything and decided about things for himself. He believed that everyone should practice religion because as humans we need something to believe in. He seemed to regularly think about religion and the meaning of life and saw value in such considerations for the rest of life. Both of these traits characterize the Adapter style of religiosity.

Michael saw himself as fairly average among his friends in Catholic school in terms of religious practice. Some of his friends attended church more than he did, some less. He went to Mass fairly regularly and prayed the rosary on Fridays. But, he said, prayer is mostly a formality for him. He did not go to youth group or on summer mission trips because those conflicted with time he usually spent with friends and football camp and practices. Michael had done a fair bit of volunteering, however, and he made sure the interviewer understood that it was not just because some volunteering was required for school. He also gave his own money to charity from time to time.

Michael reported feeling pretty close to God, but not as close as he could be. He called himself a "doubting Thomas" and said that his logical thinking sometimes got the best of him. Still, he said that his faith had an influence on how he viewed the world and on his actions. His religion teaches him that abortion is wrong, for example, so he views it as murder.

Two years later, at the time of the second interview, Michael had just returned from a family trip to see the Tour de France, where he "fell in love with Paris." He was taller, more muscular, and even more confident and opinionated. Now when asked to describe how he sees himself religiously or spiritually, Michael paused, sighed, and said he considered himself Catholic but partially agnostic or atheist. He hadn't decided yet. In the meantime he remained fairly active in his Catholicism. In fact, he said he was trying to cling to his faith but had lately sensed a lot of contradictions in religion. He attended Mass a couple of times a month with his parents. He still volunteered frequently, even over and above the school requirements. He did not report his extra volunteer work to the school, though, because he believed that taking that kind of credit for it cheapened the experience. He recently went to Mexico with Habitat for Humanity to build houses.

Michael told the interviewer he was becoming less religious. He used to have religious symbols and posters hanging in his room, but he had taken them all down. He expressed some sadness over questioning his faith. When the interviewer asked what he imagined he would be like religiously at age 25, he said, "I'll either be completely back in the church, or I will have fallen completely away. At this point, I think you've found me exactly in the middle."

We see in Michael's story the elements of a transition from Adapter to Assenter. At the time of the first interview he was expressing some doubts about his faith but still reported feeling personally close to God. He prayed regularly and believed his prayers were answered. When asked about the importance or centrality of religion in his life he said, "I'd say it's pretty important. It helps the decisions that I make." He also put a lot of thought into the meaning and purpose of life. At the time of the second interview, however, his responses to these same questions were more consistent with those of an Assenter than an Adapter. He described his Catholic identity by saying, "I don't know, I still cling to it I guess, but I'm having trouble with the clinging." The trouble he is having is that he has begun to have more consistent and problematic doubts about God and the faith required to believe in God.

Interviewer: So you don't know if you believe in God?
Michael: No.

Interviewer: What's your latest thinking about that?

Michael: It's all . . . it's all on the edge. I mean in order to believe in God, you have to take everything or nothing. And I have problems with some things. Like I'm really, it has to drag everything into question.

Although he still attends religious services a couple of times a month, he no longer prays regularly. Instead he prays a couple of times a week or "whenever the mood strikes." When asked if he thinks his prayers are answered, he returns an immediate no. The interviewer asks why he continues to pray, and he answers, "Probably clinging to it." He is still trying to maintain some connection to his religiosity but finds that his beliefs no longer support his previous level of religious engagement. As to the overall role of religion in his life, Michael says that religion is only a "somewhat little" part of his everyday life and is no longer the basis for how he lives his life. This reduced centrality of religion, along with a decrease in religious practice and belief, puts Michael on the path from Adapter to Assenter.

Assenter to Avoider

Of the 30 percent of youth who fit the profile of Assenter in 2002, most remained in that category. The most likely form of change experienced by these adolescents was to move from being an Assenter to an Avoider. Assenters became Avoiders by feeling distant from God and viewing God as less involved in daily life. They pray and attend religious services much less often and find religion much less important in general. Religion all but disappears for these youth. They are unlikely to become totally Atheist and reject belief in God, and instead to shift to a life in which religion is extremely tangential. Lindsay's story exemplifies this type of change in adolescence.

Lindsay

When we first met Lindsay, a white 14-year-old, she was living in a suburb of a southern city, in a very well-to-do subdivision of large homes, with both parents and her younger brother. They had moved there a few years earlier from a midwestern suburb. She described herself as a little odd because she says what she thinks, and some people find that obnoxious. Nevertheless she had a lot of friends, including "geeks," "cheerleaders," and "one punk friend." The interviewer noted that she seemed pretty young for her age, giggling and not always carefully considering the questions posed in the interview. The biggest change in her life at the time was that she had started liking her mother more and seeing her as a friend. She chalked this up to her own maturing.

Lindsay identified herself and her family as Methodist. She said they all had the same beliefs, but since they had moved they had not attended religious services as much. She said her parents often had work to do on Sunday, and sometimes they all would rather sleep in. Here's what Lindsay said when asked about her own religiosity in the first interview:

> *Interviewer*: Do you think of yourself as a religious or spiritual person?
> *Lindsay*: Not exactly.
> *Interviewer*: In what ways do you feel like you are and in what ways do you feel like you aren't?
> *Lindsay*: Um, I feel like I am sometimes because I observe Lent. Um, I feel like I'm not because I don't go to church all that often. And sometimes I'll do things that are like, not supposed to be done in my religion.

Lindsay's faith was not a central feature of her identity. Sometimes responsibilities such as school were more important than religion, she said. She accepted being a Methodist and said she sometimes followed what she feels is required of her by religion, but not always, and that was fine with her. She had no regrets about how religion fit into her life. She believed in God, describing her belief this way: "[He is] pretty much just like, kind of a part of my life. It's not like something that I think about all that often, just something that's like, there, underneath everything." When asked if she feels close to God, she said, "In between."

Fast-forward two years, and now 16-year-old Lindsay and her family had moved again, because of a job transfer for her father, to a medium-size town in the Midwest. Lindsay had really grown into herself. She said the move was pretty difficult, and it took about three months for people at her new school to start talking to her and get to know her. She had three friends, but they were all seniors who had just graduated, so she anticipated that the next year might be difficult again. But she had just landed the position of drum major in the marching band, so she expected that would bring people "flocking" to her. She missed her old high school, partly because it was so academically challenging, but did not miss the pressure that comes with going to a high school that is recognized as one of the best in the nation. Her grades had actually dropped a bit since the move.

After this move she and her family made little effort (beyond attending one Christmas service) to find a Methodist church to attend.

Religion took even more of a backseat than it had a couple of years earlier. When asked in the second interview if she believed in God, she said, "Yes, I believe in a sort of a super human, super force out there, some sort of a god." When asked if she prayed, she said, "Um, I, well it depends on the situation. Sometimes if I feel that I really need help, I do pray but not to one religion in particular. I just do some sort of universal prayer." Lindsay had just recently started looking into a variety of religions, especially Buddhism. She said her interest was piqued in her World History class modules on world religions. For now she considers herself something like a Unitarian, but is thinking of getting into Buddhism. She had a flute teacher who was Buddhist and had taken her to a couple of meditation services. Lindsay's mother, who she said had always been interested in foreign cultures, was supportive of Lindsay's interests in other religions.

Even though Lindsay was curious about Buddhism and other religions she said that religion is not a part of her everyday life, she does not think about it much, and religiosity or spirituality have no real influence on how she lives her life. At this point Lindsay seemed interested in some day working out what she thinks the best religion or meaning system is for her, but religiosity or spirituality was not necessarily a central or salient feature of her identity.

At the time of our first interview Lindsay was in the Assenter group. She identified herself as somewhat religious and had just finished observing Lent as part of her Methodist religious tradition. However, she did not consider religion to be a central part of her life and didn't see that her faith influenced her in many ways. She no longer identified herself as a Christian by the time of the second interview. She had been through a process of questioning her religion: "I'm exploring new things. I'm starting to question my religion and developing new theories about it based on what I've learned. . . . So right now I'm pretty much in acceptance of all different religions. I don't think that any one is right or wrong, and I'm just kind of keeping it in mind that everyone thinks that their religion is the right one, so I'm trying to figure out if there's some sort of a common bond between all of them."

Throughout this second interview Lindsay makes it clear that she no longer believes in any one religion, particularly not Christianity. However, she is not rejecting religion entirely. She still believes in God as a "sort of a super human, super force out there." She also expresses an interest in exploring other religions, mentioning both Buddhism and the Unitarian Church because it teaches the "acceptance of all religions." During the portion of the interview about religion and spirituality the interviewer asked whether she thinks of herself as more one than the other. She responded, "I don't know, I think of myself as more in between. Like I said, I don't follow one particular religion, but um, I'm also not completely spiritual. I mean I still do believe in God."

Lindsay is no longer an Assenter, agreeing with but only marginally connected to her Methodist faith. Instead she has moved into the category of Avoider, and religion is very tangential to the rest of her life. She differs from some Avoiders in that she continues to be interested in religion at some level and is minimally searching for the one that makes the most sense to her. However, we do not want to overemphasize the degree to which Lindsay is searching for a new religion. She talks of considering other religions in the interview, but she appears to be looking for an identity, a way to say "I am this," religiously speaking. Her discussion of thinking about trying a new religion is more to counter the risk that others would see her as not spiritual or as an atheist—notice how she asserts her belief in God at the end of the above quotation. Lindsay does not seem to be looking for a new religion in which to actively engage, especially publicly. Rather she has maintained a sort of religious curiosity; she is not ready to walk away from religion entirely, but is not convinced that there is one particular religion that would suit her.

Avoider to Atheist

About 17 percent of youth fit the profile of Avoiders in 2002. By the next survey, three years later, these adolescents were very likely to have stayed in that profile, though 11 percent of them were more likely to be reclassified as Atheists. Becoming Atheist over these three years involves a clear set of changes. These Avoiders decide there is no God, drop private expressions of religion such as praying, and lose any sense of being close to God. Religious service attendance and the importance of religion were already low for those who were Avoiders. The biggest change involved in moving from Avoiders to Atheists is a cognitive shift in belief about God. We see such a shift in Christina.

Christina

Christina, who was 18 at the time of our first interview, had dropped out of high school to start college. School was not interesting or challenging to her anymore, so she quit, waited the necessary three months to take her GED exam, passed it, and started at a local community college studying psychology. Christina seemed a lot older than other youth her age. She volunteered at a low-income clinic for people with AIDS and loved the experience. She had a diverse group of friends, including three about her age who had gotten pregnant in the past year. She was very social and went to a lot of parties, which had led to experimentation with lots of different drugs, including "pot, ecstasy, 'shrooms, and acid." She lived in a bedroom community of a big East Coast metropolis with her two parents and two brothers, one older and one younger. Her mother is Honduran and her father Italian American. Both parents were raised Catholic, and Christina attended Catholic school until she dropped out, but the family rarely goes to church. At the time of the first interview, when asked if she thinks of herself as a religious or spiritual person in any way, she said, "I kind of think of myself [as] more spiritual because if something bad happens to me, I'll kind of be like oh, I did something bad, God is punishing me, like when I crashed the car, I'm like God is punishing me. . . . I do believe in God, but I kind of don't. I mean, maybe I do . . . but I don't do things that would reflect somebody who believed in God . . . like praying or going to church."

Christina still considered herself Catholic and said she did believe in God, but did not engage in any religious practices. In fact her tenuous belief in God was about the only connection to religion in her life. In talking about the importance of religion in her life, she says, "I don't live by religion. I don't really think it is for me." She openly admits that religion is not important at all in her life and is unable to articulate any specific religious beliefs. She called her beliefs "wishy-washy" and said that she "thinks one thing one minute and another thing the next minute." Like other Avoiders in our interviews she did not consider herself to be religious, but neither was she willing to claim a nonreligious identity. She seemed to be avoiding identifying as either religious or not religious.

During the time between our first and second interviews Christina transitioned from an Avoider profile to an Atheist profile. At the second interview she felt much more comfortable identifying as irreligious. She appeared increasingly confident in her claim that she has no religious beliefs and that religion is not a part of her life. When asked how she would describe herself in terms of religiosity or spirituality, she said, "Nonexistent." If people ask, she says she is Catholic to avoid explaining that she is not religious, but she said that being Catholic means nothing to her. She does not believe in God and views the Bible as "a fairy tale." She has no interest in exploring any other religions or being spiritual at all.

Christina is an example of the youth in our study who move from Avoiders to Atheists. These youth may hang on to an outward religious identification and express some degree of belief, but with little salience or practice connected to it. As time passes they realize or become accepting of the fact that they do not believe in or connect with any aspect of religion or spirituality. For these youth this process is part of becoming an autonomous being, of making the transition to adulthood and being comfortable with who they are. As Christina demonstrates, religion is not a central part of their life at either interview. Acknowledging a nonreligious identity and no belief in God reflect the transition from the Avoider profile to the Atheist profile.

Atheist to Avoider

Only 3 percent of our youth respondents were classified as Atheist in 2002. People with a public identity that involves a disavowal of religion and God are uncommon in the United States. Most Americans openly criticize atheism, making it difficult for people to announce their non-belief in most social contexts.[13] Of the youth who fit into the Atheist profile at the time of the first survey, 52 percent remained there at the second. The most common group to which they move is the Avoider group, which has similar behaviors and attitudes but does register some belief in God. Atheists also had a slight probability of moving into the Assenter or Adapter groups.

Many of the youth who might register as Atheist at one point in time may also register as unsure about the existence of God at other times. For example, James was raised in a nonreligious home and reports no religious beliefs or practices.

Interviewer: Do you think of yourself as a religious or spiritual person?
James: No.
Interviewer: Do you believe in God?
James: Uh, I'm not sure yet. I mean, I can see that a person might not believe in God until, until, you know, you see "this is God," but I haven't had any experience like that.
Interviewer: So there's no particular understanding or feeling that you have about what God is like?
James: No.
Interviewer: Okay, do you consider yourself to be a part of any particular religion?
James: No.

Interviewer: Okay, so do you have any religious beliefs?

James: No.

During the second interview James discusses the possibility of the existence of God in similar terms: "At times I just have the general, sort of, feeling when, well, when studying biology, actually. It just seems so amazing that um, that this can all come about without, you know, some sort of, you know, divine plan for it all. But those are pretty fleeting moments." This young man says he is not religious and has no trace of religiosity in his upbringing or present life; throughout the two interviews he seems fairly confident in his nonreligious identity. However, he expresses some fleeting doubt about his worldview and is not able to say with absolute certainty that God does not exist. As we mentioned earlier, truly stable Atheists (at least those who are willing to say so in a telephone survey or in-person interview) are fairly rare in the United States. Among the youth that we interviewed there were only a handful of self-professed atheists. Some that are categorized as Atheist in our analysis, however, have not closed the door entirely on the possibility of the existence of a higher power. Like James, these youth may vacillate over time between the Atheist and Avoider profiles.

Summary

Between middle and late adolescence there is not much switching between religious profiles. Even though certain dimensions of religiosity, especially public religious practice, are likely to decrease at this point in the life course and there is some change in the centrality of religion, changes in religiosity are not large scale enough to create much movement between profiles. It appears that the types of religiosity that adolescents live are fairly stable between middle and late adolescence. Following these same youth through the transition to adulthood will allow us to see if and how this set of religious profiles changes. These same five profiles may also fit the adult population in the United States. Once a person finds a profile that fits her well she may be likely to stay within the parameters of the profile for life, a question for future research to examine.

The stability in profile membership does not, however, mean that youth who stay in a given profile are not experiencing change and adjustment in their personal religious mosaic or the components therein. In fact many youth who appear religiously stable describe tangible change in their religiosity over time. As part of the 2005 NSYR telephone survey we asked our respondents, "Over the past three years, have you become more religious, less religious, or stayed about the same?" More than half said their religiosity stayed about the same. For those who report having experienced some change, surprisingly a greater number say they have become more religious (26 percent) than say they have become less religious (16 percent). This seems paradoxical given that comparing measures of religious content, conduct, and centrality at both time points suggests more downward than upward change. These self-reports of religious change raise the question of how adolescents themselves experience or process their own religiosity or religious development and why their own assessments and narratives seem to differ from what is revealed by comparing their survey reports over time.

5

When Down Is Up: Complexities in Adolescent Religious Change

Interviewer: Over the past couple of years, do you think you've become more religious, less religious, or stayed about the same?
Participant: More, but more in the way I think, and less in that I don't go to the temple that much. (18-year-old Hindu male)

As mentioned in the previous chapter, there is somewhat of a paradox in our data when it comes to observed change and adolescents' perceptions of religious change in their lives. Looking at aggregate survey data we see that average levels of definitive religious belief, religious service attendance (as in the case of the young man quoted above), prayer, and the centrality of religion in life all drop by small but significant amounts over time in our sample of American adolescents. This matches what most would predict happens, on average, in the period of adolescence—that adolescents become preoccupied with school, work, and socializing with peers in ways that do not always fit well with the organization or ethos of religious institutions. On the other hand, when in the second survey we asked adolescents whether they have become more religious, less religious, or stayed the same over the past three years, the majority said they stayed the same, and 26 percent said they became *more* religious in the past three years, like the young man quoted above. Only 16 percent of our nationally representative sample of adolescents reported becoming less religious in the past three years. Why do adolescents report slightly decreasing levels of beliefs, practices, and salience at the same time that most of them tell us they either stayed the same or got more religious over the past three years? The answer lies in our qualitative data from in-person interviews with these adolescents, where they reveal what religiosity means to them and the dynamics they have experienced in their faith over time. In our analysis of these interviews, we pay close attention to the dimensions of religiosity adolescents themselves identify and the weight given to each dimension in describing the dynamics of their own religious histories. Their answers tell us something about how adolescents understand their own religious lives and how they weigh the different facets of religiosity in assessing their religious development.

In the second in-person semistructured interviews we conducted with a subsample of NSYR respondents, we asked specific yet open-ended questions about whether there had been any change in their religiosity or spirituality between the two time points. We also asked several questions regarding what being religious or spiritual means to them personally. A large part of our analysis focused on these directly relevant conversations. We were particularly interested in how participants answered questions that directly probed how their religiosity had changed (or not) through time and their assessment of that. However, we did read entire transcripts multiple times to get a full sense of participants' lives and experiences. We draw insight from both what they are saying directly about religion in their lives and what emerges in between the lines of their discourse throughout the interviews.

When these adolescents do explicitly talk about their religiosity and its dynamics over time, they often focus on one of the three dimensions of religiosity (content, conduct, and centrality) as the anchor for describing how they have either stayed the same or become more or less religious over time. For this reason we have organized this chapter in a way that demonstrates how adolescents rely on certain dimensions of religion to evaluate themselves and to describe themselves to others. Table 5.1 lists the number of interview respondents who tell us they have stayed the same religiously, gotten more religious, or gotten less religious over the past three years by the primary dimension of religiosity on which they focus when describing the dynamics or stability of their own religiosity.[1]

How Religious Conduct Factors into Narratives
of Religious Change

Often public religious practice, or religious service attendance, is the yardstick by which one person measures whether or not another

Table 5.1. Reported Direction of Religious Change or Stability by Dimension of Religiosity Used in Semistructured Interview Discourse

Direction of Change/Stability	Dimension of Religiosity				
	Conduct	Content	Centrality	Mixed/ Unidentified	Total
Stayed the same	3	8	3	39	53
Became more religious	5	3	20	7	35
Became less religious	16	4	2	1	23
Total	24	15	25	47	111

Source: National Study of Youth and Religion, Wave 2 semistructured interviews, 2005.
Note: Measures of religious change/stability and dimensions of religiosity presented in this table were coded from responses to an open-ended question in the semistructured in-person interviews. Only the 111 interviews that provided a response to the question about religious change are included in this table.

person is religious and if or how a person's religiosity is changing. For about 22 percent of the youth we interviewed this was the main dimension of their own religiosity used in describing religious stability or change in their lives. In our study some youth pointed to patterns in their religious service attendance as evidence of having experienced each of the three types of directionality in their religious or spiritual lives (staying the same religiously or having become more or less religious).

As in the telephone survey, the majority of the subsample of semistructured interview participants reports staying the same religiously between our first and second interviews. Some of these youth used the regularity in their frequency of attending religious services to illustrate how they are the same religiously. Of those who say they stayed the same religiously, 6 percent focus on consistent religious practice to describe this stability, while many more include this as one element in a larger package of religious stability. For example, a 16-year-old Asian American Hindu girl who best fits the religiosity profile of an Abider at the time of both surveys said she had stayed the same religiously over the past three years; when asked to expand, she explained that she still goes to the temple weekly and does *puja* (a Hindu form of worship) daily. In some cases the stability of attendance patterns serves as evidence of religious stability even though respondents might describe changes in other aspects of their religious lives. One 17-year-old white Latter Day Saint girl who fit the Assenter category in both surveys explained how her religious beliefs have gotten stronger: "I think I believe stronger in what I believe now because I'm more knowledgeable of what it really means to me." In spite of her stronger beliefs, however, her church attendance pattern has remained very much the same since the first interview: attending only on holidays or when invited by friends. When asked if she had become more or less religious, she reported that she had stayed the same and immediately began to talk about religious service attendance. Her response indicates that even though she has experienced some strengthening of her religious beliefs, it is the consistency of her sporadic religious service attendance that drives her answer to our question about religious change in her life.

Another group of youth identifies changes in the frequency of their religious service attendance as the basis for their reports of religious change in their lives. For some this change in religious service attendance was accompanied by changes in other aspects of their religious lives, such as a change in their religious beliefs or in the importance of religion in their lives. However, for other youth changes in religious service attendance were not necessarily tied to other aspects of their religious lives. For example, when a 16-year-old white Lutheran girl who used to be a regular church attendee was asked if she had stayed the same or become more or less religious since the last interview, she said, "Probably a little less because we used to go to church a little more, but we don't really anymore." She fit the Assenter profile of religiosity at the time of both surveys. Another girl, who is 18 and identifies as Latina, black, and Pentecostal, cites religious service attendance to describe why she has become less religious: "I used to go to church with my great-grandmother, but ever since she passed I haven't been to church." Based on her survey answers in 2002 and 2005 she is classified as an Adapter. She goes on to say that her religious identity and religious beliefs have remained the same. Thus her report of becoming less religious appears to be rooted in the reduction of her involvement at church, and not in the strength of her beliefs, which she reports have stayed the same.

Referencing religious service attendance when describing an overall change in religiosity was the most common response among those who reported having become less religious (16 out of 23 respondents). Take, for example, one 17-year-old white boy who best fits the Avoider category, identifies himself in the interview as Christian (giving no specific denominational affiliation), and had the following exchange with the interviewer:

> *Interviewer*: Over the past couple of years would you say you've become more religious, less religious, or stayed about the same?
>
> *Participant*: Less.
>
> *Interviewer*: Is there a reason why you think you've become less religious?
>
> *Participant*: Naw, I think it just fades. . . . I guess it's just because, I mean, other things will start to take up more time in my life, so I just cut that out, 'cause it was never really that important in the first place. . . . We used to attend services semiregular and then we just slowly stopped, and now we just don't attend anymore, and that was just about it.

This boy goes on to describe decreases in prayer, feeling less close to God, and religion being less important or relevant to the rest of his life. He says his religiosity has been dropping off since about age 9 or 10. He still considers himself Christian and believes in God, but he says, "I really don't have a religious point of view." In most cases of this type of all-around decrease in religiosity, adolescents start by describing a gradual decrease in religious service attendance. In many cases, as in this one, a decrease in an adolescent's religious practice is accompanied by a decrease in parental attendance as well.

It was less common for a youth to identify an increase in religious service attendance in order to describe how he became more religious. Only 5 out of the 35 participants who claimed they had become more religious cited religious service attendance as the barometer for their increased religiosity. Instead attendance patterns appear to be most often cited by those who are explaining religious stability or decreases in religiosity. There are a couple of reasons why overall stability or decreases in religiosity may be described mostly in terms of attendance and increased religiosity is not. First, as we noted earlier, attendance is what often initially comes to mind as a representation of religiosity. It is a public action that is easy to discuss, quantify, and recognize as a core piece of religiosity. Particularly for those youth who are not very engaged in religion, discussing attendance does not require any specialized religious knowledge or familiarity with particular religious languages or beliefs. Therefore in cases where there is consistent decline across multiple dimensions of religiosity it seems that youth most readily gravitate toward a discussion of religious practice. Further, when discussing religiosity in an interview setting our

youth participants may find it less controversial to say that their attendance dropped off than to admit that they find religion less relevant in
their life or that they are discounting religious belief. In a society
where public rejection of religion, especially Christianity, can draw
skepticism and condemnation, the average person may not want to
run the risk of appearing to be atheist.[2]

One of the few participants in our study who does attribute his
more religious answer to religious service attendance illustrates these
tendencies as well as youth reporting stability or decrease. This
20-year-old Catholic male who best fits into the profile of an Assenter
in both surveys is pretty clear about not being all that into religion.
When asked about his religious identity and various practices, he
repeatedly replies with the line, "I just don't think about that stuff all
too much." He believes in God, but he is much more interested in
detailing his drinking, drug use, and sexual exploits than discussing
religion. However, when the interviewer asks whether he believes he
has gotten more religious, less religious, or stayed the same in the past
three years, he says, "I guess more, just because I go to church more.
I'm not that like nonreligious, I go with my grandma to church and
shit." He has recently moved for college to the same town in which his
grandmother lives, so now he drives her to church every Sunday. He
has very little connection to religion in his life and does not appear to
be conversant in religious language and beliefs. However, he also does
not particularly want to be identified as nonreligious. Therefore he
draws on his increased level of religious service attendance to claim an
increase in religiosity.

Among scholars and lay audiences alike religious service attendance
remains an appealing measure of religious commitment. Measures of
levels of attendance have sparked many debates about the state of religion in our society.[3] And many youth seem to echo this sentiment that
religiosity and religious change are anchored in how often you attend
religious services. However, some youth were very specific about the
fact that religious service attendance alone does not define one's religiosity. One 16-year-old white girl who identifies as Christian said,
"I don't believe you have to go to church to be Christian. You don't
have to. You just have to pretty much believe in God." According to
her survey answers, she fit the Abider profile in 2002, but was most
likely to be an Assenter in 2005. Similarly Chelsea, who we talk about
in the introduction and who is classified as an Assenter in 2002 and
2005, said, "I don't think I need to go to church to prove that I'm a
Christian and I believe in Jesus Christ as my Lord. I think people that

say that you have to go to church . . . It's a ridiculous statement." A white Presbyterian girl who is 18 and best fits the profile of an Adapter in both surveys said, "I think I'm a religious person even though I don't go to church every Sunday." These youth seem to be suggesting that there are other factors besides attendance that better answer questions about how religious a person is. Although they reject the notion of religious service attendance as the yardstick for religiosity, built into their responses is a perception of how common it is to equate participation in organized religion with personal religiosity. Consider the interview of an 18-year-old Catholic Latina who is most like an Adapter at both time points:

> *Interviewer*: Over the past couple of years, do you think you've become more religious, less religious, or stayed about the same?
> *Participant*: Um, I don't know if you'd call not going to church less religious.
> *Interviewer*: Do you consider it less religious?
> *Participant*: No I don't.
> *Interviewer*: Okay.
> *Participant*: Yeah, I think I'm the same religiously, but I just don't go to church. I think I've stayed as religious as I was. Like according to the church I would be less religious, but . . .
> *Interviewer*: Well I just want to know what you think. So do you think you've changed?
> *Participant*: No.
> *Interviewer*: Do you go to Mass less?
> *Participant*: Yeah.
> *Interviewer*: Okay. Would other people you've known well over the past couple of years, like friends or family, say you've changed religiously or spiritually?
> *Participant*: No, I don't think so.
> *Interviewer*: Why would you say that?
> *Participant*: I mean, I've just been the same.

She acknowledges a decrease in attendance at religious services and suggests that although the church might consider this a sign of becoming less religious, she does not. For this girl, declining attendance does not equate to a decline in how religious she perceives herself to be. Beyond that she does not believe that other people in her life would consider her less religious as a result of her declining attendance at Mass. Her beliefs and the extent to which religion fits into her life have not changed, so she believes she is the same religiously speaking.

At a time in their life when adolescents are facing increasing demands on their time as well as increasing autonomy from parents, religious involvement has great potential to be dialed back. A small number of adolescents are relieved by the decrease because they didn't much enjoy attending services and not going anymore fits their overall move away from religion. Another small group regrets the decrease and wishes they could be more disciplined about going, but most are rather pragmatic about and accepting of their declining attendance. They say there just isn't time or they would much rather be getting more sleep on weekend mornings. Numerous studies have shown that adolescents do become more and more preoccupied with school, work, and socializing and that biologically they require more sleep.[4] Both phenomena compete with regular religious involvement. For some adolescents this decline in religious participation translates into a life narrative about "becoming less religious." For others it is a practical reality, but not necessarily a defining feature of their personal religious identity.

Relying on the Content of Beliefs to Frame Religious Stability or Change

For many of the youth we talked to, religious conduct in the form of religious service attendance is not the main criterion they use to evaluate the role of religion or the level of religiosity in their lives. In our interviews we also heard youth rely on the two other Cs: the content and strength of religious beliefs and the centrality of religion to their life.

Most of the youth we interviewed described their religious beliefs in very broad and vague terms. Yet however unspecific these beliefs may be, they serve as the glue that holds a minority of adolescents to their religious identity and the criteria by which they assess change in their own religiosity. One such subset of adolescents reports that they have not changed religiously in the past three years, and they support this answer by pointing to the fact that they still hold all of the same religious beliefs that they did in the past. Sometimes this consistency of belief is accompanied by a consistency of religious practice, but this is not necessarily the case. For example, a white 17-year-old Baptist boy who best fits the Assenter profile was asked to describe himself religiously and answered, "I have a strong hold and belief in it and I try to stick to that firm hold and beliefs." Later in the interview he said that for the past year and a half he has been working with his uncle on weekends to build a house and has therefore stopped attending church. In spite of this change in his religious participation, however, he reports that he has stayed the same religiously since the previous interview. In this case, his assessment of religious change is based on the constancy of his religious beliefs and not on the conduct of his religiosity through church attendance. Similarly, an 18-year-old white girl who was a devoted Wiccan and fit the profile of an Adapter at the time of the first interview, but who was most likely to be an Avoider at the time of the second survey, reported the following about the religious changes in her life:

> *Participant*: I still believe all the stuff that I believed before. I'm just not really active. I just don't do anything anymore.
> *Interviewer*: Over the past couple of years, do you think you've become more religious, less religious, or stayed about the same?
> *Participant*: Are you asking how I've changed religiously?
> *Interviewer*: Yes, do you think you've changed, religiously, much over the last couple of years?
> *Participant*: No, I still believe the same things.
> *Interviewer*: So just a change in activities?
> *Participant*: Yes, the intensity went down, you know.

The important issue for this girl seems to be that the content of her beliefs and worldview has remained the same. She minimizes the decline in her attendance at Wiccan functions and personal rituals and emphasizes that she still holds the same religious and spiritual beliefs.

A few youth report becoming more or less religious as a result of changes in their religious beliefs. One young man continues to attend Catholic Mass every week with his parents because they require it, but he has come to reject his former religious beliefs and now considers himself an atheist. When asked about religious change in his life, this 16-year-old white boy, who made the transition from being most likely to be an Assenter to best fitting the Atheist profile, reports that he is less religious than he was two years ago. He attributes this to the changes in his religious beliefs.

> *Interviewer*: Describe to me over these past couple of years, if you think you've become more religious, less religious or stayed about the same?
> *Participant*: Less religious.
> *Interviewer*: Okay, and in which ways have you become less religious?
> *Participant*: Um, I've gone from having minor doubts to atheism.

Interviewer: Okay, so two years ago how would you have described yourself to me religiously?

Participant: Um, I would have said that I have a few doubts, like a few questions about religion, but overall I would have said I still believe.

Interviewer: Okay, and what's been behind the change from then until now?

Participant: Because like all, all, like the questions that I had couldn't really be answered, and if they did it was like just have faith, you just have to have faith, which I found unacceptable, and so, I mean, if just . . . I found so many holes in it.

His overall assessment of becoming less religious reflects changes in the content of his beliefs, which are under his control, not his weekly Mass attendance, which was controlled by his parents. There were also a small number of adolescents who linked becoming *more* religious to a change in their religious beliefs. One example is a 19-year-old Asian American Buddhist boy who reported the following:

Participant: I'd say I probably became more religious, because I really didn't think that way when I was in high school. So now that I kind of realize that, uh, I guess I'm a little more religious now.

Interviewer: Okay. So you feel more religious even though you haven't upped your temple attendance or anything like that?

Participant: Yeah.

Just prior to this the boy had been talking about some of his particular religious beliefs: "You bring about your own misery. If you're unhappy, you made yourself unhappy. I kind of really believe that one. . . . You have to have a better understanding of what's going on around you. . . . Like, um . . . you should accept others for who they are." When he is asked to assess his own religious change he points back to these beliefs that have developed more strongly within him and now guide his life to support the claim that he is more religious. As the interviewer clarifies, his perception of becoming more religious is not connected to any change in how often he goes to a temple.

These examples illustrate cases in which youth point to the content of their religious beliefs as the main marker of their religious stability or change. We present these cases to show the full range of how youth draw on different dimensions of religiosity to describe their religious trajectories, but remind readers that sizable change in the content of religious beliefs during adolescence is fairly rare. Although some adolescents discussed religious beliefs in their assessment of religious change, particular religious beliefs do not appear to be a significant factor when the majority of youth assess levels of religious change in their lives. Part of this might be explained by the fact that specific religious beliefs are not particularly central to the religious identities of adolescents. With some notable exceptions, questions in our interviews about specific religious beliefs drew vague generalities or even blank stares. Earlier research with adolescents found that they are not particularly proficient when it comes to articulating detailed religious beliefs.[5] Youth are not highly invested in the particularities of their religious traditions and tend instead to report very general versions of religious beliefs. If there is not much thought or evaluation going into the specific content of religious beliefs, then it should come as no surprise that youth do not draw very often upon their religious beliefs to discuss religious change in their lives. Also, because there is not a specific focus on the particulars of belief, a change in belief would almost require a wholesale acceptance of new beliefs or rejection of current beliefs. This type of radical change is very rare, as religious beliefs tend to remain fairly stable over time.[6] Some youth certainly did come to a clearer statement of their religious beliefs in the second interview, but most continue to be satisfied with the same general version of their religious tradition, or what Smith and Denton refer to as Moralistic Therapeutic Deism. When religious beliefs are the primary gauge for religious change, the overriding response is that there has been no change.

The Centrality of Religiosity as a Touchstone

In listening to the voices of youth so far, we have heard them define religiosity and any change therein in terms of participation in religious services and religious belief. A third dimension of religiosity that we heard youth refer to as they responded to the question about religious change was religious centrality or salience. This manifests in the interviews as the broad array of language used to express how being religious is important, is internalized as a core piece of their identity, and serves as a reference point for everyday life. The centrality of religiosity to one's identity was cited by our interview participants with similar frequency as religious conduct to explain religious change. However, this explanation of religious change was found most prominently among those youth who said they had become more religious; 57 percent of youth who reported becoming more religious pointed to an increase in religious centrality as the primary explanation for this change.

A prominent theme among those who report becoming more religious during adolescence has to do with their making a faith of their own. For these youth the main criterion for assessing religious change in their lives was the extent to which they had embraced and personalized the religion in which they were raised. For many youth, religion is a part of their life from a young age. But as we mentioned in an earlier chapter, adolescence is a time of cognitive development that often results in youth making decisions about what worldview, beliefs, and values they will carry forward into young adulthood and beyond.[7] Many youth who are raised in a religious tradition at some point find themselves with the freedom to decide for themselves whether or not to continue in that tradition.[8] For those who do decide to continue on in the faith tradition of their family, this can become a defining characteristic of their faith, the point at which the faith becomes their own decision based on their own understanding of the world. This is not necessarily a specific moment that they can point to. But asking them whether they had become more or less religious or had stayed the same seemed to be an opportunity for them to reflect on their own personal religious or spiritual refinement. We heard youth report that they considered themselves more religious now than in the past specifically because they had adopted their family's faith as their own, taken responsibility for their own religious life, or were experiencing some level of personal spiritual growth.

In some cases adolescents taking ownership of their religiosity has a strong element of practicality. As youth get older they become more responsible for their own religious lives—deciding for themselves whether or not to go to religious services, for example, and being responsible for following through on these decisions. One white Baptist boy who is 16 and fits the profile of being an Abider at the time of both surveys supported his claim of becoming more religious by describing the actions he took to maintain his faith: driving himself to church and making decisions based on his religion. These actions indicate to him, and others, that being religious is something he is choosing for himself.

> *Interviewer*: In the last couple years would you say you've become more religious or spiritual or less religious or stayed about the same?
> *Participant*: Probably more religious or spiritual.
> *Interviewer*: How's that?
> *Participant*: I guess I've matured more, and I've started taking my own time to do more with the church and stuff. Because I drive to church

activities and my parents don't have to take me or tell me to do it. . . . I can make my own decisions about stuff based on my religion, so I feel more with it.

Some adolescents described developing a deeper understanding of their religion. This is a time in the life course when youth are developing greater levels of abstract thinking and are better able to understand and process the tenets of religion.[9] Learning more about their religion and being able to better understand their faith results in a more salient connection to their religious tradition. For example, one 18-year-old black boy who attends a Baptist church and is also most likely to be an Abider across time attributes his increase in religiosity to his better understanding of church teachings. This has allowed him to make religiosity his own choice instead of his mother's.

> *Interviewer*: Over the past couple of years, do you think you've become more religious, less religious, or stayed about the same?
> *Participant*: Um, the past couple of years, more religious, because like I said, when I moved from the old church to the new church, I was able to understand everything better, which has made me more religious. [At the old church] I didn't really understand what was going on. I was just going through my mama's thing.
> *Interviewer*: I see, so now it's become your thing?
> *Participant*: Yes.
> *Interviewer*: Has religion become more or less the basis of your life and how you live your life?
> *Participant*: More.
> *Interviewer*: Again, why would you say these changes occurred?
> *Participant*: 'Cause with me being able to understand the Word better and applying it to my everyday life.
> *Interviewer*: How big of an impact would you say that religion and spirituality have on your life?
> *Participant*: A great impact.
> *Interviewer*: In what ways?
> *Participant*: Because, like I said, with me being able to understand it more, it helps me to make the choices I've made. . . . Just everything I do involves that, making the right choice and things.

For still other youth the increasing centrality of religion is expressed in terms of spiritual growth or getting closer to God. Listening to their descriptions of religious change we get a sense of religion becoming more meaningful and personal in their lives. Here is how a 15-year-old white Christian and Missionary Alliance boy who is classified as an Abider at both time points conveys it:

> *Interviewer*: Over the past couple of years, do you think you've become more religious, less religious, or stayed about the same?
>
> *Participant*: I think I've gotten more religious because I've been able to go on a lot of church camps and stuff like that that have really made me grow more in my spiritual faith.
>
> *Interviewer*: What kind of growth specifically have you seen?
>
> *Participant*: Maybe just realizing how important God needs to be in my life and how I should make him, how sometimes I can like put other things in front of him and stuff, like money or whatever, and it just really made me realize how God's the most important thing.

A 17-year-old white girl who attends a nondenominational church and is also best classified by the Abider profile across time says, "I think I've become closer to God, yeah I think I definitely have. Just as I learn more about myself, and as I learn more about God, and I feel more established in who I am. It's easier to kind of like, it's easier to grow. Like when you don't feel so sporadic, so I feel like I have grown in my relationship [with God]." When the interviewer asks, "Is there any way in which you think you've changed in terms of your beliefs or practices in the last couple of years?" the girl responds, "No, I haven't, I mean, I've learned more but I haven't changed, I haven't changed something that I used to believe into something different."

Similar to other youth we heard from, this girl reports that there have been no major changes in her religious beliefs or practices, yet she has clearly experienced an increasing sense of religiosity in her life. In her response she packages growing up, learning more about herself, and gaining a stronger sense of self with learning more about God, feeling closer to God, and growing in her relationship with God. Religion—or at least her relationship with God—appears to be playing a more important role in her life than it has in the past. This is not due to any changes in behavior or belief, but is the result of an internal process of increasing religious salience.

Increased Need

For another subset of youth increased salience was related to an increase in their felt need for religion. As youth get older many are faced with more challenges in their lives. These challenges can some-times serve as a catalyst that reaffirms or strengthens their religious faith. For example, one of the young men in our study who is 20, white, affiliated with the Brethren denomination, and fits the profile of an Abider at the time of both surveys, reports that being out on his own has been instrumental in his becoming more religious over the past couple of years.

> *Interviewer*: Do you think that over the last couple of years you have become more religious, less religious or stayed about the same?
> *Participant*: I'd say more religious just because being out on my own I have had to rely on myself and rely on God a lot more. I'm just looking for guidance and direction in that aspect. I have become more reliant on God. But other than that I would say that there hasn't been much of a change.
> *Interviewer*: Have any of your beliefs changed in the last couple of years? It doesn't sound like any of those things have changed.
> *Participant*: Right. I mean I've learned more about [my beliefs]. I'd say that I've definitely learned more about things that are religious. So in discussions and stuff I can just kind of say, hey, this is why I believe how I believe and just kind of have reason for it more so than just, well, I just felt like it.

He notes that there hasn't been much change in his religious life, but he has come to rely on God more for guidance and direction. This increased reliance on God appears to be the reason he considers himself to have become more religious. It is the increased need for and use of religion—not a change in religious practices or beliefs—that has led to this increase in perceived religiosity. In other words, religion seems to be becoming more central to other aspects of his life, serving as a point of reference in making decisions about what to do.

Personalization Even in the Face of Declining Religious Involvement

These examples illustrate that youth often perceive themselves to be more religious even when outward appearances would suggest that they have remained very similar religiously. For another group of youth, the perception of becoming more religious persists in spite of acknowledged *decreases* in religious practices. When asked to report about religious change they respond in ways that suggest that not only can one become more religious without increasing religious practice, but one can become more religious even if one's actual religious practices decline. In these cases, changes in religious salience strongly outweigh measures of religious participation or practice as these youth assess their own religiosity. As a girl we quoted earlier stated, "I think I am a religious person even though I don't go to church every Sunday."

When asked about religious change in her life, a 19-year-old white Latter Day Saint who fits well in the category of Abider at both waves of the survey reports that she has become more religious: "I think I have become more religious just because there's been so many things, while out on your own, that you need more than when you're sheltered and you just, you need someone who's always there and God's always there." Like the young man above, she explains how she has become more religious by pointing to being out on her own as the catalyst for the change. However, when the interviewer asks about changes in religious participation and practices, she says, "It's gone from more involved to a little bit less." Her religious involvement is declining, at least somewhat, but when asked to report on her overall religiousness she says that she is more religious now than three years earlier. What explains this apparent contradiction? It seems that the rubric she is using to assess the religious change in her own life must not consider a decline in religious participation as being equivalent to becoming less religious. Instead the increase in her felt dependence on God signals to her an increase in religiousness. Religion appears to have become more salient to this young woman. Regardless of her actual involvement in religious practices, she believes herself to be more religious because she "feels" her religious need more acutely now than in the past; in other words, religion is now more relevant to her.

When Taking Greater Ownership Means Becoming Less Religious

Defining one's religious self does not always result in retaining and then personalizing the style of religiosity experienced in one's upbringing. A small number of youth also experienced a transition related to the personalization of faith, but one that resulted in resignation of their religious upbringing. In these cases the autonomy that comes with age resulted in making decisions to distance themselves from their religious past. This type of religious change is reflected in comments like the following, from a white, 19-year-old Baptist girl who best fits the category of Assenter at both waves of the survey: "I just heard it in church, 'cause I grew up in church, and then when I was older I decided I didn't want to go and I didn't have to." Other participants describe this type of change in religiosity in more detailed terms.

The next two boys (a consistent Assenter and a consistent Adapter, respectively) talk about being freed from parental control of religious service attendance.

Interviewer: Over the past couple of years, have you become more religious, less religious, or stayed about the same?

Participant (an 18-year-old white boy who was raised as a Latter Day Saint): Ah, probably less religious.

Interviewer: Do you mind me asking what was behind the change?

Participant: Um, I can finally do what I want. I just, my father had forced me to go to church and practice certain things in the church, and if you're gonna tell me to practice certain things, and do certain things, the more I don't want to do them. The more I'm going to rebel. So now that I'm actually on my own, I can actually rebel, and not do those things.

Interviewer: In the past couple years, has your attendance at church gone down or been just about the same, about once a month?

Participant (a 16-year-old Latino who was raised as a Catholic): It's gone down, I think, because when I was younger, my mom used to, you know, just make me go every Sunday, but I was like, I have a choice. So I think it's gone down.

Interviewer: Okay. What do you think makes you less likely to go?

Participant: Just lazy. Being lazy. Not being able to wake up.

For some youth the religion in which they were raised—or at least their understanding and experience of it—begins to lose relevance for their lives. As their lives become more fast-paced and busy, religion slides down the list of priorities. When asked to think about religious change in their lives, these youth reply that religion no longer seems relevant or urgent. Whether or not they continue to hold particular religious beliefs, religion loses salience in their lives. It becomes less influential, receives less consideration, and they participate less frequently. As a result these youth tell us that they have become less religious over the three years between interviews.

Adolescence is a time when youth repeatedly talk about what they decide, what they choose, that they are on their own and do what they want to do. This increased autonomy and sense of self can translate into becoming more or less religious. Adolescents desire autonomy and ownership over their personal religiosity. This can lead to affirmation of the beliefs and practices they were involved in as children or adaptations into higher or lower levels of religiosity.

Complexities in How Youth Describe Religious Change

So far we have categorized youth by the dimension of religiosity on which they primarily rely in their discourse regarding religious change and stability in their own lives. The reality is that it is not always easy to identify a single dimension of religiosity in their discourse, and it is even more difficult to predict which dimensions a given youth will pick to describe her religious life.

We were surprised by how many youth did immediately focus their answer in a particular direction and describe their own religious change or stability in relation to one particular element of religiosity. These responses teach us something about the dominant categories in which youth tend to think about their religious lives (or at least the categories on which they draw when asked by a relative stranger interviewing them to think about their religious lives in this way). We can also learn something from those youth who struggle to provide an overall assessment of religious change in their lives and acknowledge in their responses that it is not so straightforward. The youth whose responses include some level of ambiguity generally reflect the same themes as those already discussed. They illustrate well the complexity of measuring or assessing religious changes in light of the multiple dimensions of religion. This further reinforces one of the main positions of this book, that a person-based or typology-centered approach to categorizing religiosity helps us to better summarize the main ways that youth are living religion in their lives.

Recall the young man quoted at the start of this chapter, an 18-year-old Hindu whose parents immigrated to the United States from India. Based on his survey data he had transitioned from being most likely to be an Adapter to best fitting in the Assenter profile. He had a hard time choosing between the content of his beliefs and religious conduct as the main touchstone for defining religious change in his life.

> *Interviewer*: Over the past couple of years, do you think you've become more religious, less religious, or stayed about the same?
> *Participant*: More, but more in the way I think, and less in that I don't go to the temple that much. . . . I'm more of a practical . . . I more practice in the way I act than . . .
> *Interviewer*: Okay, so you think about things more?
> *Participant*: Yeah.

A 16-year-old white girl who is a Latter Day Saint and best characterized as an Abider deals with this issue by labeling practices as "religious" and beliefs as "spiritual." Similar to the Hindu boy, however, when asked to assess religious change in her life she makes a distinction between religious practice, such as service attendance, and religious beliefs.

> *Interviewer*: You said earlier that you felt you've become maybe a little less religious and a little more spiritual?
> *Participant*: Yes.
> *Interviewer*: What do you mean by that?
> *Participant*: Like I constantly am, you know, I follow God's will and I believe in him and that sort of thing, but like my practice has gotten a little waning, probably because of high school, because I'm so busy I don't have time, or I forget to pray, you know, or stuff like that, or maybe I don't go to as many church activities as I did before. But I think spiritually I'm strong because I've never waned on that. I've never not believed in it or questioned it. Well, you know, you're supposed to question, but I've never like denied it or anything, so I think I've always been strong in that point, so I don't think I'm worried about that.

Recall the Catholic Latina who distinguished between her view of what it means to be less religious and the church's view of this issue:

> *Participant*: Yeah, I think I'm the same religiously, but I just don't go to church. I think I've stayed as religious as I was. Like according to the church I would be less religious, but . . .
> *Interviewer*: So do you think you've changed?
> *Participant*: No.

A 19-year-old Latina attending a nondenominational church, who is best characterized as an Abider, asks directly what the question means. When told to define it herself, she talks about maturing in faith.

> *Interviewer*: In the past couple of years do you think you've become more religious, less religious, or stayed the same?
> *Participant*: Well, probably more religious, although I don't know what you mean by more religious.
> *Interviewer*: However you would define that.
> *Participant*: I think, I define it as maturing more in my faith and yeah, I'm definitely maturing more. . . . A huge part of it is where I'm working right now 'cause I'm with kids all day long, I'm with Christians all day

long, and every night we have a worship service, and we read the Bible and we have staff devotionals every morning, so like whether I want to or not I have to be there and I'm going to be in the Word.

Interviewer: Would other people you've known well over the past couple of years, like friends or family, say that you've changed religiously or spirituality, become more or less?

Participant: Yeah, I think that people have definitely noticed that I've matured more.

Interviewer: What would they have seen in you to make them think that?

Participants: Hopefully by my actions, in the way that I treat people, like I hope that they see that I treat people better, that I can be encouraging to them, be a leader.

Interviewer: Have any of your beliefs changed?

Participant: No.

Interviewer: Has your level of attendance at religious services or groups gone up or down?

Participant: Uh, it's probably gone up.

Interviewer: Has your involvement with any youth groups or college-age groups gone up or down?

Participant: Yeah, up.

Interviewer: Do you pray more or less?

Participant: I don't know. It's probably the same.

Interviewer: Do you think you read the Bible more or less?

Participant: Probably read it more . . . just it's something that I want to do more for myself.

Interviewer: Okay. Has religion become more or less of the basis for how you live your life?

Participant: More.

Her need to ask how the interviewer is defining *religious* highlights the ambiguity that is inherent in this type of questioning. Part of the strategy of not providing more clarity about the definition is that we wanted to understand how youth themselves understand and define the concept of religious change and what words they would choose to use. But this does create a situation in which different youth are in effect answering different questions (i.e., the question they perceive us to be asking). What we do gain from this approach is a better understanding of what youth draw on when asked to provide a global assessment of their religious journeys.

Religious Profiles and Self-reported Religious Change

We have described hearing youth talk about taking ownership of their faith and that some consider themselves to be either more or less religious as a result. When we go back and look at the religious profiles of these youth, we find an interesting pattern. Youth who pointed to religious centrality as a marker of increased religiosity were almost always Abiders or Adapters. In addition, these were youth whose religious profile remained stable across both surveys.[10] We think that this suggests a couple of interesting points. First, it adds some insight to the question of which youth are moving toward and away from religion in their lives. In chapter 3 we saw that although the typical movement is toward religious decline, there is in fact movement in both directions among the youth in our study. Listening to the voices of youth talk about religious change suggests that increases in religious centrality might be most common among those youth for whom religion is already highly salient. Youth for whom religion is less salient at the time of the first survey are not likely to be among those youth who talk about moving toward more incorporation of religion in their lives.

Second, our interviews allow us the opportunity to assess religious change from yet another perspective. We have seen that youth themselves report religious change that is not visible simply by looking at transitions from one religious profile to another, or among the five *A*s. At least some of the religious change they talk about is happening within religious profiles and does not necessarily result in movement between the five profiles. Although the overriding theme is religious stability, it appears that youth continue to make subtle shifts in the arrangements of conduct, content, and centrality tiles in their religious mosaics. Consider Ashley, the Abider we met in chapter 2. As she has gotten older the tiles that reflect religious practices, such as youth group, youth choir, and church attendance, have been shifted around to make room for tiles that reflect ownership of her religiosity, such as the initiative to seek out a new church rather than drop out when her congregation was no longer a comfortable place for her. Though the emphasis on the various dimensions of religion may have changed, the overall pattern of her mosaic is still that of an Abider.

These two themes are illustrated in Table 5.2, using NSYR survey data. Here we see how stability and change within the religious profiles compare to responses to a survey question asking if youth have become

Table 5.2. Religious Profiles and Survey Reported Religious
Change (Percentages)

	U.S.	More religious	Less religious	Stayed the same
Religious profile remains stable, Wave 1 to Wave 2	73	29	11	59
Abiders	19	52	07	41
Adapters	18	34	07	58
Assenters	20	20	16	64
Avoiders	15	10	15	75
Atheists	1	00	14	86
Religious profile changes, Wave 1 to Wave 2	27	18	27	54

Source: National Surveys of Youth and Religion, 2002, 2005.

more religious, less religious, or stayed the same in the previous three years. The table compares those youth who remained in the same religious profile with those who made a transition from one religious profile to another between the first and second surveys. Youth whose religious profile changed between surveys are more likely to report becoming less rather than more religious. Examining change within religious profiles we see that the majority of the youth whose religious profile remained stable report that they have stayed the same religiously. However, 29 percent of these youth identify themselves as more religious three years later, and only 11 percent report becoming less religious. Specifically it is the Abiders and Adapters who are most likely to report becoming more religious. Again we see that youth belonging to a religious profile characterized by relatively high levels of religious centrality are the most likely to report an increase in their overall religiosity. In addition we see significant perceptions of religious increase among those youth whose religious profiles suggest stability. Of all of the youth who were Abiders at both points in time, 52 percent identify themselves as more religious three years later, and 34 percent of stable Adapters do so.[11] Taken together, Abiders and Adapters who report that they have become more religious in the past three years account for nearly 16 percent of all of the youth in our study.[12] Thus, a sizeable proportion of American adolescents claim religion is central to their lives and becomes increasingly so during adolescence.

Summary

We have explored the variety of ways youth talk about religion in their lives, specifically the dimensions they rely on when considering or reporting overall religiosity and change in their lives. Supporting the approach taken in this book to view religiosity as a person-based characteristic that is not easily summarized from low to high at one point in time, or averaged into a unidimensional trajectory over time, youth reveal a wide range of approaches in choosing a touchstone for assessing their overall religiosity. They do tend to rely on some mix of the three Cs (religious content, conduct, and centrality) when describing their religiosity, reinforcing the value in this conceptualization of religiosity. Some have an easier time than others in choosing between the content of religious beliefs, religious conduct, and the centrality of religion in their lives to support their evaluation for how religious they have been over time. Some give us the ups and downs in the various dimensions of religion and express ambivalence about which change marks the basis of overall religious change in their lives.

There is no single definition of overall religiosity among these adolescents, but we do find some interesting patterns. A substantial number of youth use religious practice as a measure of religiosity, yet others specifically reject this emphasis. What is it that leads to these different responses? The answer to this question is no doubt as complex as the youth themselves. It seems, however, that at least one difference between those who report religious practice as a measure of religious change and those who do not is the level of religious commitment in their lives. The youth most likely to cite religious attendance were those for whom religion was not a particularly salient or central feature of their lives at either time point of the study. Most often these responses were from youth who reported that they had become less religious in recent years and pointed to declining religious service attendance to explain their answer. It is not always possible to know whether declining practice leads to reduced salience or reduced salience leads to declining practice. In all likelihood they are inextricably linked. Not surprisingly many youth themselves were unable to untangle these elements. It is also likely that when youth are disengaging from religion on a number of levels, attendance is the easiest or most readily accessible way to discuss their religious decline, particularly for those who do not have a strong connection to religion and may not have language to talk about religious decline in terms of religious beliefs or religious salience.

On the other hand, youth for whom religion was a central part of their identity or played a significant role in their life appeared less likely to rely on changes in attendance patterns to assess changes in their overall religiousness. When religion or a change in one's religiosity is highly salient, the issues of ownership and personalization appear more likely to be the focus of youth reports about their religious lives. In fact among youth for whom religion is highly salient modest declines in religious practice do not seem to alter their own perceptions of themselves as religious individuals. Levels of religious practice seem to be less significant to youth who are engaged in working out the particulars of their religiosity or personalizing their own connection to religion, whether it is in a move toward or away from religion.

Although there are some discernable patterns in the terms that youth themselves use to talk about religious change in their lives, it appears the various components or dimensions of religiosity do not average neatly into a global religiosity. This makes us skeptical about what highly generalized indices of religiosity from survey data really tell us, and cautious about using one particular measure of religiosity as a gauge for overall religiosity, as so many studies do. Instead we posit that youth see distinctly the multiple dimensions of religion and are comfortable packaging them together in various ways, even when their intensity or importance is not always consistent. Using the different colored tiles of religious conduct, religious content, and religious centrality, adolescents choose how to balance the various colors and patterns of their mosaics.

However, we must also note our finding that not all adolescents start the mosaic-building process with the same number or combination of colored tiles. The tiles from which an adolescent can choose to create his religious mosaic are shaped by his family background and other social contexts. In other words, it is not all about adolescent agency or choice. The way they build their own mosaics is influenced by their exposure to different types of religiosity in childhood and adolescence and the examples that are available to them. Their mosaics are also influenced by the social context in which they live. Life events such as a residential move or a school transition can create disruptions in their religious lives, uprooting them from a religious community or providing them with access to a new religious community. Practical constraints such as transportation availability and the demands of school and jobs can also influence the way different youth are able to piece together the tiles of their religious life.

Adolescent religiosity is extremely complex and nearly impossible to summarize in one dimension (i.e., high, moderate, or low). Even adolescents themselves resist averaging across the three main dimensions of religion to describe change. They are quite comfortable talking about various dimensions decreasing while others increase. The evidence presented here further suggests that a useful way to envision and holistically study religiosity in adolescence and its dynamics is through the mosaic analogy and the identification of religious profiles that share commonalities in the patterns of their mosaics.

6

Scaffolding for Religious Refinement in Adolescence

Consider the master chess player competing in a tournament. He or she is unquestionably engaged in an intellectual activity as he or she deliberates over strategies and plans moves. However, the master's intense concentration and deliberate actions are supported by emotions such as heightened arousal, a desire to win, joy in playing, and so forth. The social dimension is apparent in the competition, most obviously in the moves of the opponent. But it is also evident in the nature and conventions of the game itself. Violations of these conventions would disqualify the player. From a historical perspective, the opponents' actions reflect the society and culture in which the game was developed and also that in which the player learned to play.[1]

This description of a master chess player, which the psychologist Mary Gauvain uses as an analogy for the complexity of cognitive development in general, is also a good analogy for the continual process of refining one's religious mosaic. Individual cognitive ability, emotions, and social context all intertwine to shape religious development, or what we prefer to call the refinement process.[2] Youth have the agency and increasing capacity to move the chess pieces, or make moves in regard to the content of their religious beliefs, the conduct of their religious lives, the centrality of their faith, and how the three interlace. However, they are raised in families, peer contexts, and religious institutions that vary in the extent to which the game is even introduced as a worthwhile activity, let alone how it is played and which moves are emphasized over others. As scholars have argued, humans have an innate desire to explain the unexplainable and connect with other human beings in exercises that produce meaning and moral order.[3] These processes are akin to choosing strategies and moves for a chess game. The social contexts in which youth live influence their religious refinement. This helps explain why some youth shift religious profiles over time and what factors lead to refinements occurring within the profiles.

We have shown that adolescents have ever-refining, mosaic-like religious profiles. For the vast majority these multidimensional, subtly dynamic mosaics maintain relatively stable forms with similar color patterns and structures over time. However, slight adjustments do occur and not always consciously. The most common adjustments in adolescence are the waning of religious practice and some increase in the balance of the mosaic devoted to personal spirituality, or a more deeply felt connection to that which is sacred. Adolescence is a time of increasing autonomy across a number of life domains, and for many this autonomy building stretches into the domain of religion as well. Youth who experience this personalization describe their faith as having become stronger or having stayed the same despite declines in other dimensions of their religiosity.

As would many adults, youth struggle to articulate their religious identities to our interviewers, so we do not mean to suggest some sort of *über*-religiosity in adolescence that is going unnoticed.[4] We do, however, want to emphasize that youth are, to varying degrees, processing (or at least attempting to process) their religiosity and spirituality. The social contexts in which they do this plays an important role. Parents and other influential adults, peers, and religious institutions facilitate and at times stymie this process.

Scaffolding in the Lives of Adolescents

In our in-depth analysis of the NSYR in-person, semistructured interviews, we could not help but notice the varying degrees (and often absence) of a phenomenon described by some social scientists as *scaffolding*. The term is most often used in the study of teaching, learning, and tutoring children to describe a process whereby adults help children solve problems by creating a context in which the child can participate at a level just beyond his current capabilities.[5] In the best applications of scaffolding, an adult acts on observations and information about the child's abilities, needs, and interests to create a situation in which the child can concentrate on aspects of the task that are within his grasp. Then the child can learn about the task by participating in it and experience a sense of accomplishment and ownership through the process.[6]

The psychiatrist Ronald E. Dahl extends the discussion of scaffolding to the support adolescents need as their neurobehavioral systems mature: "It is crucial for adolescents to have the appropriate social *scaffolding*—the right balance of monitoring and interest from parents, teachers, coaches and other responsible adults—in which to develop the skills of self-control while still being afforded sufficient support and protection. Ideally this scaffolding should gradually fade, allowing adolescents to make increasingly independent decisions without placing them in situations that they are not yet ready to handle."[7] Within this metaphor of scaffolding children are buildings with relatively weak internal supports. They need social scaffolding as they strengthen their core cognitive abilities and extend upward into young adulthood able to make well-informed, consistent, and sustainable decisions for their mental and physical health and well-being. Part of this process is the unfolding of personal religious identity, whether in a form that embraces religion or disengages from it. Both approaches involve the refinement of a meaning system over time, and this refinement is aided by appropriate social scaffolding. Key sources of social scaffolding for the refinement of religious identity in adolescence are parents, other influential adults, peers, and religious institutions.

In the application of the social scaffolding approach to tutoring children a critical feature is that it is adjusted over the course of a problem-solving interaction to take into account the degree of a child's skills and confidence. The child's actions and expressions of emotion signal the level of support and intervention she needs, and adults should use this information to modify their interaction with the child. This process is called *contingent responding*.[8] Through these contingent responses adults create scaffolding that supports the unique needs of the individual child.[9] We find that youth who are doing best in life as a whole, as well as those who are the happiest with the state of their religious and spiritual lives (no matter which type of religious profile they have), are those who are well scaffolded by at least one parent figure, friends, or members of their religious congregation. This is supported by a long line of sociological research on religion suggesting the vast importance of social ties in the maintenance of religious beliefs.[10]

The Role of Parents in Trajectories of Religious Refinement

Parents and parent figures are by far the most influential people in the religious lives of American adolescents.[11] Our participants make that very clear in their interviews. Parents socialize their children directly and indirectly through modeling religious beliefs and behaviors. These processes have been well established elsewhere, so we extend this line of thought by considering the context in which parent religious socialization is more or less successful.

Two adolescents in our study who were particularly good at articulating their ideas about religion and who have fairly consistent levels of belief, practice, and salience over time are Ashley, who fits the category of Abiders, and Samantha, who fits the Atheist profile.[12] Extensive descriptions of their personal profiles of religiosity are given in chapter 2. What is also strikingly similar about Ashley and Samantha is that neither fits the stereotype of the average "popular" student at school. Ashley has short brown hair with bleached blonde bangs and three piercings in each ear, wears all black clothing, and is dealing with a pretty serious case of depression. Samantha is extremely introverted, spends most of her time reading alone, and only has a couple of friends. Despite their distinctive personalities and what many parents would consider issues to be promptly addressed, their parents seem to "get" them and successfully scaffold them. Ashley's parents are supportive of the friends she has and do not criticize her goth style. Samantha's parents fully supported her when she became impatient with her public school's inability to challenge her academically and keep her engaged. When the school tried to suspend her for absenteeism, her parents helped her rebut the punishment with a lawsuit over teachers' inabilities to keep her challenged with schoolwork. Samantha ended up switching from regular school to homeschooling with an online high school program that she finished at age 16. She then began taking college courses and is now excelling academically.

When it comes to religion Ashley's mother and father (who are married, as are Samantha's parents) seem to both be religious in an Abider fashion. They all attended a large megachurch together until Ashley started having interpersonal problems with another young woman in the church. This other young woman would confront Ashley at youth group, make hurtful accusations in front of others, and talk behind Ashley's back. Ashley had never felt truly comfortable at this church, and this behavior did not help matters. After talking things over with her parents Ashley decided to begin attending another, smaller church with a friend. Her parents saw that she was uncomfortable and supported her decision to go elsewhere. When the interviewer asked whether her parents were bothered that she goes to another church, she said, "They knew that for me it had never been, like, I didn't feel that I belonged there. It was a very, very large church. And I just didn't belong there. I just never connected, and it was just too large. And then this one girl just came to the church who didn't like me. And I was just like, I think I'll find a happier place." Ashley still goes to church with them on occasion. The family still does devotionals together, helps each other memorize Bible verses, and prays together. For them this arrangement works. We gather from our interview with Ashley that her parents have been contingent responders, making decisions and fashioning their support of her based on exactly what she needed to continue the refinement of her religiosity and spirituality.

Samantha's parents also resemble her in religious terms. They are all atheists, so to return to the chess game analogy, she had a set of strategies to follow, and religious engagement was not a strategy modeled in her household. However, if Samantha did begin to question her atheism it seems likely that her parents would be there to support her, as they did when she had problems in school or when she asked to move out on her own. When she was only 16, but taking college courses, she asked if she could get her own apartment. She had a job and wanted her own space. The family home was noisy during the day due to her parents' day care business, and Samantha is not particularly fond of young children. At first her parents explained that they were uncomfortable with her moving out at such a young age, but when she turned 17 they agreed to start discussing it more and looking for apartments. Eventually she moved out, and she is very happy with her current living arrangements. She still goes home to visit at least weekly. This is another example of parents understanding their child's capabilities and what the child might need to build autonomy, maturity, and a sense of self. Very few children could manage to move out on their own at 17 and be responsible for rent, bills, cooking, and everything else, but Samantha could, and it built her confidence. Her parents recognized this and supported her desire.

Diego, the young man described in chapter 2, has the religious profile of an Adapter at the time of both the 2002 and 2005 NSYR surveys; religion is very central to his life, but his institutional participation is rather low. Diego lives with both parents, and comparing his mother and father shows the difference between a properly scaf-folding and an overscaffolding parent. During our second interview with him Diego goes to great lengths to describe what he feels is a wonderful relationship with his mother. They are very close. On the occasions when Diego attends church he goes with his mother and grandfather, who attend a Catholic church almost weekly. Even though he is not particularly fond of this church he views attendance as a family affair.

> *Diego*: I would only go with my parents, or with my mom, you know? She's the only one I would go with and she goes where my grandpa goes. . . . Like, if I could go to another place, I would. I really would.
> *Interviewer*: Is it about transportation or . . . ?
> Diego: No, I would only go with somebody else and definitely some-body in my own family. And, so I go wherever they go.

When it comes to the refinement of his religious beliefs Diego cites his mother and her close relationship to him as vital. Here is what he says about her and how he compares her to his father:

> In the past two years, we've grown closer. I think she understands me a little bit more, and with my mom . . . she's more open. She's like "I can understand this, or I can understand that." You know, but um, I think my dad is a little more traditional, more afraid to question anything like that. My mom's maybe a little more, she's like, she'll hear the ques-tion and she'll think about it and, you know, she'll recognize its incon-sistency or whatever. Sometimes I'll ask my mom a question on religion. I had a European Civilization class focused on different reli-gions, and there was a lot of stuff that I didn't realize, you know, and I was asking my mom, and she was like "Yeah, that's true." And I think that's maybe the one thing that maybe we have like an actual discussion on religion. And where I had some questions about the words in the Bible or, you know, um, the function of the apostles and the different accounts, and how come some of them conflict, you know, and I think that's one question, that's one thing that we did have. But I didn't dis-cuss them with my dad because, you know, he would have tried to call a priest to exorcise me or something.

Diego's mother is taking an interest in where he is cognitively and emotionally, and she supports his questioning. She is honest with him when she agrees that it is difficult to understand apparent inconsis-tencies in the Bible. It seems his father is quick to dismiss his questions and doubts and condemns him for them. This suggests that his father is overscaffolding him, trying to get him to believe exactly what he does and not letting him process various challenges to his beliefs. In this case Diego is more appreciative of the approach his mother takes. He values her opinion, and to this point it has helped him strengthen his beliefs and maintain his Adapter approach to religiosity.

Michael, on the other hand, was an Adapter in 2002 and by 2005 was classified as an Assenter. As we learned in chapter 4, Michael's religiosity was in flux by the time of the second interview, and it seemed as if he was leaning toward atheism. His parents were still married, and both seemed to be religious in an Assenter fashion: occasional practice and relatively little salience for the rest of life. Based on Michael's description, they were unable to provide the scaffolding he needed to process the doubts he was having. Michael, much like Samantha, is a very intellectual adolescent. He senses how he differs from others and knows that not all adults are comfortable debating grand ideas with him. From what he says, it seems his mother has trouble understanding him and his intellectual struggles. He described a recent incident with her over religious beliefs:

> I tried to talk to my mom about religious beliefs once, but she started crying. She gets really emotional about stuff. I told her I thought the Bible was more like . . . not literal but figurative in the way it was written, and my mom got real upset. And I was like, okay no more of that with Mom. I could with my dad, but you know, I'm not really going to get anywhere with him.

Michael would like to be able to talk to his mom and dad about his beliefs and the way he understands the Bible, but he senses that neither of them would appreciate the discussion or support his exploration. It sounds as if they would both become exasperated and expect him to just accept what he has been taught. This is overscaffolding, or putting up extensive and strong supports far above the place at which an adolescent is in the process of religious refinement. Such extensive or overreaching supports feel confining to an adolescent who is trying to think through what it is he wants his religiosity to be. Michael feels his parents are not providing space for him to grapple with and talk through his doubts and thoughts with them.

Unfortunately we see in the interviews that when parents overscaffold it tends to backfire. Parents think they are setting an example and boundaries that will lead to a religious identity like their own. However, by preventing their child from processing what he believes parents may send him the message that religion is inflexible or simplistic and critical thinking is not tolerated. To be sure, we do not have the parents' side of the story in our data, and our participants may be misperceiving the situation. We recognize that most parents make every effort to provide the proper level of scaffolding and support autonomous religious or spiritual development. Our intention is not to blame parents in cases where they are disappointed with the results of their religious socialization efforts. Rather, we are suggesting that the scaffolding process is likely to be most effective when parents' supportive efforts are in tune with and well matched to their child's current abilities, understandings, and desires in the realms of religiosity and spirituality.

Underscaffolding is detrimental to the adolescent process of refining religiosity as well. A good example of this is Kayla's situation. Kayla is the young woman we introduced in chapter 4 who has lived since infancy with an older foster mother who is much like an Abider herself. Kayla was also an Abider at the time of our first survey. She attended church often, believed in a personal God, had exclusivist views, and found religion to be very central to life. A few years later a lot had changed in her life, including a growing skepticism of organized religion and doubts about the relevance of her faith. At that point she resembled an Assenter. There were growing signs that Kayla's foster mother was not providing adequate scaffolding in many areas of Kayla's life. She had begun to let other youth from the neighborhood live with them; some of them were stealing money and using drugs, and she did not enforce any consequences for them. Kayla was spending more time with friends who were into drugs and crime. She was getting into trouble at school and had been sent to an alternative high school. She talked a lot about how she felt no one understood her and had an especially hard time getting along with other young women. She had dated a string of boyfriends from her neighborhood who were all seven to ten years older than she. She first met her most recent boyfriend at the bus stop. She was in love with him, but he had lately become very jealous. Her mother had let him move into the house (in his own room) when he became homeless. At one point he angrily broke Kayla's cell phone because he suspected other men were calling her, but then cheated on her himself. Kayla's mother refused her request to kick him out of the house, so Kayla moved into a friend's house. Unlike Ashley's parents, who listened and helped her work through her struggle to feel comfortable at church, Kayla's mother paid little attention to the fact that Kayla was struggling with the phoniness she perceived in others at church.

Interviewer: Do you have any doubts? Have you had doubts about your religion in the past two years?
Kayla: Yes.
Interviewer: What have those doubts been?
Kayla: Is he really real? Is Jesus really real? If he is, why are certain things happening? A lot of stuff.

Interestingly the interviewer remarks in her field notes, "She was pretty open and honest with her answers. Unfortunately I don't think she has the tools at this time to best leverage the 'good head on her shoulders.'" The interviewer can sense that this is a bright and strong young woman who is not surrounded by adults who can give her the necessary tools, or provide the appropriate scaffolding, to come to well-reasoned and informed conclusions about life and the role of religion in it for her. On the other hand, maybe even with a parent providing more contingent responding, or recognizing what kind of support would be best tailored to her needs, Kayla would continue to view the congregants at her church as phony and feel as if Jesus is not real. We cannot say for certain how Kayla would process the struggles she is having with her faith, but it does seem as if she is being let down to some degree by the adults in her life and that this may have an impact on the type of religiosity she lives.

Kayla's case may seem particularly extreme to many readers of this book, but a surprising number of youth in our nationally representative sample face equally difficult challenges in their lives. Often parents and guardians are overwhelmed with personal and community problems (e.g., drugs, violence, interpersonal conflict, or economic despair) that drain the mental, social, and economic resources parents need to provide adequate social scaffolding for their offspring. Although it is important for parents to be self-reflective about the extent to which they scaffold their children in matters of religion and spirituality, it is also essential that youth-serving programs, religious or not, consider how to best support and train parents or provide additional scaffolding to benefit youth.

Contingent responses involve expending effort to understand the current capabilities and emotions of adolescents and gearing one's support toward bolstering adolescent efforts to develop well-founded autonomy. As these examples of parental scaffolding show, when adults provide these contingent responses adolescents do work to some degree at refining their own religious faith. Often this leads to a personalization of the faith in which one was raised, and occasionally it results in adolescents expressing that they feel more religious because they have processed what it is they believe and how they see religious conduct and centrality fitting into their lives. Sometimes the personalization of religion means that it becomes less essential, practice decreases, and its centrality declines. We are not making a judgment here about which degree or direction of religious refinement is preferable. We are showing that refinements that involve tailored support or scaffolding from parents seem to result in adolescents feeling that they have made well-reasoned choices in the design of their own religious mosaics. These youth express far less regret, sadness, or hesitation over any changes that they have made to their mosaics of religiosity.

A greater understanding of the importance of parental scaffolding and contingent responses emerged from our in-person interviews. We also have evidence from the survey data to suggest that parental characteristics are related to religious change in youth. Youth were asked in the first survey to report on how much they feel understood by their parents and how much freedom their parents give them to develop and openly express their own views on important issues. Feeling understood by parents and being given the right amount of freedom to express their thoughts are indicators of parents who are in tune with and providing adequate scaffolding for their adolescent children. The majority of youth remained in the same religious profile over the three years of our study. However, as we saw in chapter 5, many can and do identify various ways in which their religious lives are undergoing change and refinement. In the second survey we asked our participants to provide us with an overall assessment of this process, reporting whether they had become more religious, less religious, or stayed about the same since the first interview. In table 6.1 we divide youth into the five religious profiles and examine the extent to which their reports about their parents are related to their assessments of religious change in their own lives.

The results in table 6.1 demonstrate the importance of youth feeling understood by their parents during the religious refinement process. The magnitude of this relationship varies across the religious profiles. The first row of numbers for each religious profile represents the percentage of youth within that profile who reported being more, less, or the same religiously. We can compare the distribution of types of religious change (more, less, the same) for each profile to the distribution of types of religious change within each response category for the question about feeling understood by parents. Abiders and Adapters who at

Table 6.1 Parental Scaffolding at Wave 1 and Survey Reported Religious Change at Wave 2 (Percentages)

	Became more religious	Became less religious	Stayed about the same
Abiders	46	12	42
How much do parents understand you?			
A lot	48	9	43
Some, a little, or none	44	15	41
How much freedom do you have to express your own views?			
Too little	42	16	41
Right amount	47	10	43
Too much	25	56	20
Adapters	29	14	57
How much do parents understand you?			
A lot	30	8	61
Some, a little, or none	28	18	53
How much freedom do you have to express your own views?			
Too little	33	14	53
Right amount	29	13	58
Too much	30	18	52
Assenters	20	20	60
How much do parents understand you?			
A lot	18	19	63
Some, a little, or none	21	21	59
How much freedom do you have to express your own views?			
Too little	13	22	64
Right amount	21	20	59
Too much	20	18	62

continued

Table 6.1 (*continued*)

	Became more religious	Became less religious	Stayed about the same
Avoiders	12	16	72
How much do parents understand you?			
A lot	10	18	72
Some, a little, or none	12	16	72
How much freedom do you have to express your own views?			
Too little	11	15	73
Right amount	12	15	73
Too much	12	34	54
Atheists	4	16	80
How much do parents understand you?			
A lot	9	11	81
Some, a little, or none	3	17	80
How much freedom do you have to express your own views?			
Too little	10	28	63
Right amount	3	11	86
Too much	7	43	50

Source: National Surveys of Youth and Religion, 2002, 2005.
Note: Percentages may not add to 100 due to rounding.

the time of the first survey report that their parents understand them a lot are less likely than other youth in these profiles to say they have become less religious over time. For example, 14 percent of all Adapters report becoming less religious. Among Adapters who feel understood by their parents, however, only 8 percent report declining religiosity. For Abiders and Adapters there appears to be a relationship between being understood by parents and maintaining or intensifying their religiosity. Among Avoiders, however, feeling understood by parents is associated with a slightly higher percentage of youth becoming less religious over time. When analyzing this pattern it is helpful to remember that contingent responses by parents can facilitate refinement and ownership of religious identity. We found that Avoiders often maintain some level of obligatory connection to religion in spite of being almost totally disengaged from or disinterested in religion. In these cases, having understanding parents might be one factor that contributes to these youth feeling comfortable moving further away from religion in their own lives.

The second question we examine is how youth perceive the freedom they are given to develop and express their views on important issues. The large majority of youth report that they are given the right amount of freedom. However, reports about having too little or too much freedom might be indicative of over- or under-scaffolding on the part of parents. Examining these results in relation to self-reported religious change, we see differences among those youth who report the underscaffolding response of having too much freedom to express their own views. For example, 12 percent of all Abiders report that they have become less religious. However, of the Abiders who thought their parents gave them too much freedom in 2002, 56 percent report becoming less religious by 2005. With the exception of Assenters, we find a similar pattern among the other religious profiles as well. Among Assenters we see that it is overscaffolding, or having too little freedom of expression, that is associated with a slightly higher number of youth becoming less religious. It appears that parents who leave youth to grapple with important issues on their own or who constrain the opportunities for discussing these issues may make it more difficult for them to connect to and identify with the religious traditions in which they were raised.

The relationships we see in these survey data between parenting and youth religious change are more subtle than dramatic. However, they are statistically significant in a consistent direction, and they lend support to the patterns we saw in our in-person interviews. In the process of trying to understand religion and its role in their lives youth rely on the examples set for them by their parents as well as the extent to which their parents support them through this process. Like Michael, youth whose parents try to enforce a particular belief structure without allowing them to wrestle with religious doubts might be more likely to drift further away from religion in the process. And youth whose parents exhibit a more hands-off approach, like Kayla's foster mother, also have difficulty in their process of religious refinement, finding little support when their questions about faith bump up against the challenges of adolescence.

The Importance of Friends

Parents and other adults play a significant role in the religious lives of youth and continue to be the strongest predictor of youth religiosity in middle to late adolescence.[13] However, the role of peers is not insignificant and must also be considered as a source of scaffolding in the lives of adolescents.[14] For the most part adolescents in the NSYR do not know much about the religious lives of their friends and claim to rarely talk about religious or spiritual topics with them.[15] However, some youth do have friends with whom they talk about religion and share common religious views. Friends who understand each other's perspectives, allow opportunities to talk about things important to them, and encourage thinking about religion can provide another source of scaffolding for youth.

During the semistructured interviews we asked youth to identify people who had influenced their faith in recent years. Ashley's immediate answer to this question was, "Just some of my friends. Yeah, I mean, nothing like horribly dramatic. Just like reaffirming things." Her response suggests that there is something significant about having friends who share her religious views and commitments. In her own words, this support is not "dramatic," but rather steady affirmation of her religious identity. Many of her friends come from the youth group at the smaller church she moved to after having problems at the large church her parents attend. Ashley is very clear that her friends' religious experiences impact her as well. Here is how she describes one such experience.

> *Ashley*: I have a friend who just came back from a really destructive path. And that was really, really exciting, and so I definitely see that as a God thing, 'cause I mean, I really, I had really no hope that she would turn things around. So I mean that.
> *Interviewer*: Did that have an influence on your own faith?
> *Ashley*: Yes, I mean not a ton, but it was just . . . it was really just nice. It was a miracle, so sure, in that way it was kind of a booster to my faith.

Jared, an Assenter at both surveys, credited his girlfriend with his recently renewed interest in his faith at the time of the second interview. She and her mother talked with him regularly about religion, and their dating relationship seems to have motivated him to attend services more regularly and take his faith more seriously. This encouragement provided critical scaffolding for Jared, prompting his desire to maintain a connection to religion. After describing her family as regular churchgoers he says, "[I'm] starting to believe more because of what my girl embodies, it just makes me want to go more because I know that I don't want to lose her over something like that."

In addition to his girlfriend Jared is aware of the influence that religion has on his other friends. At the time of the second interview he had recently been cleaning up his life and trying to disengage from some destructive behaviors. Of his friends he says, "We like brothers. We always look out for one another . . . they always, they support me, like when I stopped doing a lot of stuff that I was doing, they wasn't throwing it in my face. They supported me for it." Jared valued the support of his friends in his efforts to clean up his behaviors. At the same time, however, he recognized that this particular group of friends is not ready to adjust their behavior like he is, and he attributes at least some of this to religion: "I notice that my religious friends, they're more positive people you know, they doing school and they not into, involved in a lot of other stuff . . . as opposed to my friends who's not so religious. . . . They having rough sex and . . . not using condoms, they using drugs, you know, they drinking." While he professed loyalty to his less religious "brothers" and appreciated their support of him, he also expressed some desire to spend more time around his religious friends, who might be better able to help him stay out of trouble. The scaffolding provided by Jared's old friends certainly could have been more problematic for him if they had not been supportive of his decision to stop partying. But it is also likely that continued association with this group could present a challenge to his desire to maintain the recent changes in his life.

For Ashley, Jared, and others, peers can be an important source of scaffolding that affirms their identity and supports their efforts to maintain their religious profiles. In contrast Kayla's situation provides an example of the way a lack of support from peers can make more difficult the process of refining religious identity, especially because she is not getting optimal social scaffolding from her parent figure either. She expresses frustration with not being able to relate to other girls her age because of all the "drama." Getting into physical altercations with other youth has caused her to be suspended from school. Missing so much school resulted in being held back twice, and eventually Kayla was transferred to an alternative high school. She describes herself as having very different views on religion than most youth: "A lot of people my age don't really think about religion." She assumes that if she were to bring up religion other youth would make fun of her, but she admits to never really trying.

Unlike Jared, Kayla feels that very few of her friends have her back and support her endeavors, especially when they are different from their own. Unlike Ashley, Kayla does not seem to have friends willing to share what they are thinking about religion. Kayla's foster mother does not appear to be providing good scaffolding, and Kayla does not appear to have access to good peer scaffolding either. This means any religious refinement that she could potentially achieve is not well supported.

In terms of peer networks, youth's ability to refine their religiosity benefits from the support of peers who understand them, accept them for who they are, encourage them, and communicate openly. Using the measures of peer characteristics available in the NSYR survey data, we examined how the number of close friends a youth has and whether he talks to his friends about religion related to his reports of religious change over time, but we found no statistically significant results. It may be that the influence of friends is so minor that we do not observe it in the survey data. It is also possible that more specific measures of the social scaffolding friends provide, such as the degree to which youth feel understood by their friends and free to express their deepest thoughts without ridicule, would allow for more rigorous tests of these relationships. Future studies should continue to explore these friendship dynamics and their relationship to how youth refine religious faith during adolescence.

How Religious Institutions Matter

Religious institutions provide another potential source of social scaffolding. For adolescents who grow up with some connection to a church, synagogue, or temple, the leaders, congregants, and programs available through religious institutions also provide scaffolding that props up particular systems of meaning and ways of religious practice that inform adolescents as they adjust their religious mosaics. In the analysis of the interviews we find certain characteristics of religious institutions that seem to facilitate the refinement of religiosity in adolescence as well as issues within religious institutions that frustrate and turn off adolescents. Religious institutions that adolescents speak positively about are made up of adults and youth who are honest and loving and genuinely work to interact with others in a way that reflects their beliefs and priorities. Adolescents are especially willing to stay involved at religious institutions when they feel that the people there understand them. Scaffolding in these cases works in much the same way as it does in the cases of parents and friends. When an adolescent feels the contingent responding and senses that others in her life are working to understand exactly who she is and what she needs, she seems to thrive. This same dynamic applies to youth experiences in religious organizations. Youth are drawn to congregations where they feel genuinely valued, loved, and cared for and where the relevant concerns of their lives are taken seriously.

Most of the youth we heard from in the survey and interviews have favorable opinions of their religious congregations and seem to be well supported by their religious communities. However, there is a minority of youth for whom characteristics of their religious congregations present barriers to their religious engagement and involvement. Their stories are illustrative of the potential for over- or underscaffolding by religious congregations. Adolescents are keenly aware of the motives of those around them, and when they perceive a lack of care for them or honesty about their issues they are dismissive of those involved. Similarly when youth sense that a program or activity is not developed with an eye toward their needs or the general needs of the group they are turned off. They criticize teaching that is overly simplistic or presented as black and white with no freedom to explore complexities.

Diego has problems with some of the content of programs in the youth group of his church. He used to attend youth group and was tapped to be a leader for other youth, but he has since stopped attending.

> I didn't really want to be there anymore. There were some things that I didn't agree with, and I just, I remember one time they showed this video, and there was this like evangelical lady, and she was telling everybody that abortion is wrong—that anybody who does it is wrong. They're being touched by the devil, and I don't know. And it was like these horror stories and they were showing videos of mangled fetuses coming out and I was like . . . I thought "This is some twisted stuff." Most of the people in youth group were already this close [he holds a thumb and forefinger close together] to dropping out of high school. And I, you know, I hate to be judgmental, but I'd say a lot of them are on their way to being teen moms and dads, you know, it was going to be a waste for them. And it's sad to say, but you know, they're in that kind of environment where nobody cares about them. They're doing whatever they want, smoking, drinking. And so, I thought, "These

people are your future teen moms and teen dads and stuff. You got to stop this. And, and maybe abortion isn't the perfect thing, but I don't think you should put this guilt trip on them and force it down their throat, and show them this one-sided, twisted view of things, you know?" Yeah, it's a big decision but, you know. And I think that's the one thing that made me step back. I don't want to be part of something that's, you know, sending out this message of "This is what you have to follow, and if you don't follow it, you're going to go to hell." 'Cause that's what that lady was saying. You know, I couldn't believe it. And I think that's what threw me off.

Diego could sense that the adolescents in his youth group had so many more immediate concerns in their lives, many of which, if addressed, could prevent the pregnancies that lead to a decision about abortion. He felt that they were pitching the wrong message for that time and place and was frustrated by the tone of the presentation and the threats about going to hell. This reflects his feeling that the message was not being conveyed with more love and concern for the youth and a desire to help them understand the reasons behind the anti-abortion message. This is an example of overscaffolding on the part of the church: trying to transfer a set of beliefs without engaging the struggles these youth were dealing with. In other words, the leaders of the youth group did not seem to be in tune with what a contingent response for Diego and others might be.

Michael, the young man who made a transition from being an Adapter to being an Assenter, feels similarly about the youth group at his Catholic church. He calls it "trite" and says that the discussions are "outdated" and involve "stuff that just doesn't apply to life." He says it "irritates" him, so he stopped going: "Who needs more irritation in life?" In addition Michael cites the other youth in the group as a reason for why he no longer attends: "Um, they just, like, I don't know how to put this, the kids who do this are kind of like lemmings, they just follow, I don't do that. . . . It doesn't make sense to me." He is also frustrated with how another religious institution, his Catholic school, "crams things down people's throats." Michael argues that the strictness and the way that students are told what to believe creates more religious doubts in him and his Catholic school peers than those who attend public school. Adolescents want to believe that the issues they face are appreciated and that adults are interested in helping them deal honestly with their questions about the role of religion in their lives. They do not want to feel threatened or misunderstood.

Youth also value honesty and sincerity in their religious congregations and are turned off by what they perceive as pretense and hypocrisy. Kayla, who was a regular church attendee in 2002, connects her drop-off in attendance by 2005 to her disdain for the "phony people" at her church. Here is how she describes their impact on her.

> I love, like, the message at church, the message that the preacher sends. I love the message, you know, I love, I love being in that place, that I feel like no harm can come to me, but it's so many phony people that go to church these days. And it . . . it just makes me look at people like, with no respect, and when I go to church, I look at certain people like, "You're so phony," you know, and it makes me have ill spirit, and I don't feel like I need to bring that to church.

Christina is a rarely attending young woman whom we described in chapter 4 as typifying the transition from being an Avoider to identifying as an Atheist. She has attended church with a friend, but has no desire to go back:

> After going to church with my friend and her mother once, I was actually like, whoa, I'm glad I don't do this every weekend. But she goes every weekend. But it doesn't make any sense to me, like, she's like, she sins all the time and then you go to church? And her mother goes to church, but her mother is the mother that is like the most unhelpful person on earth, as far as her kids go. She's at church every week and, like, you should be with your daughter, looking at colleges, or something.

Christina senses inconsistencies between the behavior of her friend and her friend's mother at church and outside of church, so it does not appeal to her. She is particularly disturbed by her friend's association with an organization that is incongruent with her other actions. This is similar to what Kayla perceives as phoniness in fellow congregants. Drawing on survey data we know that not all youth are concerned about hypocrisy in their congregations. Nearly 73 percent of youth affiliated with a congregation say that few or none of the adults there are hypocrites. However, the remaining youth (27 percent) report that at least some of the adults in their congregations are hypocrites.

The accuracy of youth's perceptions of churchgoers could be debated, and it is possible that this argument about hypocrites is a particularly easy narrative for youth to latch onto in rationalizing why they are not frequent attendees. But many of the youth who show declines in religious activity express these types of perceptions.

In research on other areas of social life, scholars have found that it is perceptions of one's social interactions and not some objective measure of the quality of the interactions that influence individuals. For example, it is the perception of fairness in the division of household labor, not an objective assessment in the hours each spouse contributes, that is most related to high reports of marital quality.[16] As long as spouses are satisfied with how household tasks are distributed, it does not matter what an outsider may observe in terms of the fairness of the arrangement. In a similar way it is not necessarily an objective measure of how phony or hypocritical a congregation is, but the perception that youth have that influences their desire to be religiously involved. Religious institutions might engage these youth by encouraging adult members to hold public conversations with them about what it means to be religious and involved in a religious institution and how that should be carried through in other aspects of life.

Various other issues can present barriers for youth involvement in religious congregations. Diego complains that his mother's church is a "huggy, touchy, feely church," and he is "not really all that into it." Here is an example of congregants who seem to be trying to express a certain type of support to Diego, but it is not in a style to which he is very receptive. That does not mean the church is doing anything wrong. Maybe Diego would feel more comfortable at another type of church, and maybe the "huggy, touchy, feely" style is what other youth in that parish need. The type of emotion and support shown within a religious institution is something leaders could consider in terms of whether it is meeting the needs of members. It is also something that families might consider when looking for a religious congregation that fits the needs of all family members, including adolescent children. In addition to feeling uncomfortable about the display of emotion and affection in church, Diego also struggles to understand the Salvadoran priest who performs the Mass in Spanish. Diego says, "My Spanish isn't perfect, but the priest has a weird accent. I don't get anything. So I guess I just go and I try to pick up as much as I can, but usually it's just fragments. They also have a horrible audio system." Of course these examples are unique to Diego and don't necessarily indicate a need for change on the part of the religious congregation. But they do serve to highlight the fact that congregations that do not accurately assess the needs of their youth might reduce the effectiveness of any scaffolding these congregations may be trying to offer.

These examples highlight cases in which youth are turned off by religious institutions and feel unsupported in their efforts to personalize their faith and refine their religious beliefs and identity. Overall, however, youth who are involved in religious institutions have favorable opinions of them. The NSYR survey data show that in both 2002 and 2005 between 70 and 80 percent of adolescents who attend religious services find their religious congregations to be warm and welcoming and report that they usually inspire them to think. For many youth religious congregations serve as important sources of social scaffolding and lend stability to their efforts at religious refinement. Their stories highlight the benefits to youth of congregations who are able to offer contingent responding within their communities.

One way that congregations offer contingent responding is by helping youth to act out their religious commitments in ways that are salient and meaningful to them. For example, Diego speaks highly of the priest at his family's church and likes the fact that the priest "really calls people to action." Here is one incident he describes to reflect this:

> One week the priest had asked everybody to bring a blanket, 'cause it was right around Christmas time, and they were going to be handing them out to the poor people that live nearby. And they asked everybody to bring an old blanket, a new blanket, whatever you have, you know. And I remember the next week, only one person brought a blanket. And I remember the priest was so insulted. He was like, where are the others? And he was really like laying it on thick, you know? And I think that was something that I really liked. He really put the guilt trip on them and really forced them, not maybe to preach their beliefs or, you know, to take something and swap it, but really to just make an act, you know, give something, you know? But, uh, that's probably the one thing that I like about the church.

Diego is not alone in getting excited about a religious leader who calls people to action and promotes volunteer work or social action. Several other youth expressed a passion for volunteer and service opportunities within their church, such as mission trips to Mexico and working at homeless shelters. These are examples of religious institutions succeeding at "igniting passions" in youth, as Dahl described it. Because of the brain development process under way during puberty youth have a natural inclination toward novelty, arousal, and excitement. Society generally laments the social problems that can result, but the "emotional tinderbox" of adolescence also creates a great opportunity for harnessing these emotions in the service of positive goals.[17] To the extent religious institutions can do this, they will attract adolescent involvement.[18] A detailed description of ways to achieve the engagement of adolescents can be found in Lytch's book *Choosing Church: What Makes a Difference for Teens.*

Congregations also provide social scaffolding through the relationships that are fostered with and among youth. Ashley, the young woman who is an Abider and whose parents supported her in switching churches, feels very comfortable at the church she now attends with friends.

> Over time, I have become more comfortable with the people and the atmosphere at my new church. Just because, for me, being at a small church is more reassuring. Somehow, at the old church, I ended up with friends who are the kind of people who wanted drama, and I don't like that. And there was no way to stop that. So for me it's a lot more comfortable being at a church where people aren't concerned about that, and I don't have to deal with that.

When asked to describe what it is she likes about her youth group, she said:

> Well, it's just, it's really nice to be with people who, you just kind of build each other up, 'cause you can ask questions, you can discuss things, and people come from the same basic background. So it's just, it's a really good time to kind of explore what you believe and get taught more. I enjoy just kind of the attitude, I don't know. Groups, especially groups of kids, have a definite feel to them, and I just, I enjoy how this one is more laid back and less socially elitist. It's just there isn't nearly as much of a clique thing going on.

She explicitly mentions her appreciation of the freedom to ask questions and openly discuss issues. Feeling that people in this group build her up is a very different experience from the struggles that other youth have described.

Although he does not attend as much as he (or his mother) would like, Jared, the young man described as typifying the Assenter category, attends church a little more often at the time of his second in-person interview. Part of the reason for this is how much he enjoys being around the people at church and the support and acceptance he receives there.

> I feel like church is a good place to be, like, even if it is true that there isn't a God and all that stuff, it's like the people there who do believe are such good people that, why wouldn't you want to be around them?

And they always looking to help out. Everybody there love me. They're supportive, like, they like to hear me talk about going away to Costa Rica [for a study abroad program] or starting school. They're supportive of all that. They like to hear me doing positive things.

Much like Ashley, Jared seems to respond well to a small and intimate church body: "I like the size, like, it's not a big church. It's pretty small, it's like a storefront church but because there's so few people there, the people there really want to be [there] and, like, you get to know everybody on a personal level and I think that's a good thing, like everybody's, like, it's like a little community of our own when we come there." Jared seems especially drawn to his pastor: "It's like we're friends, you know. It's not like, 'Oh that's Pastor so and so, let me not say anything, let me watch my mouth,' but it's cool. My pastor made a donation to my trip to Costa Rica, just because I am part of the church—nothing more, nothing less."

In Ashley's and Jared's descriptions of their churches it is clear that they feel engaged, loved, and accepted. This seems to put them at ease and increases the possibility that they will feel comfortable exploring their beliefs and personal faith. In much the same way as with parents and friends, religious institutions can scaffold adolescents by engaging and understanding them, giving them the freedom to refine their systems of meaning in a supportive environment. Results from the NSYR survey data support these conclusions. Youth who were affiliated with a religious congregation at the time of the first survey were asked a series of questions about their congregation. Two questions offer insight into the extent to which youth feel engaged by their religious communities: "Is your church boring to you, usually, sometimes, rarely or never?" and "Are there any adults in your congregation, other than family members, who you enjoy talking with or who give you lots of encouragement?"[19] In table 6.2 we explore how youth responses to these questions in 2002 are related to youth reports of religious change in 2005.

Youth were fairly evenly distributed in their opinions about church being boring. About 24 percent of youth affiliated with a congregation reported that it is never boring to them. The congregations of these adolescents appear to be engaging them in relevant ways and keeping their interest. For other youth, like Michael, this is not the case. About Mass at his Catholic church he says, "After eighteen years of it, you've heard it all before. There's nothing new after eighteen years. It's like, okay, I've heard this before." Table 6.2 shows the youth from each religious profile who in 2002 say church is never boring

Table 6.2 Evaluation of Religious Congregations at Wave 1 and Survey Reported Religious Change at Wave 2 (Percentages)

	Became more religious	Became less religious	Stayed about the same
Abiders	46	12	42
Is your Church boring to you?			
Never	53	7	40
Usually, sometimes, or rarely	43	14	43
Are there adults who talk with or encourage you?			
Yes	46	12	42
No	40	17	43
Adapters	28	15	57
Is your Church boring to you?			
Never	30	10	59
Usually, sometimes, or rarely	26	18	56
Are there adults who talk with or encourage you?			
Yes	26	16	59
No	37	14	49
Assenters	18	23	59
Is your Church boring to you?			
Never	18	21	61
Usually, sometimes, or rarely	18	23	59
Are there adults who talk with or encourage you?			
Yes	20	21	59
No	12	29	59
Avoiders	9	30	61
Is your Church boring to you?			
Never	33	20	47
Usually, sometimes, or rarely	6	32	62
Are there adults who talk with or encourage you?			
Yes	10	29	61
No	6	32	62

Source: National Surveys of Youth and Religion, 2002, 2005.
Note: Percentages may not add to 100 due to rounding.

compared to those have experienced being bored at church. In 2005 youth for whom church was never boring are more likely to report that they have become more religious and less likely to report that they have become less religious during the intervening period. Assenters are the exception to this pattern; there is no difference in the percentage of Assenters who become more religious. However, a smaller than average percentage of those who are never bored report becoming less religious three years later.

Boredom at church captures something about the extent to which congregations are engaging youth with the content of their programs and services. The second question taps into the interpersonal connections that youth might have with the adults in their congregations. Abiders, Assenters, and Avoiders who do not have supportive adults in their congregations are less likely to become more religious than those who do have supportive adults in their churches. They are also more likely to become less religious over time. Having engaging adults in their congregation does not appear to increase Adapters' likelihood of becoming more religious.[20]

Most of the youth in our study spoke positively about their congregations and seem to be satisfied with their experiences there. These positive experiences provide yet another layer of support as they move through adolescence. Far less common are youth who are affiliated with but not engaged by congregations. These youth appear to be more likely to drift away from religion as they move through adolescence. We are not suggesting that a lack of congregational scaffolding is the only or even the primary reason for a movement away from religion. However, in the process of religious refinement, congregations are one more potential source of scaffolding for adolescents, and every layer of scaffolding contributes to the complex support system surrounding adolescents. Some youth have sufficient scaffolding from parents, family, and friends such that the absence of congregational scaffolding may not have a significant impact on their lives. There may be other youth, however, for whom the absence of a supportive religious community compounds the effects of an already weak support system in their lives.

Summary

Throughout this chapter we have explored the importance of social scaffolding for youth as they move through adolescence and engage in a certain degree of religious refinement and personalization.

Adolescence is a time of dramatic change and development across a variety of domains. For youth today this is compounded by the complexity of a society in which youth are exposed to a dizzying array of competing opinions, values, options, and opportunities. They are at a point in the life course where they are gaining autonomy and preparing to emerge into the arena of adulthood, but still are not fully prepared to manage it alone. It is in this context that many youth are also trying to sort out this thing called religion and are faced with questions about its importance in their own life.

Parents are the most important source of social scaffolding for most youth during this complex period of their lives. Our interview respondents have shown us some of the problems that arise when parents are not able to engage in contingent responding and instead over- or underscaffold their children. A restrictive approach that does not allow youth to be honest about their questions and doubts can make it difficult for them to sort out the many competing messages they receive in our culture and to develop informed thinking about these issues. For some, like Michael, the result is to regretfully (or not so regretfully) wave the white flag and back away from a religion that they cannot reconcile with the rest of their lives. The hands-off approach of underscaffolding also makes it difficult for youth to navigate the complicated waters of adolescence and emerging adulthood. Without guidance from caring and understanding adults they may be left rudderless and more likely to be pulled in the direction of the currents that surround them.

Adolescents can and do thrive, however, when surrounded by social scaffolding that offers both space to grow into their newly acquired autonomy and guidance to help them figure out what to do with it. When this type of scaffolding is present in the course of religious refinement it often results in youth who go through a process of personalizing the faith in which they were raised. In our survey analysis we see this in the stability of religious profiles over time. It appears that the majority of youth have social scaffolds that facilitate religious stability with respect to their religious profiles. We also see evidence of stability in youth self-reports of overall religious change. In addition to the majority who report staying the same religiously, a significant percentage of youth report becoming more religious in spite of overall declines in our survey measures of religious content, conduct, and centrality. It is apparent through the in-person interviews that at least some of what is happening among these youth is a process through which religion becomes more salient to them as they come to better understand and take ownership of their faith. At the same time some youth with the proper social scaffolding ultimately decide that religion is not for them. They develop a nonreligious system of meaning that is salient to them. The process of religious refinement in a supportive context can lead to religious change in a variety of forms and directions. Whatever the result, the process seems better informed and more positive for an adolescent's overall well-being when parents provide contingent responding and appropriate levels of scaffolding.

In addition to parents, peers and congregations have the potential to strengthen the overall social scaffolding during adolescent religious refinement. Effective social scaffolding reflects a complex interweaving of different sources of support in the lives of youth. The extent to which parents, peers, and congregations contribute to this structure and the effectiveness of each type of support varies for different youth.

For some youth, like Ashley, peers provide an important source of scaffolding as they refine their religiosity during adolescence. For many youth, however, peers are not clearly related to this process. In fact most youth don't make connections between their peers and their religious lives. They are relatively unaware of the religious lives of their friends and don't often discuss religion with them. Their ability to compartmentalize religion from other areas of their lives extends to their friendships as well.[21] From the perspective of most of the youth we talk with there are many functions of friendship, but support for religious development and exploration is not one of them. Regardless of youth's awareness of the impact of their peers, friendships do have the potential to shape their religious lives. As youth work out their religious identities during adolescence, some draw tremendous encouragement from their friends and peer networks. For others friends may knowingly or unknowingly discourage them from engaging in a serious consideration of religious issues and questions. So although peers are not a primary source of scaffolding they do have the potential to facilitate or detract from the religious development of youth. This is a point on which parents, religious institutions, and youth programs in general should reflect. Encouraging and guiding the development of peer-to-peer religious discussions during adolescence is likely to bolster the social scaffolding available to youth.

For those youth who consider themselves to be affiliated with a religious congregation, their experiences within these religious communities can be formative in their process of religious refinement. Youth recognize the support of adults in these institutions, thrive on personal relationships with adults and peers in youth groups that express acceptance and encouragement, are energized by opportunities for social service, and appreciate personal and intellectual challenges from their religious institutions. They criticize hypocrisy, oversimplification of theology, and a condescending tone. As the metaphor of social scaffolding implies, they desire religious institutions that are good at assessing the needs of a variety of youth and providing programs and services that give them tools that help them push forward in the process of refining their faith.

Stepping back to think of the adolescent population as a whole, what we have shown in this book is that their religious profiles, mosaics, or identities are relatively stable and are highly reflective of the religious tradition in which they were raised. The generally subtle changes that do occur tend to be in the form of youth personalizing their beliefs and practices as well as determining how salient religion is to the rest of their lives. This process of religious refinement is more active at some points of adolescence than others and is often subconscious and not well articulated. We do not mean to assert that there is a wave of obvious spiritual renewal sweeping the nation's youth. What we do mean to posit is that adolescents, given the general cognitive development and establishment of autonomy taking place, are not opposed to thinking about and refining their religiosity. Many adults and religious institutions make the assumption that adolescents are uninterested in matters of religion, and either ignore or chastise adolescents based on this account. What we find is that when adults, peers, and congregations meet adolescents where they are in this process of examining their beliefs, adjusting forms of practice, and fitting religion in with their many other activities and identities, adolescents are more likely to engage in well-founded work on their religious identities. For those invested in helping youth process their religious identities it is important to recognize this key opportunity and respond accordingly.

Conclusion

Youth are heated by Nature as drunken men by wine.
Aristotle

Children today are tyrants. They contradict their parents, gobble their food,
and tyrannize their teachers.
Socrates

I would there were no age between ten and three-and-twenty, or that youth would sleep
out the rest; for there is nothing in the between but getting wenches with child,
wronging the ancientry, stealing, fighting.
Shakespeare

As the roaring of the waves precedes the tempest, so the murmur of rising passions announces
the tumultuous change. . . . A change of temper, frequent outbreaks of anger, a
perpetual stirring of the mind, make the child almost ungovernable.
Jean-Jacques Rousseau

These quotes from prominent thinkers going back centuries demonstrate the long history of society's generalizing the period of adolescence as turbulent and full of risk. G. Stanley Hall, widely recognized
as the first scientist of adolescence, adopted the term "storm and stress"
as a descriptor of adolescence, a time, he said, when youth are likely
to question and contradict their parents, be particularly moody, and
have a propensity for reckless and deviant behavior.[1] Many parents of

teenagers are probably enthusiastically nodding their heads right now, but some are not. Some are saying, "That's not *my* daughter" or "That's not *my* son." People tend to stereotype adolescents in general as unstable and frustrating, but often categorize the ones they know and love as unique in positive ways.

Adolescents view themselves as unique as well. We asked the adolescents who participated in the NSYR in-person interviews how they think adults in society view teenagers, whether that view is accurate, and whether they themselves are viewed by adults in the same way as teenagers in general. The replies were surprisingly similar.

> *Interviewer*: How do you think adults in this society view teenagers in general?
>
> *Participant*: Um, I think one word sums it up. Pretty much hellions. [laughs] I don't know how else to say it, um, even people in the church describe youth groups like that, but there are some adults who see kids as opportunity and potential, and some adults see them as just nothing, like they can't hold the future.
>
> *Interviewer*: The adults that see them as hellions, do you think that's accurate?
>
> *Participant*: I, I think so, yes.
>
> *Interviewer*: How do adults in your life view you, in particular? Do they think of you as a hellion or . . . ?
>
> *Participant*: No. I would think not. [laughs] Um, everyone I meet, I tell them about my faith, and I smile the whole time, um, I have two jobs right now and this one, I work at a theme park and they ask me to do the trash run, and if you knew the trash run at the theme park, it's not very good, but I smiled and sang the whole time and um, one of the vice presidents of the park was like, "You're the only person I've seen happy to do the trash run." I hope they don't see me like that—a hellion.

Almost all of the in-person interview participants reported that adults see most adolescents as rebellious troublemakers. They believe this assessment is somewhat accurate, but they think there are plenty of youth who are responsible, mature, and prosocial, themselves included. It was rare for anyone to admit to being an unruly teenager.

These sentiments parallel where social scientists stand today on the character of adolescents and adults' perceptions of them. Instead of viewing adolescence as universally and inevitably full of storm and stress, scholars such as Jeffrey Arnett posit that adolescence is not a challenge for *all* adolescents, but that it is the time in which struggles with authority, emotional volatility, negative moods, and risky behaviors are most likely to occur.[2] Society and its scholars conclude that adolescence is a time ripe for conflict with parents and other adults, impulsive moods, and unsafe behavior, but there is great variance in the extent to which individual youth themselves experience these issues. We can extend this general narrative to a discussion of adolescent religiosity as well. Although most adults and even youth might assume that adolescents avoid or shun religion or engage with it to a lesser degree than those at different points in the life course, we reveal a different reality in this book. It is time we set aside the overly vague and misleading notion that adolescence is a time of dramatically declining religiosity. Instead we must focus on appreciating the complexities of how adolescents experience and live religion across time and better recognize the role of parents, social networks, and religious institutions in supporting and challenging religious refinement in adolescence. Below we highlight key points from the book and discuss their implications for scholars who study youth, adults (such as parents, teachers, and youth practitioners) who care about youth, religious institutions, and youth themselves.

Understanding the Range of Religious Profiles

What does it mean to be religious? Many scholars have argued and this book further reiterates that religiosity is multidimensional. There are many different aspects to religion, and people choose to emphasize certain aspects more than others. Three of the main components of religiosity are what we label the three Cs: the content of religious beliefs, religious conduct (or practices), and the centrality of religion in one's life. In other words, three common dimensions on which to evaluate or describe a person's religiosity are the types of beliefs he holds, the public and private religious actions in which he participates, and the salience that the beliefs and practices have for the rest of his life.

Social scientists have done a thorough job of delineating the many dimensions of religiosity.[3] Ethnographers have deftly conveyed the complexities of everyday religion as lived by people.[4] Research using survey data to show patterns of religiosity in the population has been more limited in addressing the complexities of multidimensional religiosity for a couple of reasons. First, although dozens of high-quality survey measures exist to gauge the various dimensions of religiosity, it is difficult to know how to put all the measures together to summarize a person's religiosity in a holistic way. We have argued throughout this book that a unidimensional conceptualization of religion does not adequately capture the complexity of religion as it is lived out in people's lives. Many individuals think about religion in linear terms: either someone is very religious, not very religious, or somewhere in between. This linear thinking oversimplifies reality. Religiosity, unlike height or weight, cannot always be summarized on a scale running from low to high values. Our focus has been on adolescents, but our approach to measuring religion is one that can inform scholarship about religion across a variety of populations. A person-centered approach, such as that provided by the latent class analysis we use, allows us to account for the many dimensions of religion and how people piece these dimensions together in unique ways.

To say that religion is multidimensional and complex is not to say that there are no identifiable patterns at work in the religious lives of youth. On the contrary, the five religious profiles reflect relatively discrete and discernable patterns in the religious mosaics of youth. *Abiders* are those who are very religious on virtually every measure of religiosity we use. They are especially institutionally engaged. *Atheists*, like the Abiders, have religious mosaics that represent a consistent balance across the dimensions of religion. In this case, however, the tiles reflect consistent distance from religion. Atheists do not believe in God and do not identify with the various dimensions of religion. The religious mosaics of *Adapters* are notable for their emphasis on religious centrality, private religious conduct, and adaptive enactments of religiosity, such as helping others and thinking about the meaning of life. Their mosaics are more variable in the extent to which tiles of public religious practice are included in the design. The religious mosaics of *Assenters* are also variable along the dimension of religious conduct, both private and public. The common pattern among Assenters is that while their mosaics tend to reflect belief in a personal and involved God, they do not include tiles of intense religious centrality. Assenters are unlikely to say that religious faith is very important to them. *Avoiders* are those youth who maintain a very tenuous connection to religion in their lives, most often in the form of a belief in God. They avoid atheism as well as any notable religious engagement. Identifying these five religious profiles highlights the range of religious expression that exists in the adolescent population. In addition the profiles allow us to better understand the nuances of religiosity by moving away from a linear conception to a person-centered understanding of the unique ways people combine the various elements of their religious lives.

What do we learn from these five profiles of religiosity in the population? The multiple dimensions of religiosity are not always congruent in individuals' lives.[5] Any one individual may have within her religious mosaic tiles of religious devotion and tiles of relative disengagement. To be sure, this is not the case for all; there are plenty of youth who do demonstrate congruence across religious content, conduct, and centrality. But it is important to recognize and allow for the possibility that these dimensions may not always operate in concert. To better study and understand religiosity and its consequences for adolescents we need to appreciate its various forms.

Different from previous work that identifies ideal types of more congruent forms of religiosity in the population, identification of the five *A*s highlights two groups in particular that have been difficult to summarize and study: Adapters and Atheists. In the past the Adapters and Assenters and the Avoiders and Atheists have tended to be lumped together, yet we find important distinctions between them. The Adapters see religion as more salient to everyday life than do Assenters, even if they do not attend religious services more often. The cultural and family backgrounds of these two groups are also very different. Adapters are more likely to be African American or Latino, so cultural characteristics of their religious institutions are at play.[6] Adapters also tend to have parents with lower education and less income. They are more likely to have experienced family disruption such as divorce or residential moves. Compared to Assenters, Adapters face more barriers to becoming actively involved in public religious practice.

Adapters are an important group to consider in the larger scope of adolescent religion. When we examined alternative expressions of religion in the form of helping behaviors and time spent thinking about the meaning of life we found that these measures were a significant part of the overall profile of religiosity among the Adapters. This suggests that perhaps we need to expand our understandings of religious expression, not only among adolescents but among the adult population as well. It is possible that there are other behaviors or attitudes that are rooted in or related to religious expression that go unmeasured and unobserved when the focus is on conventional religious expressions such as religious service attendance, prayer, and particularistic religious beliefs. Increasing interest in social justice and increasing suspicion of institutional religious organizations might be encouraging people to find new ways to act out their religious inclinations.[7]

The recognition that there are alternative ways of expressing religiosity should urge scholars of religion to continue to explore the religious meanings behind attitudes and behaviors previously not included in our rubrics of religion in an attempt to more accurately assess the role religion plays in people's lives. For those who work with and are concerned with the lives of youth, we suggest they take seriously adaptive forms of religiosity. Youth who are not engaged in institutional religious practice are not necessarily uninterested in religion. Recognizing religious interest and commitment expressed in adaptive ways will allow a more complete understanding of the religious lives of youth while at the same time making more effective the outreach efforts and programs directed at youth.

It does seem that being an Abider is more protective than being an Adapter when it comes to outcomes such as substance use, sexual activity, and depression. This could be because the more regular institutional involvement of Abiders results in benefits tied to competencies and coping developed within religious institutions.[8] It is likely also the result of certain social characteristics that make it easier to become and stay Abiders (see paragraph below). Thus although we argue that it is important to acknowledge the diverse ways in which religion is lived, we are not claiming that all types of religiosity are equally associated with adolescent well-being.

In addition to expanding our conceptualization of religiosity, the Adapters in our study raise another important issue for consideration by scholars as well as religious communities. We found that although Adapters report high levels of religious salience, they are no more likely than Assenters to engage in public religious practice. There are certainly multiple explanations for this; one that is worth highlighting is the social position of Adapters. As a group Adapters appear to face a greater number of life challenges: their parents have lower than average income, education, and residential stability; although they report being close to their parents, they are the least likely of the five As to be living with both biological parents. These life challenges and disruptions may discourage or limit engagement in public religious practice. The adaptive forms of religiosity we see among Adapters are likely a response, at least in part, to the social contexts and family backgrounds that shape their lives. The implications of this finding will vary for different readers of this book. Scholars will see the importance of considering individual lives in social context and the need to account for socioeconomic factors that can have such powerful influence in so many areas of people's lives. Religious communities may be compelled to think more seriously about the potential barriers to religious engagement that are experienced by marginalized populations in our society. For some this may lead to a reevaluation of the extent to which religious communities are accessible to and welcoming of people whose lives may not conform well to current program content and schedules. For others this finding might encourage a deeper commitment to addressing inequalities that exist in our society and working to reduce those structural barriers that make it difficult for some adolescents to engage in religious communities.

We are not suggesting that structural barriers are the only issues involved in the less consistent religious involvement of Adapters. We are also not suggesting that the goal is necessarily to make Adapters look like Abiders. But for those Adapters who would like to be involved in or benefit from involvement with a religious community, it is certainly an issue that needs to be considered. The main point is that we should not assume that all religious disengagement is the result of personal choice or agency. There is often a complexity of factors at work.

The second religious profile that stands out in our analysis is that of the Atheists. The obvious distinction between Atheists and Avoiders is that Avoiders have some professed belief in God and Atheists do not. Beyond this difference, however, Atheists tend also to have thought more seriously about life and the meaning of it. They can clearly articulate their beliefs and tend to be very intellectual.[9] On the other hand, Avoiders do not think much about religion. Although these groups are distinct in many ways, most analyses of how religiosity relates to other life outcomes use survey measures of religiosity that combine these two groups. The experiences of Atheists, a very small part of the overall population, are then overshadowed by the experiences of Avoiders. Yet, our analysis in chapter 3 reveals differences in the well-being of these two groups. For example, Atheists are less likely to be depressed and have much higher educational aspirations than Avoiders. By separating out Atheists and studying them more carefully scholars will be better able to assess when religion and religious involvement offer unique contributions to the lives of youth who are engaged in them, and when religion operates similarly to other order-imposing systems of meaning and belonging such as atheism.

The distinctions between Avoiders and Atheists and their relative proportions in society are important for religious institutions and youth ministers to understand as well. In our data Atheists make up only from 3 to 5 percent of the adolescent population at the two survey points. Therefore, rather than being overly alarmist about the relatively small risk that youth will abandon all belief or become anti-religious, religious institutions may want to focus more on the much larger proportion of youth who claim a belief in God even though religious conduct or centrality in their life is virtually nonexistent. These are the youth who seem to also struggle in other realms of life like subjective well-being, risky behaviors, and educational aspirations.

In general knowing the types of religiosity that are lived by adolescents and the other life characteristics and outcomes that go along with living a certain type of religiosity clarifies the range of adolescent experience. Then, instead of relying on larger group stereotypes— such as that all adolescents are "hellions," "tyrannize their teachers," or are uninterested in thinking through their beliefs—those who study or work with youth can take a more tailored approach.

Acknowledging Adolescent Perceptions of Change

One of the strengths of the National Study of Youth and Religion is its incorporation of both survey data and in-person interview data. By drawing on both sources of data we can more fully assess the religious lives of the youth we study. There is much to be learned from the statistical analysis of survey data; our survey has generated a picture of overall religious stability among youth with some instances of religious change. Throughout this book, however, we have also allowed the voices of the youth themselves to inform our analysis and interpretation of the data. We believe that the in-person interviews are essential for uncovering some of the nuances and contradictions that can't be resolved with survey data alone. By listening to youth talk about their faith we gain more insight into their own perceptions of religious stability and change in their lives. In particular it is through the voices of youth that we come to a better understanding of one of the puzzling paradoxes of our survey data: that in spite of average declines across a number of individual measures of religion, the majority of youth report religious stability or even increased religiosity in the years between the two time points of our study.

Paralleling the general sense of cognitive development that youth experience in adolescence, our interviews reveal that adolescence is a time when many youth begin to feel more ownership over their religiosity.[10] What used to be beliefs and practices that they accepted from parents and other adults are recast as more personal. Numerous participants said they now "understand" things better or make their own decisions about their faith. Youth appear to value this personalization process, feeling more connected to a faith that they can claim as their own. However, this increased ownership of their faith rarely translates into higher levels of practice or religious engagement. In fact, as we discussed in chapter 5, ownership of one's faith appears to be distinct from issues of religious belief or practice and may even accompany a decrease in practice. Regardless of the content of their religious beliefs or the practices in which they engage, a significant number of youth appear to have a more autonomous approach to religion as they move through adolescence.

As we outlined in chapter 5, this shift in perspective to ownership of one's faith does not occur for all youth and results in a variety of outcomes when it does occur. It is debatable just how deep and consequential this shift is during adolescence; there are certainly youth who may personalize or take ownership of their faith in a way that is of little consequence in their lives. But for some, particularly Abiders and Adapters, for whom religion is already highly salient, the process of religious refinement appears to be significant and reflects an increase in religiosity that may not be captured by standard survey measures. Their reports of religious intensification offer yet another way to understand movement in the religious lives of youth, one we might not see if we limit our analyses to standard religion measures available through survey data. Though some youth are connected to religion by the thinnest of threads, others are highly engaged and desire to grow in their personal commitment to religion. Efforts to study, understand, and interact with the religious lives of youth must account for the full range of religious experience among adolescents. Much energy has been focused on religious decline among adolescents, yet many youth are maintaining their religious lives or even cultivating them further. They ought not to be overlooked either by the scholars who study them or the adults who care for them.

Those who are interested in the religious lives of youth—scholars, parents, religious leaders, and practitioners who work with youth— bring to the table their own understanding of what religiosity looks like and what constitutes religious change. Listening to youth talk about religious change and stability in their lives offers an opportunity to learn some important things from their responses. Whatever one thinks about the accuracy of their self-assessments, there is insight to be gained by listening to *how* they talk about religion and faith. We hear in their responses the complexity of religion. Some are able to articulate this far better than others, but youth in general seem quite aware of the multiple dimensions of religious experience and expression, though few would use this type of language to talk about it. More significant, as we listened to them discuss their religious lives we were reminded once again of the fallacy of congruence and the oversimplification that can result from assuming that people live out the different facets of religion in consistent ways. Youth are quite able to combine varying levels of content, conduct, and centrality in ways that may or may not make sense in a traditional framework of low to high religiosity. The variety of adolescent perceptions of religion reaffirms our commitment to a person-centered approach to studying religion, one that can account for this multidimensionality as well as the complexity and variation in how the dimensions are packaged together.

Beyond the study of religion these conversations with youth highlight for other interested parties the importance of taking seriously adolescent perceptions of religion. Religious communities, parents, and others who hope to engage youth in conversations about faith would do well to recognize these issues and leave room in the conversation for youth to come with their different mosaics and grapple with the complexity that these mosaics present. We heard youth say that a better understanding of their religion is one important aspect of taking ownership of their faith. Rather than serving as a threat to a preconceived notion of what constitutes religiosity and religious development, adolescent self-assessments and the incongruence they entail can serve as an opportunity to engage youth in conversations about their faith and help them better understand their religious traditions. Traditions will vary in their emphasis on the different dimensions of religion and their responses to the different mosaic patterns that emerge among their youth. By taking seriously the ways that youth view their own religious lives, adults may be better able to meet youth wherever they are in the process of religious refinement and guide, challenge, and support them through the process.

Scaffolding Adolescents to Thrive

We anticipate that many who read this book will be interested in the factors that relate to shifts over time across the various profiles or waxing and waning within profiles. Given that many before us have done comprehensive analyses of survey data to locate key characteristics of youth and experiences that seem tied to religious change, we focus on a unique but resounding theme that emerges from the NSYR interviews.[11] As we reported in chapter 6, youth are most likely to make well-founded and sustainable refinements to their religious identities when they are well scaffolded in the process by parents, peers, and religious institutions.

Social scaffolding is the process whereby influential others serve as a support system while adolescents strengthen their internal sense of being.[12] This involves knowing where youth are in the religious refinement process (e.g., are they currently perplexed by any particular belief issues, and if so, which ones?) so that scaffolding can be located right at the base of that particular process. This allows the youth some freedom in refining what she believes, as well as support to fall back on and models to observe. Being close enough so that youth know that the scaffolding is there, but far enough away to allow them some freedom in exploration and expression seems key to the process. This finding again highlights the importance of recognizing key forms of variance in youth.

Prior research has shown that family religious background and experiences in youth are significantly related to religious change during adolescence and young adulthood. The more parents attend religious services and value religion's role in everyday life, the more likely their child will be and remain religiously involved and engaged.[13] However, when there is religious conflict or disagreement between parent and child (especially when a parent is very religious on every dimension and the child is not), evidence suggests that parent-child relationships are strained and youth are more likely to participate in delinquent behavior.[14] Thus parental religiosity can be perceived in a variety of ways. As the scaffolding perspective suggests, when parents are able to model a high level of religiosity in combination with warmth and support, children are more likely to feel able to make their own informed decisions about their personal religious mosaics, and this usually leads them to choose to maintain an engaged faith. As scholars continue to study factors that are associated with religious change in adolescence, consideration must be given to the social context, networks, or quality of relationships in which major life changes or key events (e.g., the death of a loved one, moving away from home, being exposed to new friends with different belief systems, becoming sexually active) are experienced. It is often these systems of social support that determine whether critical life experiences bolster or threaten the religious profiles youth have developed.

On the practical side parents, adults who work with youth, and especially religious institutions should consider the forms of social scaffolding they provide. Is the appropriate level of social scaffolding in place? Do they have a thorough understanding of where the youth they care for and work with are in terms of religious and spiritual refinement as well as in other realms of life? Have they provided enough space for youth to feel that they are able to make autonomous decisions and develop a faith they can call their own? Some adults are more comfortable than others with providing youth this space. Our analysis of the NSYR data suggests it is vital that adults recognize the importance of youth feeling that they have some space to explore their own beliefs and sources of meaning with loving and honest adults and peers providing guidance and support.

Youth seem to thrive when they feel loved for who they are and trusted to explore their own beliefs, especially when they have role models from whom to draw advice and support. Youth especially struggle when no one seems genuinely interested in them as a unique individual, and when either little or no scaffolding is provided or scaffolding is overapplied. An example of overscaffolding is Michael's mother, who melts into tears when he tries to vocalize doubts he is having over God's existence. She is understandably frustrated that he is not accepting what she has taught him about God, but the result of her behavior is Michael's feeling that he cannot trust her with his faith struggles in the future. If forced to admit it, Michael's mother has probably had many of the same doubts herself. Being honest with him about this (as Diego's mother was with him) and providing him the support to process his doubts is likely to be better for him and their relationship. In addition the opportunity to verbalize his doubts and have his mother's help in thinking through his questions could facilitate a better understanding of the faith he has begun to question. Instead his mother's attempt to force him to accept what she wants him to believe has contributed to Michael's turning away from a religion that produces doubts he can't reconcile.

Youth themselves can make use of these findings as well. When it comes to their own faith journeys, they can look to the adults and institutions around them for the scaffolding they need. When they are not being fully understood or getting the appropriate level of support they may be able to talk with the adults around them to ask for modifications in the scaffolding. Youth can also learn to serve as scaffolding for each other. In fact in many ways adolescents understand each other better than adults can. They are experiencing many of the same life changes at the same moment in history and can offer encouragement to one another in the process of religious refinement.

Final Thoughts

This book is about getting beneath the surface, pushing past generalities and stereotypes, and trying to really understand the primary profiles of religiosity in adolescence, how they are refined over time, and other life characteristics that go along with these unfolding forms of faith and meaning. Youth are not all hellions, and they do not all walk away from religious beliefs and practices in adolescence. Neither are the majority of youth extremely religiously or spiritually engaged. Adolescents exhibit an interesting variety of religious mosaics, and many struggle to sort through how beliefs and practices form and are formed by their lives and understanding of the world. For scholars, parents, practitioners, or religious institutions to assume any less, or to oversimplify their approach to reaching the variety of youth refining their ideas about religion, is to shortchange themselves and the youth they care about.

APPENDIX A

Methodological Design and Procedures for the National Study of Youth and Religion, Wave 2

Background Information

The National Study of Youth and Religion (NSYR) is a longitudinal mixed-method research project designed to examine the religious lives of Americans from adolescence into young adulthood. The data analyzed in this book is based on NSYR Wave 1 and Wave 2 data: two waves of a telephone survey with a nationally representative sample of American youth and two waves of in-person semistructured interviews with a subsample of the original survey respondents. Survey data collection for the study began with the first wave of the project in July 2002, fielded by FGI Research, and was completed in April 2003. The first round of in-person interviews was conducted between March and August 2003. In 2004, with NSYR funding granted for a second wave, the study became longitudinal. The survey for Wave 2 was fielded by the Howard W. Odum Institute for Research in Social Science from June 2005 through November 2005. The in-person interviews were conducted between June and September 2005.

This appendix describes the methods and procedures involved in the Wave 2 data collection. A full description of the methodological design and procedures for the Wave 1 data is available in appendix B of *Soul Searching* by Smith and Denton. The survey instruments and in-person interview guides are available by Internet download at the NSYR website, www.youthandreligion.org/research/.

National Study of Youth and Religion
Telephone Survey, Wave 2

The second wave of the NSYR longitudinal telephone survey was designed to be a reinterview of all Wave 1 youth survey respondents. Parents of the youth respondents were not reinterviewed. At the time of this second survey the respondents were between the ages of 16 and 21. Like the Wave 1 survey, the Wave 2 survey was conducted by telephone using a Computer-Assisted Telephone Interviewing (CATI) system.

For this second wave of the survey we conducted interviews only in English. Four youth respondents did not participate in the Wave 2 interview due to their not being able to understand or speak English. We did translate our presurvey mailing into Spanish for respondents we knew to have Spanish-speaking parents or guardians. Additionally a call center staff member was available to conduct the verbal parental consent in Spanish.

The Wave 2 telephone survey questionnaire covers many of the same topics as the Wave 1 questionnaire. Many of the questions are identical so that change can be measured precisely. However, the Wave 2 questionnaire was designed to take into account changes in the lives of the respondents as they began to enter young adulthood. The Wave 2 survey includes new questions pertaining to behaviors occurring during the transition to adulthood, such as nonmarital cohabitation, educational and career aspirations, pregnancy and marriage.

To test the Wave 2 survey instrument and to give interviewers the opportunity to practice interviewing, a pretest was conducted with seventy-eight respondents, seven of whom were also pretest respondents in Wave 1. The remaining seventy-one were recruited by calling from a list of telephone numbers provided by a national sampling group, Survey Sampling International. A targeted-age sample was obtained, which allowed us to limit the calling to numbers that included a household member in a particular age bracket (16–21 years). A call script was developed, which included text for obtaining verbal consent from the potential respondent and a parent or guardian if needed. This consent and call script was reviewed and approved by the Institutional Review Board at the University of North Carolina at Chapel Hill. Pretest callers were recruited from a group of experienced telephone interviewers. Each interviewer spent several hours receiving training from the project manager before being given the list of numbers to begin calling. If any parent or adolescent refused participation he was given further explanation of the study and its importance, and if he continued to refuse he was not recontacted. The pretest respondents' full names, phone numbers, preferred calling days and times, and any relevant notes were given to the survey programmer to be preloaded into the survey instrument. After approximately one month of calling, project staff were able to successfully recruit and receive consent from 109 pretest respondents. Of those, seventy-one completed the survey. Each pretest respondent was paid a modest incentive for survey completion. Based on the pretest results and interviewer feedback, final revisions were made to the survey instrument.

Survey interviewers were hired by the Howard W. Odum Institute for Research in Social Science at the University of North Carolina at Chapel Hill, the survey organization contracted by NSYR to field the survey in Wave 2. Survey interviewers participated in four days of project-specific and general interviewing skills training. Training topics included obtaining cooperation, understanding bias, using probing methods, using the CATI system, and resolving respondent questions. A variety of methods were used in training, including written exercises, role-playing, and practice with the CATI system. For part of their training project interviewers were required to take part in a "Human Participant Protections Education" session and received a certificate verifying their understanding of the ethical issues involved in human subjects research. Throughout the entire survey data collection period interviewers were monitored remotely by Odum supervisors and by project staff for quality control. The interviewers were also routinely evaluated on their performance.

Telephone calls to respondents were spread out over varying days and times, including weekends. Every effort was made to contact and survey all original NSYR respondents, including those out of the country, in the military, or on religious missions. In addition respondents were able to initiate the completion of their survey interview at their convenience by calling a toll-free number provided in mailings and in occasional voice mail messages left by interviewers. On average fourteen phone calls were made to each respondent (including those who completed the survey). Of the cases where no contact with a human was ever made, sixty-five calls were made to the household on average. Of the cases where contact was established with the household but the survey was not completed, on average there were forty-six attempts to reach the respondent by telephone. A total of 2,604 respondents participated in the survey, for a final NSYR Wave 2 overall nonweighted response rate of 78.6 percent.

Prior to conducting all Wave 2 survey interviews each respondent's verbal consent was obtained. In addition, for all respondents under age 18, parental consent was obtained through the return of a signed form before the start of the survey or verbally by phone with a survey interviewer. The respondent's identity was confirmed using name and date of birth. If a respondent was unable to correctly answer one or all of the screening questions a call center supervisor was notified. The supervisor then attempted to identify whether the answer discrepancy was due to a keying error made in the Wave 1 survey (if the birth date was off by one day, for example) or whether it was in fact questionable that the interviewer was speaking with the correct respondent. If the supervisor had any question about the identity of the person on the phone the interviewer broke off the survey and notified the respondent that she would call back at a later time. The supervisor then recorded the details of the situation and informed project researchers. The NSYR researchers made the final determination of whether the survey interview should be completed with the respondent.

Every attempt was made to resurvey the 3,364 original youth respondents (3,370 Wave 1 respondents minus six respondents whose contact information was not collected), including those who were out of the country or serving in the military. The entire survey was completed in Wave 2 by 2,581 respondents, for a full retention rate of 77.9 percent (2,581 of the 3,312 eligible respondents). The overall retention rate is 78.6 percent, which includes the twenty-three respondents who partially completed the survey. Therefore the total attrition in Wave 2 was 766 respondents. The predominant source of attrition was nonlocated respondents (see table A.1). The overall combined response rate for Waves 1 and 2 of the NSYR telephone survey, calculated by multiplying the Wave 1 and Wave 2 response rates, is 44.8 percent. Of the original Jewish oversample of eighty, seventy-four completed the Wave 2 survey (92.5 percent).

The Wave 2 cooperation rate was 89.9 percent. This was calculated by dividing the number of completed cases (including partials) by the number of respondents who were successfully contacted ($N = 2,865$). The categories making up the noncontacted cases ($N = 505$) are the following: no human contact (38), nonlocated military or job corps (15), nonlocated out of the country (4), other nonlocates (390),

Table A.1 Sources of Attrition in Wave 2

	N	%
Total possible respondents in Wave 2	3370	100
Total respondents participating in Wave 2 survey	2604	78.6
Attrition in Wave 2	766	22.7
Sources of attrition (N=766)		
Respondents not located	390	50.9
No human contact	38	5.0
Military or job corps	15	2.0
Out of country	4	0.5
Respondent incapable	1	0.1
Institutionalized	16	2.0
Respondent language barrier	4	0.5
Respondent deceased	5	0.7
Questionable respondent eligibility	2	0.3
Successfully contacted incomplete	129	16.9
Refusals	132	17.2
Discovered to be DOB outliers	30	3.9

Source: National Surveys of Youth and Religion, 2002, 2005.

and ineligibles (58). The ineligible group consists of deceased respondents (5), respondents who were institutionalized throughout the entire data collection period (16), respondents with language barriers (4), cases where the identity of the respondent was too questionable to proceed with the survey (2), and one case where the respondent was incapable of completing the survey. In addition to these are thirty cases that were taken out of the Wave 2 data after the survey had been fielded when it was discovered that the date of birth reported by these respondents put them outside of the age criterion for the study. When a situation like this arose, where the DOB reported in Wave 1 and Wave 2 differed, the birth date was checked with the respondent several times by the survey interviewers. Additionally, before taking these thirty respondents out of the data, the study project manager contacted the respondents to confirm the dates of birth one last time.

Comparisons of the two surveys reveal only minor differences between the Wave 1 and Wave 2 responders (see table A.2). Only minor differences exist in the percentage of those Wave 1 and Wave 2

Table A.2 Comparison of Wave 1 Respondents, Wave 2 Respondents, and Wave 2 Nonrespondents on Key Lifestyle Characteristics (Percentages)

Wave 1:	W1 Respondents	W2 Respondents	W2 Nonrespondents			
			No Contact	Contacted, No Refusal	Contacted, Refusal	Total
Never drinks alcohol	62	62	60	55	70	61
Never uses marijuana	74	77	61	68	73	65
Smokes cigarettes regularly	8	7	14	9	8	12
Nights per week eats dinner with one parent (mean)	5	5	5	5	5	5
School type attending						
Public	87	87	86	86	89	86
Private religious	7	7	4	6	8	5
Private secular	2	2	2	2	0	2
Home-schooled	2	2	3	1	1	2
Missing	3	2	5	5	2	5
Attends religious services weekly or more	39	41	32	31	31	32
Never attends religious services	18	17	24	13	25	22
N	3,290	2,530[a]	438	127	132	697

Source: National Surveys of Youth and Religion, 2002, 2005.
Note: Percentages may not add to 100 due to rounding.
[a] N does not include ineligible respondents or the Jewish oversample cases

responders who attend religious services weekly or more and those who never attend. However, when analyses were run comparing the Wave 2 responders and nonrespondents it was found that nonrespondents are more likely to never attend religious service and are less likely to attend religious services weekly or more than responders. This is consistent with findings from other social science research that indicate that more religious study participants are more likely to cooperate with research studies than nonreligious participants.[1] On key demographic characteristics only small differences between Wave 1 and Wave 2 respondents were found (see table A.3). Longitudinal weights were calculated for use when analyzing data from Wave 1 and Wave 2 of the NSYR survey data (excluding data from the Jewish oversample).

The refusal rate for Wave 2, calculated as the number of eligible respondents (N = 3,312) who refused to take part in the survey, was 4.0 percent. For each initial respondent refusal some attempt was made to persuade survey participation. The reason for the refusal was clearly noted and any conversion attempts were specific to the respondent's (or guardian's) concerns. When appropriate, a project staff member would contact a respondent directly to give more detailed information about the project. Letters were drafted to address concerns about data security, sensitive questions, and confidentiality as well as to persuade those respondents who reported being "too busy" or "not interested." Each respondent was reminded that his participation was important to the success of the project, and every attempt was made to address each respondent's questions. Of the 132 refusals forty-five were indirect, meaning that the refusal was given by a parent, guardian, or other adult household member, not the respondent. In situations where the person giving the refusal was not a legal guardian of an underage respondent, the cases were treated as "blocked." All efforts were made to contact the respondents directly in these situations, and when those attempts were unsuccessful project staff tried their best to persuade the blocking adult to allow us to communicate with the respondent. Every effort was made in the NSYR project design, instrument construction, interviewer training, and survey fielding to produce the best possible results.

The analyses in this book are based on the survey responses of the 2,604 youth who completed both Wave 1 and Wave 2 of the survey. The nonrepresentative Jewish oversample (n = 74) was excluded from the analysis in this book, resulting in a final sample of 2,530.

Table A.3 Comparison of Key Demographic Characteristics, Wave 1 and Wave 2 (Percentages)

	W1 Respondents	W2 Respondents	W2 Nonrespondents			
			No Contact	Contacted, No Refusal	Contacted, Refusal	Total
Census Region						
Northeast	15	15	15	17	14	15
Midwest	23	24	17	17	27	19
South	42	41	46	39	40	43
West	20	20	22	27	18	22
Gender						
Male	51	50	51	51	63	54
Female	49	50	49	49	37	46
Age						
13	19	19	17	15	17	17
14	20	20	17	20	18	18
15	21	22	21	13	27	20
16	20	20	20	28	17	21
17	20	19	26	23	21	24
Teen Race/Ethnicity						
White	65	69	48	50	74	54
African American	17	16	23	20	15	21
Latino	12	10	22	23	5	19

Asian/Pacific Islander/ American Indian/Mixed/Other	5	5	6	7	5	6
Missing	1	1	1	0	0	0
Family Structure						
Lives with two biological/ adoptive parents	50	55	27	34	50	33
Household Income						
Less than $10K	3	3	7	5	3	6
$10K–20K	7	6	11	14	4	10
$20K–30K	12	11	19	17	8	16
$30K–40K	13	12	16	18	21	18
$40K–50K	13	14	13	7	14	12
$50K–60K	11	11	8	13	11	10
$60K–70K	7	8	5	2	4	4
$70K–80K	6	7	4	7	6	5
$80K–90K	5	6	1	1	6	2
$90K–100K	4	4	3	4	5	3
More than $100K	11	12	6	9	13	8
Missing	6	6	7	4	6	6
N	3,290	2,530[a]	438	127	132	697

Source: National Surveys of Youth and Religion, 2002, 2005.
Note: Percentages may not add to 100 due to rounding.
[a] N does not include ineligible respondents or the Jewish oversample cases

National Study of Youth and Religion In-person Interviews, Wave 2

The second phase of the Wave 2 data collection involved in-depth personal interviews with 122 youth. The purpose of the interviews was to provide extended follow-up discussion about youth's religious, spiritual, family, and social lives, especially in contrast to the responses they might have given in Wave 1. The interview guide included many items from Wave 1, with the addition of several new subjects of interest and the elimination of some sections that had not proved helpful in analysis. Interviews were conducted almost exclusively in person and were digitally recorded. They lasted an average of 107 minutes with a range of 43 to 237 minutes. Respondents were given a $40 cash incentive to complete the interviews. The majority of the in-person interviews were conducted between June and September 2005; several were conducted during December 2005. All interview subjects were selected from the 267 youth who had given in-person interviews in Wave 1; additionally all subjects were required to participate in the NSYR telephone survey before they could complete the in-person interview.

Our sampling strategy was to replicate the Wave 1 sample distribution, which varied across a range of demographic and religious characteristics and took into account region; urban, suburban, and rural residence; age; sex; race or ethnicity; household income; religion; and school type. We clustered the respondents with whom we were still in contact into geographic areas for ease of travel in interviewing. The time lapse between a youth completing the Wave 2 telephone survey and completing a personal interview ranged from one day to four months. Therefore for some the Wave 2 personal interview came two years after the Wave 1 interview, and for others the interviews were nearly three years apart. Thus the Wave 1 age range of 13 to 18 became 15 to 21, with a mean age of nearly 18.

Sixteen different interviewers conducted interviews in twenty-eight states, each interviewer conducting between three and seventeen interviews with a mean of seven. Twelve of the original interviewers returned for Wave 2, and respondents were matched with their original interviewers as often as possible. The majority of the 122 Wave 2 interviews were matched on gender and race or ethnicity, and all of the black respondents in the sample were interviewed by minority interviewers. Because of the sensitive nature of the interview questions, prior to interview data collection the NSYR renewed the Certificate of

Confidentiality from the U.S. National Institute of Child Health and Human Development, obtained in Wave 1, to protect the data from subpoena.

All sixteen interviewers participated in a day-long training, which covered the logistics of the interview process, procedural requirements, Institutional Review Board concerns, the protection of human participants, safety and liability concerns, a review and discussion of the interview questionnaire, keys to interview success, and the proper use of the digital recording equipment. In addition to this training all interviewers were required to obtain a Human Participants Training Certificate through the U.S. National Institutes of Health website.

The sixteen project interviewers were assigned to sets of specific geographic locations around the United States. Each interviewer was provided with contact sheets for the youth in their assigned geographic areas. The contact sheets included respondent name, respondent nickname (if known), parent name, address, phone number, respondent birth date, respondent gender, respondent race or ethnicity, household income, religious affiliation, and religious denomination or tradition. The contact sheet included space to note any changes to the contact information provided (new phone number, additional email address, etc.) and provided a call record. Interviewers recorded each household contact, noting the date, time, with whom they spoke, and the content of each contact. In addition to the original sample, as the project progressed through the interviews the priorities shifted somewhat according to the types of respondent interviews still needed. In this way we attempted to match the demographics of Wave 1.

In addition to the demographic information on the contact sheet interviewers were asked to review the transcript of the Wave 1 in-person interview. Because the Wave 2 survey was conducted concurrently with the in-person interviews, the respondents' survey information was not available at the time of the interviews. If the interviewer had not conducted the Wave 1 interview with a particular respondent, the Wave 1 transcript provided background information to help facilitate a smooth interview.

Using a standard call script provided by the NSYR, interviewers made contact with potential interviewee households. Interviewers were required to obtain verbal consent from the respondent to conduct the interview and, if the respondent was under 18, from both a parent and the respondent. If parents or respondents seemed hesitant about participating an additional script provided more information about the project and offered the phone number for the principal investigator, whom they could (and sometimes did) call with questions or concerns. In addition interviewers offered to mail to hesitant respondents written information about the project and then call back in a few days. Interviewers worked hard to obtain consent from the parents. In a very few cases, when a respondent seemed reluctant to participate or was hesitant about the time commitment, an additional incentive was offered. However, in cases where respondents refused to participate even after being offered additional information, interviewers made no further attempt to convert those who refused.

Upon receiving verbal consent from the respondent (and parent if necessary) and scheduling an interview time, interviewers mailed a packet of information to each household. The packet contained a cover letter from the principal investigator, multiple copies of the respondent (and parent if necessary) written consent form(s), and an appointment card including a portrait photo of the interviewer. Interviewees were required to bring a copy of the written consent form(s) with them to their interviews, signed by themselves (and a parent if necessary). Interviewers also called the respondents at least one week prior to the interview and again the day before the interview to confirm that they were still planning to participate in the interview.

Interviews were conducted in public settings that nevertheless provided confidentiality for the respondent. The ideal location for these interviews was in study rooms at local libraries. When these were not available interviews were conducted in restaurants, coffee shops, mall food courts, and outdoor settings. Interviewers were given guidelines for how to present themselves during the interviews as well as appropriate attire to wear in order to ensure consistency in the presentation of interviewers across the interviews. Specifically interviewers did not attempt to "relate" to respondents by dressing down or dressing in a more trendy fashion. Instead we built rapport by presenting ourselves as professional researchers with a sincere interest in young people's lives.

At the close of the interview respondents were given a $40 cash incentive for their participation and in appreciation of their time and effort. Interviewers also followed up interviews with handwritten thank-you notes mailed to respondents.

The final sample of interviews included 122 complete interviews selected from 245 potential contacts. Out of the remaining 123 cases, seventy were purposely never contacted, and an additional fourteen were unable to be contacted (including four who were displaced from

Table A.4   NSYR Wave 2 Personal Interview Demographics

GENDER	N	REGION	N
Female	63	Midwest	26
Male	59	Northeast	19
		South	37
AGE	N	West	40
16	33	**RELIGION**	N
17	27	Protestant	52
18	26	Baptist	15
19	24	Bible Church	1
20	12	Brethren	1
		Calvary Chapel	1
		Charismatic	1
RACE	N	Christian and Missionary	1
White	81	Alliance	
Latino	12	Christian or just Christian	9
African American	16	Church of the Nazarene	2
Asian American	5	Evangelical Free Church	1
Native American	2	Lutheran	6
Other	6	Methodist	5
		Nondenominational	5
HOUSEHOLD INCOME	N	Presbyterian	4
Less than $10K	2	Catholic	25
$10K–$20K	7	Mormon	6
$20K–$30K	11	Jewish	9
$30K–$40K	7	Buddhist	1
$40K–$50K	18	Muslim	1
$50K–$60K	13	Hindu	2
$60K–$70K	13	Eastern Orthodox	1
$70K–$80K	10	Other	9
$80K–$90K	4	Not religious	16
$90K–$100K	8		
More than $100K	23		
Don't know	3		
Refused to answer	3		

Source: National Study of Youth and Religion, 2002, 2005.

their homes after Hurricane Katrina). Eighteen could not be interviewed in person because they had failed to complete the phone survey, and seventeen interviews failed for reasons such as scheduling problems and emergencies. One interview was only partially completed. Three respondents refused to participate.

Table A.4 provides the demographics of the 122 interview participants. With the exception of race/ethnicity and income, which were only measured in the Wave 1 telephone survey, the table reflects the demographic information that was collected at the time of the Wave 2 telephone survey.

APPENDIX B

Latent Class and Latent Transition Analysis Methods

Latent Class Analysis

Throughout this book we report the results of a latent class analysis (LCA) to detect the main profiles of religiosity in the adolescent population of the United States. The main objectives of LCA are to reduce the complexity of the data by suggesting a small number of latent classes that represent the key types of people in the population, and to be able to assign each case or person in the data to one of these classes by estimating the probabilities of belonging to each class on the basis of the person's survey responses.[1] Our application of LCA is to discover what latent classes of religiosity exist among American adolescents and to calculate the probabilities each respondent has of belonging to each of the five classes. Our latent class analysis is based on eight survey questions that measure key components of adolescent religiosity. Latent class methods are well-suited for our purpose because they help reveal the existence of qualitatively different groups when membership in these groups is unknown and not easily predicted from a single measure. This is certainly true of religiosity or spirituality—complex profiles with multiple dimensions.

LCA has some advantages over using cross-tabulation methods (i.e., a priori designating profiles based on certain types of response patterns, such as picking all the highest answers, all the lowest answers, or somewhere in between) to designate groups. First, LCA uses multiple indicators of latent class membership, which provides a basis for estimating measurement error and therefore producing a clearer picture of the underlying latent variable indicating class membership. Second, LCA provides a sense of both the underlying group structure and the amount of measurement error associated with particular indicators.[2]

For the LCA in this book we use eight measures of religiosity that were collected in both NSYR surveys: two measures of religious content (belief in God and exclusivist attitudes toward religion), three measures of religious conduct (the frequency of individual prayer, religious service attendance, and helping others outside of organized volunteer work), and three measures of centrality (importance of religion, closeness to God, and frequency of thinking of the meaning of life). These eight measures are used to jointly characterize the classes (or religious profiles) that exist among adolescents in the United States. Table B.1 contains the exact wording of our eight indicators and their response options, our recoding of some response options, and distributions of each variable within our sample of adolescents who participated in both NSYR telephone surveys.[3]

We are primarily relying on measures of religiosity often applied in Western contexts (belief in God, exclusivist beliefs, prayer, attendance, importance of religion, and closeness to God), but we also incorporate two less standard and less obviously religious measures. One is a question about how often youth think about the meaning of life. This measure is included to tap spirituality, or the drive to connect to that which is sacred, in a way that does not directly reference organized religion. The second is a question about how often the respondent helps those who are needy outside of organized volunteer work. This measure is an attempt to leverage a measure of religious or spiritual practice that has no direct reference to organized religion. Clearly not everyone thinking about the meaning of life or helping others is doing so with religious or spiritual intentions, but we do consider these markers that might help delineate types of religiosity or spirituality in the population that are a bit more individual and less connected with Christian language and ritual. So although they are imperfect measures of religiosity or spirituality alone, we expect that combined with the other measures of religiosity they will help to delineate the types of religious and spiritual youth living in the United States.

Using this group of eight variables LCA identifies common patterns of responses to these questions (e.g., higher values for all questions,

Table B.1 Survey Measures Used in Latent Class and Transition Analyses

Question Wording and Response Categories	Percentage Wave 1, 2002 (Ages 13–17)	Percentage Wave 2, 2005 (Ages 16–21)
View of God (Combination of two survey questions)		
• Do you believe in God, or not, or are you unsure?		
• Which of the following views comes the closest to your own view of God: personal being involved in the lives of people today, created the world but is not involved in the world now, not personal, like a cosmic life force, or none of these views?		
Does not believe in God	3	5
Believes in an uninvolved, or impersonal God	28	29
Believes in a personal God	69	66
Exclusivism (Combination of two survey questions)		
• Which of the following statements comes closest to your own views about religion? Only one religion is true, many religions may be true, or there is very little truth in any religion?		
• Some people think that it is okay to pick and choose their religious beliefs without having to accept the teachings of their religious faith as a whole. Do you agree or disagree?		
Believes one religion is true *and* should accept all teachings	21	21
Not exclusive on either or both questions	79	79

(continued)

Table B.1 (continued)

Question Wording and Response Categories	Percentage Wave 1, 2002 (Ages 13–17)	Percentage Wave 2, 2005 (Ages 16–21)
Praying Alone		
• How often, if ever, do you pray by yourself alone? Never, less than once a month, one to two times a month, about once a week, a few times a week, about once a day, many times a day?		
Never	14	17
From less than once a month to a few times a week	48	53
Once a day or more	38	30
Religious Service Attendance		
• About how often do you usually attend religious services? Never, a few times a year, many times a year, once a month, two to three times a month, once a week, or more than once a week?		
Never	18	28
From a few times a year to two to three times a month	40	43
Once a week or more	42	29
Helping Others on Your Own		
• In the last year, how much, if at all, did you help homeless people, needy neighbors, family, friends, or other people in need, directly, not through an organization? Was it a lot, some, a little, or none?		

None to some	90	89
A lot	10	11
Importance of Religion		
• How important or unimportant is religious faith in shaping how you live your daily life?		
Extremely important, very important, somewhat important, not very important, or not important at all?		
Not at all to somewhat important	49	55
Very or extremely important	51	45
Closeness to God		
• How distant or close to God do you feel most of the time? Extremely distant, very distant, somewhat distant, somewhat close, very close, or extremely close?		
Does not believe in God	3	5
Extremely to somewhat distant	25	34
Somewhat close	35	34
Very or extremely close	37	28
Thinking about the Meaning of Life		
• How often, if at all, do you think about the meaning of life?		
Never	10	11
Rarely to sometimes	70	64
Very often	21	25

Source: National Surveys of Youth and Religion, 2002, 2005.

lower values on all questions, or unique combinations of high on some questions and low on others). The analysis then outputs the number of latent classes that best fit the data and provides characteristics of these classes, such as the approximate size of each class in the population and the probabilities of answering each question a certain way based on membership in each of the classes. We use data from all of the NSYR survey respondents who participated in both the Wave 1 (2002) and Wave 2 (2005) telephone surveys, excluding the Jewish oversample ($N = 2,530$).

Our latent class analyses suggest that the best fit to these data is a model that allows five main classes of religiosity, or what we term religious profiles. In Table B.2 we show the fit statistics for models that assume one through six classes of religiosity. The second column provides G^2 statistics, which express the correspondence between the observed and predicted response patterns in the data. For ordinary contingency table models the G^2 statistic is distributed as a chi-square; unfortunately, for large contingency table models such as the one we are analyzing here, the chi-square distribution is an inaccurate approximation of the G^2 distribution. Instead a rough rule of thumb is that a good model has a G^2 statistic lower than the degrees of freedom. Relative model fit, or deciding which of several models is optimal in terms of balancing fit and parsimony, can be assessed with the Akaike Information Criterion and Bayesian Information Criterion. Models with lower AICs and BICs are a better fit. As you can see in table B.2, the model with five classes has a G^2 statistic that is lower than the degrees of freedom and the lowest BIC.

Table B.2 Goodness-of-Fit Statistics for Latent Class Analysis Models

Number of Classes	G^2	df	BIC	AIC
1	5087.35	2577	5115.35	5197.05
2	2140.81	2562	2368.05	2198.81
3	1486.30	2547	1831.09	1574.30
4	1112.68	2532	1575.01	1230.68
5	974.10	2517	1553.96	1122.10
6	889.55	2502	1586.95	1067.55

Source: National Surveys of Youth and Religion, 2002, 2005.

Using the model with five latent classes, the results obtained through LCA specify the probability that a person with a given profile of religiosity will answer each of the eight survey indicators in a particular way. Table B.3 displays these probabilities, giving a sense of how members of each latent class of religiosity are likely to answer each of the eight indicators of religiosity.

Table B.3 Conditional Probabilities of Responses to Eight Survey Items Measuring Religion

	Abiders	Adapters	Assenters	Avoiders	Atheists
View of God					
• Does not believe in God	.00	.00	.00	.00	1.00
• Believes in an uninvolved, or impersonal God	.05	.20	.23	.75	.00
• Believes in a personal God	.96	.80	.77	.25	.00
Exclusivist Views					
• Believes one religion is true *and* should accept all teachings as a whole	.33	.89	.87	.98	.98
• Not exclusivist on either or both questions	.67	.11	.13	.02	.02
Praying Alone					
• Never	.00	.03	.04	.48	.88
• From less than once a month to a few times a week	.25	.41	.85	.48	.11
• Once a day or more	.75	.56	.11	.04	.01
Religious Service Attendance					
• Never	.01	.12	.12	.62	.78
• From a few times a year to two to three times a month	.16	.52	.63	.34	.21
• Once a week or more	.83	.37	.25	.04	.01
Helping Others on Your Own					
• None to some	.88	.83	.93	.91	.90
• A lot	.12	.17	.07	.09	.10

(continued)

	Abiders	Adapters	Assenters	Avoiders	Atheists
Importance of Religion					
• Not at all to somewhat important	.04	.24	.73	.96	.97
• Very or extremely important	.96	.76	.27	.04	.03
Closeness to God					
• Does not believe in God	.00	.00	.00	.00	1.00
• Extremely or somewhat distant	.05	.07	.32	.81	.00
• Somewhat close	.24	.31	.60	.16	.00
• Very or extremely close	.71	.62	.07	.03	.00
Thinking about the Meaning of Life					
• Never	.07	.05	.10	.17	.23
• Rarely to sometimes	.66	.54	.77	.68	.63
• Very often	.27	.41	.13	.16	.14

Source: National Surveys of Youth and Religion, 2002, 2005.

Because we are working with underlying latent classes not everyone will fit perfectly into one of the five classes. What the analysis produces is the probability that a given respondent is in each of the five latent classes based on his survey answers. The better a latent class model fits, the easier it will be to identify the one class respondents are most likely to be in. In other words, the model fits better when for most respondents one of the five probabilities is much higher than the other four. For example, in our data we find more confidence in our results given that 23 percent of our respondents have a 100 percent chance of being in one particular latent class. We also consider it a good sign that 58 percent of our respondents have greater than an 80 percent chance of being in the best fitting latent class. Only 7 percent of our respondents have less than a 60 percent chance of being in the latent class that best fits them. In other words, very few of our respondents are on the border between latent classes. For descriptive purposes and ease of interpretation throughout this book, we introduce our study participants by identifying the latent class to which they are most likely to belong and describe them as members of that class or profile of religiosity.

Latent Transition Analysis

The objective of our latent transition analysis (LTA) in chapter 4 is to assess the probabilities that a member of one class in 2002 has of being a member of that class or any of the other four classes in 2005. These results demonstrate how likely transitions are over time and which types of transitions are more common than others. Our LTA model, estimated in SAS using the *proc lta* command, is run with the ρ parameters constrained to be equal at both points in time. These are the parameters representing the probability of choosing a particular response option conditional on membership in a particular class at that point in time. In other words, the conditional probabilities in table B.3 have been set to be the same for both waves of data. We ran a statistical test to make sure this restriction was viable with the data we have, and the G^2 difference test for the nested models is 261 with 70 df ($G^2 = 14,808$ with 6,718,299 df vs. $G^2 = 15,069$ with 6,718,369 df). The difference is nonsignificant, providing evidence that the assumption of measurement invariance over time holds. In other words, we can be reasonably sure that the qualities of belonging to a particular class have not changed much over the three-year period, so we can constrain them to be exactly the same and work with results that are easier to interpret.

Notes

Introduction

1. In place of their real names, we use pseudonyms when describing or quoting from our interview participants.

2. Wuthnow, *Growing Up Religious*.

3. Lerner and Steinberg, "Scientific Study of Adolescence."

4. Smetana, Campione-Barr, and Metzger, "Adolescent Development."

5. Ibid.

6. Arnett, *Emerging Adulthood*; Steinberg, *Adolescence*; Smetana, Campione-Barr, and Metzger, "Adolescent Development."

7. Fowler, *Stages of Faith*.

8. Smetana, Campione-Barr, and Metzger, "Adolescent Development."

9. Smith and Denton, *Soul Searching*; Regnerus, "Religion and Positive Adolescent Outcomes."

10. The terms *U.S. adolescents* and *American adolescents* are used throughout the book. Both terms are intended to refer to adolescents who were living in the United States at the time of the surveys.

11. We limited the size of the in-person interview sample because our experience analyzing the 267 transcripts from the first wave of interviews suggested that our primary research questions for the second wave of the study could be addressed with a smaller set of interviews.

12. For more detailed information on the survey and semistructured interview, see Smith and Denton, *Soul Searching*, 272–310. Methodological design reports for Waves 1 and 2 are available online at www.youthanreligion.org/research; a third wave of the NSYR survey and interviews was conducted in 2007-8. Results from that phase of the project are reported by Smith and Snell in *Souls in Transition*.

13. John P. Bartkowski and Xiaohe Xu, "True to the Faith: Religion and Social Life among Latter-Day Saint Youth," unpublished manuscript; Christerson, Edwards and Flory, *Growing Up*; Schwadel, "Current Expressions"; Schwadel, "Jewish Teenagers' Syncretism"; Van Ryn, "'There's the Jewish Culture.'"

Chapter 1

1. Glock, "On the Study of Religious Commitment"; Glock, "Religious Revival"; Glock and Stark, *Religion and Society*.

2. Stark and Glock, *American Piety*.

3. D. W. Wimberley, "Religion and Role-Identity."

4. Cornwall et al., "Dimensions of Religiosity"; Davidson and Knudsen, "New Approach"; De Jong, Faulkner, and Warland, "Dimensions of Religiosity Reconsidered"; Verbit, "Components and Dimensions"; R. C. Wimberley, "Toward the Measurement"; D. W. Wimberley, "Religion and Role-Identity."

5. Stark and Glock, *American Piety*; Lenski, *Religious Factor*; M. King, "Measuring the Religious Variable"; Verbit, "Components and Dimensions"; Cornwall et al., "Dimensions of Religiosity."

6. Davie, *Religion in Britain*; Yamane, "Beyond Beliefs." In much of this chapter we discuss adolescent life in terms of the social or external influences shaping adolescents' religiosity. There is much good theory to expect this causal influence. However, we must always be mindful that individuals also assert agency and help to shape the social contexts in which they live.

7. Stark and Glock, *American Piety*; Lenski, *Religious Factor*.

8. M. King, "Measuring the Religious Variable."

9. Verbit, "Components and Dimensions"; Cornwall et al., "Dimensions of Religiosity."

10. Bender, *Heaven's Kitchen*; McGuire, *Lived Religion*.

11. D. W. Wimberley, "Religion and Role-Identity"; Cornwall et al., "Dimensions of Religiosity"; Davidson and Knudsen, "New Approach."

12. Crawford and Rossiter, *Reasons for Living*; Zinnbauer, Pargament and Scott, "Emerging Meanings."

13. Hill and Pargament, "Advances"; Wink, Dillon, and Prettyman, "Religiousness"; Zinnbauer, Pargament, and Scott, "Emerging Meanings."

14. Wuthnow, *After Heaven*.

15. Roof, "Religion and Spirituality," 138.

16. Hammond and Johnson, "Locating the Idea"; Roof, "Concepts and Indicators."

17. Chaves, "Rain Dances."

18. Smith and Denton, *Soul Searching*.

19. D. D. Hall, *Lived Religion*.

20. McGuire, *Lived Religion*.

21. Ammerman, "Religious Identities"; Cadge, *First Generation*; Kurien, *Place at the Multicultural Table*; Orsi, *Madonna of 115th Street*; Spickard, Landres, and McGuire, *Personal Knowledge*.

22. D. D. Hall, *Lived Religion*; McGuire, *Lived Religion*.

23. McCloud, "Putting Some Class"; Schwadel, "Poor Teenagers' Religion."

24. Elder, "Life Course"; Elder, Kirkpatrick Johnson, and Crosnoe, "Emergence and Development."

25. Ammerman, *Bible Believers*; Smith and Faris, "Socioeconomic Inequality."

26. Edgell, *Religion and Family*; Schwadel, "Poor Teenagers' Religion."

27. Stolzenberg, Blair-Loy, and Waite, "Religious Participation."

28. Pargament, *Psychology of Religion*.

29. Edgell, *Religion and Family*.

30. Zhai et al., "Parental Divorce."

31. Friedman, "Divorced Parents."

32. Edgell, *Religion and Family*.

33. Schachter and Kuenzi, *Seasonality of Moves*; Teater, "Factors."

34. Pendry and Adam, "Associations."

35. Denton, "Religion"; Myers, "Interactive Model"; Pearce and Axinn, "Impact of Family Religious Life"; Regnerus and Burdette, "Religious Change."

36. Ozorak, "Social and Cognitive Influences."

37. Smith and Denton, *Soul Searching*; Smith and Snell, *Souls in Transition*.

38. Brown and Francis, "Influence of Home"; Willits and Crider, "Church Attendance"; Myers, "Interactive Model."

39. Hood, Hill, and Spilka, *Psychology of Religion*.

40. De Vaus, "Relative Importance."

41. Hoge and Petrillo, "Determinants."

42. Madsen and Vernon, "Maintaining the Faith."

43. Bainbridge and Stark, "Suicide."

44. Ozorak, "Social and Cognitive Influences."

45. P. E. King, Furrow, and Roth, "Influence of Families"; Regnerus, Smith, and Smith, "Social Context."

46. Lytch, *Choosing Church*.

47. Dahl, "Adolescent Brain Development."

48. Hood, Hill, and Spilka, *Psychology of Religion*.

49. Fowler, *Faithful Change*.

50. Hood, Hill, and Spilka, *Psychology of Religion*.

51. Clydesdale, *First Year Out*; Schweitzer, "Religious Affiliation."

52. Lytch, *Choosing Church*; Regnerus and Uecker, "Finding Faith"; Smetana, Campione-Barr, and Metzger, "Adolescent Development"; Uecker, Regnerus, and Vaaler, "Losing My Religion."

53. Ellison and Sherkat, "Identifying the 'Semi-Involuntary Institution'"; Miller and Stark, "Gender and Religiousness."

54. Taylor et al., "Black and White Differences."

55. Yancey, "Comparison of Religiosity."

56. Taylor, Chatters and Levin, *Religion*.

57. Yancey, "Comparison of Religiosity."

58. Shibley, *Resurgent Evangelicalism*; Smith, Sikkink, and Bailey, "Devotion in Dixie"; Stark and Bainbridge, *Future of Religion*.

59. Kirkpatrick, "Longitudinal Study"; Zinnbauer and Pargament, "Spiritual Conversion."

60. Paloutzian, Richardson, and Rambo, "Religious Conversion."

61. Regnerus and Smith, "Selection Effects."

62. Erikson, *Identity*.

63. Marcia, "Development and Validation."

Chapter 2

1. For more information on latent class analysis, see Collins and Lanza, *Latent Class*.

2. The exact wording of the eight measures and their response options, our recoding of some response options, and distributions of each variable within our

sample of adolescents who participated in both NSYR telephone surveys are displayed in table B.1 in appendix B.

3. Edgell, Gerteis, and Hartmann, "Atheists as 'Other.'"

4. McGuire, *Lived Religion;* Chaves, "Rain Dances."

5. Bender, *Heaven's Kitchen;* McGuire, *Lived Religion.*

6. Ammerman, "Golden Rule Christianity"; McGuire, *Lived Religion.*

Chapter 3

1. The percentages shown in tables 3.1 through 3.6 represent bivariate distributions. In additional analyses available upon request from the authors, we examined these variables in a series of multivariate models that control for sex, age, race, region, parental income, parental education, family structure, residential stability, parental depression, closeness to parents, parental religion, parental attendance, parental prayer, religiousness of friends, and youth temperament. In doing so we are able to estimate the effect of a given variable while holding constant the effects of a range of other variables that we think are also associated with the religious profiles and/or the variable of interest. Footnotes in each of the tables indicate statistical significance in the multivariate models.

2. Emerson and Woo, *People of the Dream.*

3. Ellison and Sherkat, "Semi-Involuntary Institution"; Taylor et al., "Black and White Differences"; Yancey, "Comparison of Religiosity."

4. Comparing probabilities, whites have a 0.23 probability of being Adapters, compared to 0.44 for blacks and 0.35 for Hispanics.

5. Cornwall, "Faith Development"; Miller and Hoffmann, "Risk and Religion"; Miller and Stark, "Gender and Religiousness."

6. Youth were asked to name up to five friends to whom they felt closest or with whom they spent the most time. They were then asked to answer a series of questions about each of the friends they listed. The majority of youth named five friends, but some listed fewer.

7. The alternatives offered were to report that their friend was religious or not religious at all. So the bar for a friend to be religious in this instance is fairly low, thus leading to a high percentage of all friends being reported as religious.

8. Regnerus and Smith, "Selection Effects."

9. Fewer than 2 percent of Avoiders have no religious exposure, measured as never attending religious services, having no religious friends, and having parents who never attend and claim no religious affiliation.

10. LCA probabilities in separate analysis (not shown).

11. The racial association holds true even in a regression model where we control for sociodemographic factors that could potentially explain this relationship.

12. Christerson, Edwards, and Flory, *Growing Up in America.*

13. Benson and Donahue, "Religion and the Well-being"; Smith and Faris, *Religion and American Adolescent Delinquency.*

14. Cochran, "Variable Effects of Religiosity"; Pearce and Haynie, "Intergenerational Religious Dynamics"; Smith and Faris, *Religion and American Adolescent Delinquency;* Smith and Denton, *Soul Searching.*

15. Wallace and Forman, "Religion's Role."

16. Lammers et al., "Influences on Adolescents' Decision"; Regnerus, "Shaping School Success"; Regnerus and Elder, "Religion and Vulnerability."

17. Smith, "Theorizing Religious Effects."

18. Manturuk and Pearce, "Sacred Mirrors"; Regnerus and Smith, "Selection Effects."

19. Regnerus and Smith, "Selection Effects."

20. Axinn and Pearce, *Mixed Method*.

21. Using a lagged dependent variable (LDV) controls for the level of the measured outcome at the time of the first survey. In doing so, we are measuring the likelihood that a youth with a given religious profile will experience change in the outcome between the first and second surveys compared to a youth in another religious profile. For example, including a control for whether or not they smoked at the time of the first survey accounts for the fact that Atheists were already more likely to be smoking at the time of the first survey. An LDV model measures whether or not Abiders are significantly less likely than Atheists to switch from nonsmoker to smoker between the surveys. This is a more conservative estimate because it holds constant levels of the outcome prior to the time of the first survey.

22. The multivariate regression results are available by request from the authors. Models include controls for sex, age, race/ethnicity, region, parental income, parental education, family structure, residential stability, parental depression, closeness to parents, parental religion, parental attendance, and parental prayer.

23. Although the bivariate percentages are similar, a multivariate analysis controlling for other factors shows that Adapters are significantly less likely than Assenters and Avoiders to have had sex by the time of the first survey.

24. Fosse and Haas, "Validity and Stability."

25. Multivariate analysis does not reveal any statistically significant differences between the BMI averages of the five religious profiles.

26. In multivariate regressions Abiders but not Atheists have life mastery scores that are significantly different from Adapters, Assenters, and Avoiders ($p < 0.05$).

27. Smith and Denton, *Soul Searching*.

28. Allport, *Personality*; Donahue et al., "The Divided Self"; Sheldon and Kasser, "Coherence and Congruence."

Chapter 4

1. Clydesdale, *First Year Out*.

2. Machaceck, "The Problem of Pluralism"; Wuthnow, *Saving America?*

3. Trinitapoli, "I Know This Isn't PC."

4. Of course some of the individual change in answers results from survey measurement errors and not actual individual-level change. See Groves et al., *Survey Methodology*.

5. See, for example, Good, Willoughby, and Fritjers, "Just Another Club?"; Kerestes, Youniss, and Metz, "Longitudinal Patterns"; Nooney, "Religion, Stress"; Uecker, Regnerus, and Vaaler, "Losing My Religion."

6. It is also important to keep in mind, however, that different religious traditions place different emphasis on different sorts of practices, so not all teens will value equally the role of private prayer.

7. See, for example, Ozorak, "Social and Cognitive Influences"; Wallace et al., "Religion and U.S. Secondary School Students"; Nooney, "Religion, Stress."

8. Clydesdale, *The First Year Out*; Regnerus and Uecker, "Finding Faith."

9. For further information on latent transition analysis, see appendix B; Collins and Lanza, *Latent Class*.

10. In our sample there was only one case of an Abider transitioning to an Adapter, representing 0.2 percent of this group.

11. Bell, *Velvet Elvis*.

12. Smith and Snell, *Souls in Transition*.

13. Edgell, Gerteis, and Hartmann, "Atheists as 'Other.'"

Chapter 5

1. Of the 122 interviews, only 111 provided a response to the question about religious stability and change. Table 5.1 is based on these 111 interviews. It is also important to note that our in-person interviews are not nationally representative. We present the coded counts from the interviews to represent the extent to which these themes occur in the interviews, but we are not suggesting that the distribution of responses from the interview analysis is generalizable to the larger adolescent population in the United States.

2. Penny Edgell, Gerteis, and Hartmann, "Atheists as 'Other.'"

3. Hadaway, Long Marler, and Chaves, "Overreporting Church Attendance"; Olson, "Religious Pluralism"; Woodberry, "When Surveys Lie."

4. Larson and Verma, "How Children"; Carskadon, *Adolescent Sleep Patterns*.

5. Smith and Denton, *Soul Searching*.

6. Uecker, Regnerus, and Vaaler, "Losing My Religion."

7. Eisenberg and Sheffield Morris, "Moral Cognitions."

8. Fowler, *Stages of Faith*.

9. Eisenberg and Morris, "Moral Cognitions"; Fowler, *Stages of Faith*.

10. The quotations were not selected on this basis. The interview analysis was completed without respect to religious profiles, and the profile information was added later.

11. Forty-six percent of all Wave 1 Abiders and 29 percent of all Wave 1 Adapters report becoming more religious at the time of the Wave 2 survey.

12. Throughout this analysis we acknowledge that we are dealing with youth self-assessments of religious change. This is one way of analyzing and understanding change in the religious lives of youth that needs to be contextualized within a larger analysis of survey and interview data. As with all data we recognize that youth self-reports of religious change may include elements of social desirability, lack of self-awareness, wishful thinking, and the like. However, there is still something valuable to be gained by taking seriously the language that they use to talk about religion. Whether or not their self-assessments match up with other empirical observations of their religious lives is not the focus of this chapter. Instead we are interested in identifying youth perceptions of religious stability and change and understanding how this does or does not map onto scholarly conceptualizations of religiosity.

Chapter 6

1. Gauvain, *Social Context*.

2. The term *religious or spiritual development* has a hierarchical connotation implying that individuals move from basic to more developed levels of religious

identity and suggests that there is a preferable style of religiosity toward which everyone should aspire. As we have demonstrated in this book, religiosity is better conceptualized as having different styles that are not necessarily easily ranked in universal terms of effectiveness. It is true that many people have meaning systems that do promote one particular style for themselves and others. However, we leave these issues to others and focus this chapter on how families, peers, and religious institutions seem to influence youth whose lives fit all of the various profiles of religiosity, including those who switch profiles over time.

3. Smith, *Moral Believing Animals.*

4. Smith and Denton, *Soul Searching.*

5. Wood, Bruner, and Ross, "Role of Tutoring."

6. Gauvain, *Social Context.*

7. Dahl, "Adolescent Brain Development," 20.

8. Gauvain, *Social Context.*

9. Eccles et al., "Development."

10. Roof, *Community and Commitment;* Stark and Finke, *Acts of Faith;* Stark and Iannaccone, "Why the Jehovah's Witnesses"; Snow and Phillips, "Lofland-Stark Conversion Model"; Sherkat and Wilson, "Preferences, Constraints"; Smilde, "Qualitative Comparative Analysis."

11. Hood, Hill, and Spilka, *Psychology of Religion;* Regnerus and Uecker, "Finding Faith"; Smith and Denton, *Soul Searching.*

12. The results presented in this chapter are based on our inductive analysis of interview transcripts to uncover characteristics of youth's lives that seem related to stability and change in their religious identities. We use examples from youth that have been introduced in prior chapters to illustrate our findings. This allows us to draw on readers' familiarity with the cases and background information developed elsewhere in the book. It is important to note that these cases illustrate larger processes and trends we saw in the entire sample of youth interview data. We use these qualitative data to drive our logical, case-based inference and supplement this with statistical, sampling-based inference using the survey data. See Small, "'How Many Cases.'"

13. V. King, Elder, and Whitbeck, "Religious Involvement"; Ozorak, "Social and Cognitive Influences"; Regnerus, Smith, and Smith, "Social Context."

14. V. King, Elder, and Whitbeck, "Religious Involvement"; Regnerus and Uecker, "Finding Faith."

15. Smith and Denton, *Soul Searching.*

16. Greenstein, "Gender Ideology."

17. Dahl, "Adolescent Brain Development."

18. Flory and Miller, *Finding Faith.*

19. In the computer-based telephone survey interview interviewers read from a script that was automatically inserted with the appropriate term for the religious congregation based on the religious identity of the youth respondent. For most youth this was *church,* but in cases where it was applicable the term *synagogue, mosque,* or *religious congregation* was used instead.

20. The measure for supportive adults in the congregation was statistically significant in a bivariate cross-tabulation with self-reported religious change. However, in a multivariate regression model supportive adults in the congregation at

Wave 1 was not statistically significant in relation to self-reported religious change at Wave 2. This suggests that there are other variables that explain the pattern we see between supportive adults and religious change.

21. Smith and Denton, *Soul Searching*.

Conclusion

1. G. S. Hall, *Adolescence*.
2. Arnett, "Adolescent Storm and Stress, Reconsidered."
3. Cornwall et al., "Dimensions of Religiosity."
4. Ammerman, "Golden Rule Christianity"; Bender, *Heaven's Kitchen*; D. D. Hall, *Lived Religion*; McGuire, *Lived Religion*.
5. Chaves, "Rain Dances."
6. Christerson, Edwards, and Flory, *Growing Up in America*.
7. Hout and Fischer, "Why More Americans."
8. Smith, "Theorizing."
9. Kanazawa, "Why Liberals."
10. Smetana, Campione-Barr, and Metzger, "Adolescent Development."
11. Regnerus and Burdette, "Religious Change"; Regnerus and Uecker, "Finding Faith"; Smith and Denton, *Soul Searching*; Smith and Snell, *Souls in Transition*.
12. Dahl, "Adolescent Brain Development."
13. Smith and Denton, *Soul Searching*; Smith and Snell, *Souls in Transition*.
14. Pearce and Axinn, "Impact"; Pearce and Haynie, "Intergenerational."

Appendix A

1. Brennan and London, "Are Religious People Nice People?"; Ellison, "Are Religious People Nice People? Evidence"; Morgan, "A Research Note."

Appendix B

1. Collins and Lanza, *Latent Class*.
2. Vermunt and Magidson, "Latent Class Cluster Analysis."
3. Because latent class methods are based on contingency table analysis, the analyses quickly fall apart if there are too many indicators or too many response options per indicator. To keep our models parsimonious, we merged some response options for some of our indicators.

Bibliography

Allport, Gordon W. *Personality: A Psychological Interpretation*. New York: Henry Holt, 1937.

Ammerman, Nancy Tatom. *Bible Believers: Fundamentalists in the Modern World*. New Brunswick, NJ: Rutgers University Press, 1987.

———. "Golden Rule Christianity: Lived Religion in the American Mainstream." In *Lived Religion in America*, edited by David D. Hall, 196–216. Princeton, NJ: Princeton University Press, 1997.

———. "Religious Identities and Religious Institutions." In *Handbook of the Sociology of Religion*, edited by Michele Dillon, 207–24. Cambridge: Cambridge University Press, 2003.

Arnett, Jeffrey Jensen. "Adolescent Storm and Stress, Reconsidered." *American Psychologist* 54, no. 5 (1999): 317–26.

———. *Emerging Adulthood: The Winding Road from the Late Teens through the Twenties*. New York: Oxford University Press, 2004.

Axinn, William G., and Lisa D. Pearce. *Mixed Method Data Collection Strategies*. New York: Cambridge University Press, 2006.

Bainbridge, William Sims, and Rodney Stark. "Suicide, Homicide, and Religion: Durkheim Reassessed." *Annual Review of the Social Sciences of Religion* 5 (1981): 33–56.

Bell, Rob. *Velvet Elvis: Repainting the Christian Faith* (Grand Rapids, MI: Zondervan, 2005).

Bender, Courtney. *Heaven's Kitchen: Living Religion at God's Love We Deliver*. Chicago: University of Chicago Press, 2003.

Benson, Peter L., and Michael Donahue. "Religion and the Well-being of Adolescents." *Journal of Social Issues* 51, no. 2 (1995): 145–60.

Brennan, Kathleen M., and Andrew S. London. "Are Religious People Nice People? Religiosity, Race, Interview Dynamics and Perceived Cooperativeness." *Sociological Inquiry* 71 (2001): 129–44.

Brown, Laurence B., and Leslie J. Francis. "The Influence of Home, Church and School on Prayer among Sixteen-year-old Adolescents in England." *Review of Religious Research* 33, no. 2 (1991): 112–22.

Cadge, Wendy. *The First Generation of Theravada Buddhism in America*. Chicago: University of Chicago Press, 2005.

Carskadon, Mary A., ed. *Adolescent Sleep Patterns: Biological, Social, and Psychological Influences*. Cambridge: Cambridge University Press, 2002.

Chaves, Mark. "Rain Dances in the Dry Season: Overcoming the Religious Congruence Fallacy." *Journal for the Scientific Study of Religion* 49 (2010): 1–14.

Christerson, Brad, Korie L. Edwards, and Richard Flory. *Growing Up in America: The Power of Race in the Lives of Teens*. Palo Alto, CA: Stanford University Press, 2010.

Clydesdale, Tim. *The First Year Out: Understanding American Teens after High School*. Chicago: University of Chicago Press, 2007.

Cochran, John K. "The Variable Effects of Religiosity and Denomination on Adolescent Self-reported Alcohol Use by Beverage Type." *Journal of Drug Issues* 23, no. 3 (1993): 479–91.

Collins, Linda M., and Stephanie T. Lanza. *Latent Class and Latent Transition Analysis: With Applications in the Social, Behavioral, and Health Sciences*. New York: Wiley, 2010.

Cornwall, Marie. "The Faith Development of Men and Women over the Life Course." In *Aging and the Family*, edited by Stephen J. Bahr, 115–39. Lexington, MA: Lexington Press, 1989.

Cornwall, Marie, Stan L. Albrecht, Perry H. Cunningham, and Brian L. Pitcher. "The Dimensions of Religiosity: A Conceptual Model and an Empirical Test." *Review of Religious Research* 27, no. 3 (1986): 226–44.

Crawford, Marisa L., and Graham M. Rossiter. *Reasons for Living: Education and Young People's Search for Meaning, Identity and Spirituality*. Melbourne, Australia: ACER, 2006.

Dahl, Ronald E. "Adolescent Brain Development: A Period of Vulnerabilities and Opportunities. Keynote Address." *Annals of the New York Academy of Sciences* 1021 (2004): 1–22.

Davidson, James A., and Dean D. Knudsen. "A New Approach to Religious Commitment." *Sociological Focus* 10 (1977): 151–73.

Davie, Grace. *Religion in Britain since 1945: Believing without Belonging*. Oxford: Blackwell, 1994.

De Jong, Gordon F., Joseph E. Faulkner, and Rex H. Warland. "Dimensions of Religiosity Reconsidered: Evidence from a Cross-Cultural Study." *Social Forces* 54 (1976): 866–89.

Denton, Melinda Lundquist. "Religion and the Relationship Quality of Parents and Adolescents." Ph.D. diss., University of North Carolina at Chapel Hill, 2006.

De Vaus, David A. "The Relative Importance of Parents and Peers for Adolescent Religious Orientation: An Australian Study." *Adolescence* 18, no. 69 (1983): 147–58.

Donahue, Eileen M., Richard W. Robins, Brent W. Roberts, and Oliver P. John. "The Divided Self: Concurrent and Longitudinal Effects of Psychological Adjustment and Social Roles on Self-Concept Differentiation." *Journal of Personality and Social Psychology* 64, no. 5 (1993): 834–46.

Eccles, Jacquelynne S., Carol Midgley, Allan Wigfield, Christy Miller Buchanan, David Reuman, Constance Flanagan, and Douglas MacIver. "Development during Adolescence: The Impact of Stage/Environment Fit on Young Adolescents' Experiences in Schools and in Families." *American Psychologist* 48, no. 2 (1993): 90–101.

Edgell, Penny. *Religion and Family in a Changing Society*. Princeton Studies in Cultural Sociology, edited by Paul J. DiMaggio, Michèle Lamont, Robert J. Wuthnow, and Viviana A. Zelizer. Princeton, NJ: Princeton University Press, 2005.

Edgell, Penny, Joseph Gerteis, and Douglas Hartmann. "Atheists as 'Other': Moral Boundaries and Cultural Membership in American Society." *American Sociological Review* 71, no. 2 (2006): 211–34.

Eisenberg, Nancy, and Amanda Sheffield Morris. "Moral Cognitions and Prosocial Responding in Adolescence." In *Handbook of Adolescent Psychology*, edited by Richard M. Lerner and Laurence Steinberg, 155–88. 2nd ed. Hoboken, NJ: Wiley, 2004.

Elder, Glen H., Jr. "The Life Course." In *The Encyclopedia of Sociology*, edited by Edgar Borgatta and Marie Borgatta, vol. 3, 1120–30. 3rd ed. New York: Macmillan, 1992.

Elder, Glen H., Jr., Monica Kirkpatrick Johnson, and Robert Crosnoe. "The Emergence and Development of Life Course Theory." In *Handbook of the Life Course*, edited by Jeylan T. Mortimer and Michael J. Shanahan, 3–19. New York: Kluwer Academic/Plenum Publishers, 2003.

Ellison, Christopher. "Are Religious People Nice People? Evidence from the National Survey of Black Americans," *Social Forces* 71 (1992): 411–30.

Ellison, Christopher, and Darren Sherkat. "Identifying the 'Semi-Involuntary Institution': A Clarification." *Social Forces* 78, no. 2 (1999): 793–802.

Ellison, Christopher G., and Darren L. Sherkat. "The Semi-Involuntary Institution Revisited: Regional Variations in Church Participation among Black Americans." *Social Forces* 73 (1995): 1415–37.

Emerson, Michael O., with Rodney M. Woo. *People of the Dream: Multiracial Congregations in the United States*. Princeton, NJ: Princeton University Press, 2006.

Erikson, Erik H. *Identity: Youth and Crisis*. New York: Norton, 1968.

Flory, Richard, and Donald E. Miller. *Finding Faith: The Spiritual Quest of the Post-Boomer Generation*. Piscataway, NJ: Rutgers University Press, 2008.

Fosse, Nathan E., and Steven A. Haas. "Validity and Stability of Self-Reported Health among Adolescents in a Longitudinal, Nationally Representative Survey." *Pediatrics* 123, no. 3 (2009): 496–501.

Fowler, James W. *Faithful Change: The Personal and Public Challenges of Postmodern Life*. Nashville, TN: Abingdon Press, 1996.

———. *Stages of Faith: The Psychology of Human Development*. San Francisco: Harper and Row, 1981.

Friedman, Nathalie. "Divorced Parents and the Jewish Community." In *The Jewish Family and Jewish Continuity*, edited by Steven Bayme and Gladys Rosen, 53–102. Hoboken, NJ: Ktav Publishing House, 1994.

Gauvain, Mary. *The Social Context of Cognitive Development*. New York: Guilford Press, 2001.

Glock, Charles Y. "On the Study of Religious Commitment." In *Review of Recent Research on Religion and Character Formation* 57 (1962): 98–110.

———. "The Religious Revival in America?" In *Religion and the Face of America*, edited by Jane C. Zahn, 25–42. Berkeley and Los Angeles: University of California Press, 1959.

Glock, Charles Y., and Rodney Stark. *Religion and Society in Tension*. Chicago: Rand McNally, 1965.

Good, Marie, Teena Willoughby, and Jan Fritjers. "Just Another Club? The Distinctiveness of the Relation between Religious Service Attendance and Adolescent Psychosocial Adjustment." *Journal of Youth and Adolescence* 38, no. 9 (2009): 1153–71.

Greenstein, Theodore N. "Gender Ideology and Perceptions of the Fairness of the Division of Household Labor: Effects on Marital Quality." *Social Forces* 74 (1996): 1039–51.

Groves, Robert M., Floyd J. Fowler, Jr., Mick P. Couper, James M. Lepkowski, Eleanor Singer, and Roger Tourangeau. *Survey Methodology*. New York: Wiley, 2004.

Hadaway, C. Kirk, Penny Long Marler, and Mark Chaves. "Overreporting Church Attendance in America: Evidence That Demands the Same Verdict." *American Sociological Review* 63, no. 1 (1998): 122–30.

Hall, David D., ed. *Lived Religion in America: Toward a History of Practice*. Princeton, NJ: Princeton University Press, 1997.

Hall, G. Stanley. *Adolescence: Its Psychology and Its Relation to Physiology, Anthropology, Sociology, Sex, Crime, Religion, and Education*. Vol. 2. New York: Appleton, 1904.

Hammond, Phillip E., and Benton Johnson. "Locating the Idea of Religion." In *American Mosaic: Social Patterns of Religion in the United States*, edited by Phillip E. Hammond and Benton Johnson. New York: Random House, 1970.

Hill, Peter C., and Kenneth I. Pargament. "Advances in the Conceptualization and Measurement of Religion and Spirituality: Implications for Physical and Mental Health Research." *American Psychologist* 58, no. 1 (2003): 64–74.

Hoge, Dean R., and Gregory H. Petrillo. "Determinants of Church Participation and Attitudes among High School Youth." *Journal for the Scientific Study of Religion* 17, no. 4 (1978): 359–79.

Hood, Ralph W., Jr., Peter C. Hill, and Bernard Spilka. *The Psychology of Religion: An Empirical Approach*. 4th ed. New York: Guilford Press, 2009.

Hout, Michael, and Claude S. Fischer. "Why More Americans Have No Religious Preference: Politics and Generations." *American Sociological Review* 67, no. 2 (2002): 165–90.

Kanazawa, Satoshi. "Why Liberals and Atheists Are More Intelligent." *Social Psychology Quarterly* 73 (2010): 33–57.

Kerestes, Michael, James Youniss, and Edward Metz. "Longitudinal Patterns of Religious Perspective and Civic Integration." *Applied Developmental Science* 8, no. 1 (2004): 39–46.

King, Morton. "Measuring the Religious Variable: Nine Proposed Dimensions." *Journal for the Scientific Study of Religion* 6 (1967): 173–90.

King, Pamela Ebstyne, James L. Furrow, and N. H. Roth. "The Influence of Families and Peers on Adolescent Religiousness." *Journal of Psychology and Christianity* 21, no. 2 (2002): 109–20.

King, Valerie, Glen H. Elder Jr., and Les B. Whitbeck. "Religious Involvement among Rural Youth: An Ecological and Life-Course Perspective." *Journal of Research on Adolescence* 7, no. 4 (1997): 431–56.

Kirkpatrick, Lee A. "A Longitudinal Study of Changes in Religious Belief and Behavior as a Function of Individual Differences in Adult Attachment Style." *Journal for the Scientific Study of Religion* 36, no. 2 (1997): 207–17.

Kurien, Prema A. *A Place at the Multicultural Table: The Development of an American Hinduism*. Piscataway, NJ: Rutgers University Press, 2007.

Lammers, Christina, Marjorie Ireland, Michael Resnick, and Robert Blum. "Influences on Adolescents' Decision to Postpone Onset of Sexual Intercourse: A Survival Analysis of Virginity among Youths Aged 13 to 18 Years." *Journal of Adolescent Health* 26, no. 1 (2000): 42–48.

Larson, Reed, and Suman Verma. "How Children and Adolescents Spend Time across the World: Work, Play, and Developmental Opportunities." *Psychological Bulletin* 125, no. 6 (1999): 701–36.

Lenski, Gerhard. *The Religious Factor: A Sociological Study of Religion's Impact on Politics, Economics, and Family Life*. New York: Doubleday, 1961.

Lerner, Richard M., and Laurence Steinberg. "The Scientific Study of Adolescence: Past, Present and Future." In *Handbook of Adolescent Psychology*, edited by Lerner and Steinberg, 1–12. 2nd ed. New York: Wiley, 2004.

Lytch, Carol E. *Choosing Church: What Makes a Difference for Teens*. Louisville, KY: Westminster John Knox Press, 2004.

Machaceck, David W. "The Problem of Pluralism," *Sociology of Religion* 64, no. 2 (2003): 145–61.

Madsen, Gary E., and Glenn M. Vernon. "Maintaining the Faith during College: A Study of Campus Religious Group Participation." *Review of Religious Research* 25, no. 2 (1983): 127–41.

Manturuk, Kim R., and Lisa D. Pearce. "Sacred Mirrors: Religion and Body Satisfaction among Adolescent Girls." Working paper. University of North Carolina at Chapel Hill, 2010.

Marcia, James E. "Development and Validation of Ego-Identity Status." *Journal of Personality and Social Psychology* 3, no. 5 (1966): 551–58.

McCloud, Sean. "Putting Some Class into Religious Studies: Resurrecting an Important Concept." *Journal of the American Academy of Religion* 75, no. 4 (2007): 840–62.

McGuire, Meredith B. *Lived Religion: Faith and Practice in Everyday Life*. New York: Oxford University Press, 2008.

Miller, Alan S., and John P. Hoffmann. "Risk and Religion: An Explanation of Gender Differences in Religiosity." *Journal for the Scientific Study of Religion* 34 (1995): 63–75.

Miller, Alan S., and Rodney Stark. "Gender and Religiousness: Can Socialization Explanations Be Saved?" *American Journal of Sociology* 107 (2002): 1399–1423.

Morgan, S. Philip. "A Research Note on Religion and Morality: Are Religious People Nice People?" *Social Forces* 61 (1983): 683–92.

Myers, Scott M. "An Interactive Model of Religiosity Inheritance: The Importance of Family Context." *American Sociological Review* 61, no. 5 (1996): 858–66.

National Survey of Youth and Religion, 2002.

National Survey of Youth and Religion, 2005.

Nooney, Jennifer G. "Religion, Stress, and Mental Health in Adolescence: Findings from Add Health." *Review of Religious Research* 46, no. 4 (2005): 341–54.

Olson, Daniel V. A. "Religious Pluralism in Contemporary U.S. Counties." *American Sociological Review* 63, no. 5 (1998): 759–61.

Orsi, Robert A. *The Madonna of 115th Street: Faith and Community in Italian Harlem, 1880–1950*. 2nd ed. New Haven, CT: Yale University Press, 2002.

Ozorak, Elizabeth Weiss. "Social and Cognitive Influences on the Development of Religious Beliefs and Commitment in Adolescence." *Journal for the Scientific Study of Religion* 28, no. 4 (1989): 448–63.

Paloutzian, Raymond F., James T. Richardson, and Lewis R. Rambo. "Religious Conversion and Personality Change." *Journal of Personality* 67, no. 6 (1999): 1047–79.

Pargament, Kenneth I. *The Psychology of Religion and Coping: Theory, Research, Practice.* New York: Guilford Press, 1997.

Pearce, Lisa D., and William G. Axinn. "The Impact of Family Religious Life on the Quality of Parent-Child Relationships." *American Sociological Review* 63 (1998): 810–28.

Pearce, Lisa D., and Dana L. Haynie. "Intergenerational Religious Dynamics and Adolescent Delinquency." *Social Forces* 82, no. 4 (2004): 1553–72.

Pendry, Patricia, and Emma K. Adam. "Associations between Parents' Marital Functioning, Maternal Parenting Quality, Maternal Emotion and Child Cortisol Levels." *International Journal of Behavior Development* 31, no. 3 (2007): 218–31.

Regnerus, Mark D. "Religion and Positive Adolescent Outcomes: A Review of Research and Theory." *Review of Religious Research* 44, no. 4 (2003): 394–413.

———. "Shaping School Success: Religious Socialization and Educational Outcomes in Metropolitan Schools." *Journal for the Scientific Study of Religion* 39 (2000): 363–70.

Regnerus, Mark D., and Amy M. Burdette. "Religious Change and Adolescent Family Dynamics." *Sociological Quarterly* 47, no. 1 (2006): 175–94.

Regnerus, Mark D., and Glen H. Elder Jr. "Religion and Vulnerability among Low-Risk Adolescents." *Social Science Research* 32, no. 4 (2003): 633–58.

Regnerus, Mark D., and Christian Smith. "Selection Effects in Studies of Religious Influence." *Review of Religious Research* 47, no. 1 (2005): 23–50.

Regnerus, Mark D., Christian Smith, and Brad Smith. "Social Context in the Development of Adolescent Religiosity." *Applied Developmental Science* 8, no. 1 (2004): 27–38.

Regnerus, Mark D., and Jeremy E. Uecker. "Finding Faith, Losing Faith: The Prevalence and Context of Religious Transformations during Adolescence." *Review of Religious Research* 47, no. 3 (2006): 217–37.

Roof, Wade Clark. *Community and Commitment: Religious Plausibility in a Liberal Protestant Church.* New York: Pilgrim Press, 1978.

———. "Concepts and Indicators of Religious Commitment." In *The Religious Dimension: New Directions in Quantitative Research*, edited by Robert Wuthnow, 1–28. New York: Academic Press, 1979.

———. "Religion and Spirituality: Toward an Integrated Analysis." In *Handbook of the Sociology of Religion*, edited by Michele Dillon, 137–51. Cambridge: Cambridge University Press, 2003.

Schachter, Jason P., and Jeffrey J. Kuenzi. *Seasonality of Moves and the Duration and Tenure of Residence: 1996*, 2002, www.census.gov/population/www/documentation/twps0069/twps0069.pdf.

Schwadel, Philip. "Current Expressions of American Jewish Identity: An Analysis of 114 Teenagers." In *Passing on the Faith: Transforming Traditions for the Next Generation of Jews, Christians, and Muslims*, edited by James L. Heft, 135–44. New York: Fordham University Press, 2006.

———. "Jewish Teenagers' Syncretism: A Research Note." *Review of Religious Research* 51, no. 3 (2009): 324–32.

———. "Poor Teenagers' Religion." *Sociology of Religion* 69, no. 2 (2008): 125–49.

Schweitzer, Friedrich. "Religious Affiliation and Disaffiliation in Late Adolescence and Early Adulthood: The Impact of a Neglected Period of Life." In *Joining and Leaving Religion: Research Perspectives*, edited by Leslie J. Francis and Yaacov J. Katz, 87–101. Leominster, Herefordshire, England: Gracewing, 2000.

Sheldon, Kennon M., and Tim Kasser. "Coherence and Congruence: Two Aspects of Personality Integration." *Journal of Personality and Social Psychology* 68, no. 3 (1995): 531–43.

Sherkat, Darren, and John Wilson. "Preferences, Constraints, and Choices in Religious Markets: An Examination of Religious Switching and Apostasy." *Social Forces* 73 (1995): 993–1026.

Shibley, Mark A. *Resurgent Evangelicalism in the United States: Mapping Cultural Change since 1970*. Columbia: University of South Carolina Press, 1996.

Small, Mario Luis. "'How Many Cases Do I Need?' On Science and the Logic of Case Selection in Field-Based Research." *Ethnography* 10, no. 1 (2009): 5–38.

Smetana, Judi G., Nicole Campione-Barr, and Aaron Metzger. "Adolescent Development in Interpersonal and Societal Contexts." *Annual Review of Psychology* 57 (2006): 255–84.

Smilde, David. "A Qualitative Comparative Analysis of Conversion to Venezuelan Evangelicalism: How Networks Matter." *American Journal of Sociology* 111 (2005): 757–96.

Smith, Christian. *Moral, Believing Animals: Human Personhood and Culture*. New York: Oxford University Press, 2003.

———. "Theorizing Religious Effects among American Adolescents." *Journal for the Scientific Study of Religion* 42, no. 1 (2003): 17–30.

Smith, Christian, with Melinda Lundquist Denton. *Soul Searching: The Religious and Spiritual Lives of American Teenagers*. New York: Oxford University Press, 2005.

Smith, Christian, and Robert Faris. *Religion and American Adolescent Delinquency, Risk Behaviors and Constructive Social Activities*. Chapel Hill: University of North Carolina, National Study of Youth and Religion, 2002. Research report. Available at http://www.youthandreligion.org/publications/reports.html.

———. "Socioeconomic Inequality in the American Religious System: An Update and Assessment." *Journal for the Scientific Study of Religion* 44, no. 1 (2005): 95–104.

Smith, Christian, David Sikkink, and Jason Bailey. "Devotion in Dixie and Beyond: A Test of the 'Shibley Thesis' on the Effects of Regional Origin and Migration on Individual Religiosity." *Journal for the Scientific Study of Religion* 37, no. 3 (1998): 494–506.

Smith, Christian, with Patricia Snell. *Souls in Transition: The Religious Lives of Emerging Adults in America*. New York: Oxford University Press, 2009.

Snow, David A., and Cynthia L. Phillips. "The Lofland-Stark Conversion Model: A Critical Reassessment." *Social Problems* 27 (1980): 430–47.

Spickard, James V., J. Shawn Landres, and Meredith B. McGuire, eds. *Personal Knowledge and Beyond: Reshaping the Ethnography of Religion*. New York: New York University Press, 2002.

Stark, Rodney, and William Sims Bainbridge. *The Future of Religion: Secularization, Revival, and Cult Formation*. Berkeley and Los Angeles: University of California Press, 1985.

Stark, Rodney, and Roger Finke. *Acts of Faith: Explaining the Human Side of Religion*. Berkeley and Los Angeles: University of California Press, 2000.

Stark, Rodney, and Charles Y. Glock. *American Piety: The Nature of Religious Commitment*. Berkeley and Los Angeles: University of California Press, 1968.

Stark, Rodney, and Laurence R. Iannaccone. "Why the Jehovah's Witnesses Grow So Rapidly: A Theoretical Application." *Journal of Contemporary Religion* 12 (1997): 133–37.

Steinberg, Laurence. *Adolescence*. 7th ed. New York: McGraw-Hill, 2005.

Stolzenberg, Ross M., Mary Blair-Loy, and Linda J. Waite. "Religious Participation over the Life Course: Age and Family Life Cycle Effects on Church Membership." *American Sociological Review* 60 (1995): 84–103.

Taylor, Robert J., Linda Chatters, Rukmalie Jayakody, and Jeffrey Levin. "Black and White Differences in Religious Participation: A Multisample Comparison." *Journal for the Scientific Study of Religion* 35 (1996): 403–10.

Taylor, Robert Joseph, Linda M. Chatters, and Jeff S. Levin. *Religion in the Lives of African Americans: Social, Psychological and Health Perspective*. Thousand Oaks, CA: Sage Press, 2004.

Teater, Barbra. "Factors Predicting Residential Mobility among the Recipients of the Section 8 Housing Choice Voucher Program." *Journal of Sociology and Social Welfare* 36, no. 3 (2009): 159–78.

Trinitapoli, Jenny. "I Know This Isn't PC, But . . . : Religious Exclusivism among U.S. Adolescents," *Sociological Quarterly* 48, no. 3 (2007): 451–83.

Uecker, Jeremy E., Mark D. Regnerus, and Margaret L. Vaaler. "Losing My Religion: The Social Sources of Religious Decline in Early Adulthood." *Social Forces* 85, no. 4 (2007): 1667–92.

Van Ryn, Maria W. "'There's the Jewish Culture and Then There's the Religion': Exploring the Potential of Cultural Identity for Jewish Adolescents." M.A. thesis, University of North Carolina at Chapel Hill, 2007.

Verbit, Mervin F. "The Components and Dimensions of Religious Behaviour: Toward a Reconceptualization of Religiosity." In *American Mosaic: Social Patterns of Religion in the United States*, edited by Phillip E. Hammond and Benton Johnson, 24–39. New York: Random House, 1970.

Vermunt, J. K., and J. Magidson. "Latent Class Cluster Analysis." In *Applied Latent Class Analysis*, edited by J. A. Hagenaars and A. L. McCutcheon, 89–106. Cambridge: Cambridge University Press, 2002).

Wallace, John M., Jr., and Tyrone A. Forman. "Religion's Role in Promoting Health and Reducing Risk among American Youth." *Health Education and Behavior* 25, no. 6 (1998): 721–41.

Wallace, John M., Jr., Tyrone A. Forman, Cleopatra H. Caldwell, and Deborah S. Willis. "Religion and U.S. Secondary School Students: Current Patterns, Recent Trends, and Sociodemographic Correlates." *Youth and Society* 35, no. 1 (2003): 98–125.

Willits, Fern K., and Donald M. Crider. "Church Attendance and Traditional Religious Beliefs in Adolescence and Young Adulthood: A Panel Study." *Review of Religious Research* 31, no. 1 (1989): 68–81.

Wimberley, Dale W. "Religion and Role-Identity: A Structural Symbolic Interactionist Conceptualization of Religiosity." *Sociological Quarterly* 30, no. 1 (1989): 125–42.

Wimberley, Ronald C. "Toward the Measurement of Commitment Strength." *Sociological Analysis* 35, no. 3 (1974): 211–15.

Wink, Paul, Michele Dillon, and Adrienne Prettyman. "Religiousness, Spiritual Seeking, and Authoritarianism: Findings from a Longitudinal Study." *Journal for the Scientific Study of Religion* 46, no. 3 (2007): 321–35.

Wood, David, Jerome S. Bruner, and Gail Ross. "The Role of Tutoring in Problem Solving." *Journal of Child Psychology and Psychiatry* 17 (1976): 89–100.

Woodberry, Robert D. "When Surveys Lie and People Tell the Truth: How Surveys Over-sample Church Attenders." *American Sociological Review* 63, no. 1 (1998): 119–22.

Wuthnow, Robert. *After Heaven: Spirituality in America since the 1950s.* Berkeley and Los Angeles: University of California Press, 1998.

———. *Growing Up Religious: Christians and Jews and Their Journeys of Faith.* Boston: Beacon Press, 1999.

———. *Saving America?: Faith Based Services and the Future of Civil Society.* Princeton, NJ: Princeton University Press, 2001.

Yamane, David. "Beyond Beliefs: Religion and the Sociology of Religion in America." *Social Compass* 54, no. 1 (2007): 33–48.

Yancey, George. "A Comparison of Religiosity between European-Americans, African-Americans, Hispanic-Americans and Asian-Americans." *Research in the Social Scientific Study of Religion* 16 (2005): 83–104.

Zhai, Jiexia Elisa, Christopher G. Ellison, Norval D. Glenn, and Elizabeth Marquardt. "Parental Divorce and Religious Involvement among Young Adults." *Sociology of Religion* 68, no. 2 (2007): 125–44.

Zinnbauer, Brian, and Kenneth I. Pargament. "Spiritual Conversion: A Study of Religious Change among College Students." *Journal for the Scientific Study of Religion* 37, no. 1 (1998): 161–80.

Zinnbauer, Brian, Kenneth I. Pargament, and Allie B. Scott. "The Emerging Meanings of Religiousness and Spirituality: Problems and Prospects." *Journal of Personality* 67, no. 6 (1999): 889–919.

Index

person-centered approach, 32, 56, 76, 134, 139, 174, 180
phoniness, 104, 150, 161
    See also hypocrisy
Piaget, 25
prayer. *See* religious practice
Presbyterian, 1, 123, 197
Protestant(s), 8, 19, 63–64, 70, 73–74, 95
    conservative, 63–64, 73–74
    Evangelical, 19, 95, 197
    mainline, 63–64, 73
    nondenominational, 103, 130, 135, 197

race / ethnicity, 27, 58–59, 75
Rachel, 1–3, 5
region, 27
Regnerus, Mark D., 24
reincarnation, 94
religion, adolescent views of, 2, 9, 180
    ambiguity, 134–36
    necessity, 130–31
religiosity / religiousness, 12, 15, 16, 31, 39, 54, 57, 115, 118, 141, 173, 200
    conceptualization of, 4, 8, 12, 28–29, 139, 176
    definition of, 3, 4, 12, 16, 31–32, 56, 139
    dimensions of, 3, 8, 13–16, 18–19, 31–32, 38, 54, 56, 100, 118, 126, 134, 140, 144, 173–74, 180; centrality, 3, 13–16, 19, 28, 32, 38, 54, 98–100, 115–18, 127, 137–40, 143, 152, 173, 180, 200; conduct, 3, 13–16, 18–19, 28, 32, 38, 54, 96–98, 118–19, 124, 139, 143, 173, 180, 200; content, 3, 13–14, 16, 18–19, 28, 32, 54, 88–95, 116, 118, 124–27, 139, 143, 173, 180, 200; Three *C*s, 3, 9, 13–15, 18–19, 28, 55, 59, 88, 118, 137, 139, 173
    dualities of, 16, 17
    dynamics of, 16–20, 24, 87–89, 100 (*see also* religious change / stability)
    measurement of, 17–18, 31–32, 41, 44, 46–48, 50, 53, 107, 140, 174–75, 179–80, 200, 201–3
    parent. *See* parent religiosity; family religious background
religious affiliation / tradition, 64, 67–70, 94–95
religious beliefs, 13–14, 18, 32, 54, 88–89, 92–94, 117, 124–27, 135, 139, 143, 173, 200
    belief in god, 11, 38, 39, 46, 88–91
    doubt, 46, 107, 149, 151, 155, 182
    views of god, 43, 45, 46, 49, 52, 88, 90–91

exclusivism / particularity, 38–39, 41, 44, 47, 91–94, 175
    See also religiosity
religious change / stability, 2–3, 8, 9, 11–12, 20, 24, 43, 87, 93, 100, 115–18, 126, 134, 136–37, 139, 152, 168, 179, 181
    self-reported, 116, 117–18, 137–41, 152, 155, 168, 178
religious institutions / congregations, 24–26, 51, 57, 67–70, 73–74, 85, 122, 117, 145, 158–67, 169, 177, 182
religious practice, 13–15, 32, 38, 46, 51, 54, 96–98, 105, 109, 115, 118–19, 121–22, 124, 131–32, 135, 139–40, 144, 152, 173, 176, 200
    helping others, 33, 48, 49
    prayer, 46, 49, 96–97, 105, 108–9, 111, 117, 175, 200
    service attendance, 31–32, 35, 38, 51, 67–70, 96, 109–10, 117–24, 139, 140, 175, 200
    See also religiosity
religious profiles, 8, 9, 17, 19, 32–33, 38, 54–58, 76, 78, 83, 88, 100–101, 115, 137, 144, 152, 168, 170, 173–75, 183, 199, 204
    Five *As* / latent classes of religiosity, 4, 8, 33, 55–58, 70–86, 101, 137, 174–75
    transitions in, 100–115
    See also mosaics
religious refinement, 118, 128, 143–44, 150, 152, 155, 167, 170, 179, 181–83
    See also personalization of faith; ownership of faith
religious salience, 13–15, 18, 32, 38, 54, 98–100, 105, 110, 115–18, 127, 137, 139–40, 143, 152, 173, 176, 180, 200
    closeness to God, 99–100, 200
    importance of, 98–99, 113, 200
    thinking about the meaning of life, 33, 107–8, 177, 200
    See also religiosity
religious socialization, 133, 146
research methods. *See* latent class analysis; National Study of Youth and Religion
risk-aversion, 66
risk behaviors, 76–80, 83–85
ritual / ritualistic, 14
role models, 83
Roof, Wade Clark, 15
Rosary, 107
Rousseau, Jean-Jacques, 171